Navigating the Ubiquitous, Misunderstood, and Evolving Role of the Educational Leadership Program Coordinator in Higher Education

A Volume in Dimensions of Leadership and Institutional Success: Exploring Connections and Partnerships

Series Editor

Ellen H. Reames
Auburn University

Dimensions of Leadership and Institutional Success: Exploring Connections and Partnerships

Ellen H. Reames, Series Editor

Navigating the Ubiquitous, Misunderstood, and Evolving Role of the Educational Leadership Program Coordinator in Higher Education (2024)
edited by Noelle A. Paufler and Ellen H. Reames

Partnerships for Leadership Preparation and Development: Facilitators, Barriers and Models for Change (2021)
edited by Frances K. Kochan, Ellen H. Reames, and Dana M. Griggs

Creating School Partnerships that Work: A Guide for Practice and Research (2020)
edited by Frances K. Kochan and Dana M. Griggs

Rural Turnaround Leadership Development: The Power of Partnerships (2018)
edited by Ellen H. Reames

Navigating the Ubiquitous, Misunderstood, and Evolving Role of the Educational Leadership Program Coordinator in Higher Education

Editors

Noelle A. Paufler
Clemson University

Ellen H. Reames
Auburn University

INFORMATION AGE PUBLISHING, INC.
Charlotte, NC • www.infoagepub.com

Library of Congress Cataloging-in-Publication Data

CIP record for this book is available from the Library of Congress
http://www.loc.gov

ISBNs: 979-8-88730-384-0 (Paperback)

979-8-88730-385-7 (Hardcover)

979-8-88730-386-4 (ebook)

Printed in the United States of America

Dedication

This book is dedicated to Tibor and Emily. Without them, I wouldn't be able to coordinate much of anything.

With much love, Noelle.

CONTENTS

INTRODUCTION

CHAPTER 1

UBIQUITOUS, MISUNDERSTOOD, AND EVOLVING

Characterizing the Role of the Educational Leadership Program Coordinator

Noelle A. Paufler
Clemson University

Ellen H. Reames
Auburn University

While substantial research has been conducted on formalized leadership roles in academia such as the department head or chair and college dean, there is a dearth of literature on the role of the program coordinator (PC), particularly in the field of educational leadership (Coleman & Reames, 2020; Hackmann & Wanat, 2008, 2016; Ingle et al., 2018; Ingle et al., 2020; Marshall et al., 2021; Reames, 2016). Limited research on the role of the educational leadership PC is particularly problematic considering their increasing importance as models of leadership for their students, program leaders within their departments, and facilitators of K–12 school district-university partnerships, among other roles. As the authors of these book chapters suggest, the nature of the educational leadership PC role should be closely examined in current policy and practice contexts to better understand how to conceptualize, incentivize, and support PCs amidst ongoing

Navigating the Ubiquitous, Misunderstood, and Evolving Role of the Educational Leadership Program Coordinator in Higher Education, pp. 3–13

changes and challenges in higher education. In this chapter, we characterize the role of the educational leadership PC as ubiquitous, misunderstood, and evolving; discuss how current research, including these book chapters, reinforces and at times challenges this conception; and identify potential areas for future research.

Many colleges and schools of education have a formal leadership structure that in addition to a dean includes department heads or chairs who often supervise a combination of related but distinct programs (e.g., K–12 educational leadership, higher education, teacher preparation, counseling, educational foundations) within their respective departments. These department-level leadership roles are clearly defined in institutional policy with specified authority and responsibilities (see, for example, Berdrow, 2010; Hackmann & McCarthy, 2011), including faculty workload and evaluation, resource allocation, and communication with external stakeholders within and beyond the university. Given their significant supervisory, fiscal, and representative responsibilities, chairs are challenged to adequately support multiple programs within the department with limited time and program-specific expertise and experience (Hackmann & Wanat, 2008, 2016).

Existing research indicates faculty with specific expertise and experience are often enlisted to coordinate programs as a means of supporting the department chair. This quasi-administrative PC role generally lacks both a clear position description and any formal authority within the university structure (Hackmann & Wanat, 2008, 2016). The lack of clear delineation between the role and responsibilities of the PC relative to other program faculty and the department chair at many institutions (Hackmann & Wanat, 2016) and minimal, if any, formal authority to define and operationalize their role (Ingle et al., 2018; Ingle et al., 2020) makes the work of the PC challenging, particularly when undertaken by pre-tenure faculty.

Despite the ambiguity surrounding their role, PCs frequently facilitate a wide range of program activities, including engaging with, for example, students; program faculty; department, college, and university leadership; external partners; state and national accreditation agencies and entities; and professional organizations (Hackmann & Wanat, 2008, 2016; Reames, 2016). In this chapter, we argue current research supports the characterization of the PC role as ubiquitous, misunderstood, and evolving. Further, given the multifaceted, complex nature of the work of the PC, we suggest additional research is needed closely examining the role in current policy and practice contexts to better understand how to conceptualize, incentivize, and support PCs.

In the current volume, we invite you to explore three sections. Section I is the ubiquitous nature of the educational leadership PC's role. Section II involves the many misunderstandings which arise as PCs do their work.

Section III speaks to the evolving role of the PC. As the editors of this volume, we see these as the overarching themes of the chapters that follow.

Ubiquitous Nature of the Program Coordinator Role

The term *ubiquitous*, which is an adjective defined by Merriam-Webster (n.d.) as "existing or being everywhere at the same time; constantly encountered; widespread" offers an apt description of the PC role. While limited research has been conducted on the role of the PC, prior studies suggest that PCs are responsible for myriad tasks including: program development (e.g., maintaining a vision for the program and revising curriculum), facilitation (e.g., leading meetings, and scheduling and assigning courses), outreach to students (e.g., coordinating marketing and recruitment efforts, supervising the admissions process, and addressing student concerns), communication (e.g., responding to inquiries and engaging with partners), and compliance (e.g., ensuring the program meets the requirements of national and state accreditation and certification agencies and entities). Rather than suggest that PCs have a clearly delineated, finite set of responsibilities, this list offers a sampling of tasks for aspects of coordination that have been documented in existing research (see, for example, Coleman & Reames, 2020; Hackmann & Wanat, 2008, 2016; Ingle et al., 2018, Ingle et al. 2020; Reames, 2016).

In one of few studies published to date examining the role and responsibilities of PCs across institutions, Ingle et al. (2018) surveyed PCs at University Council for Educational Administration (UCEA)—member institutions. Based on survey responses from 92 PCs (a response rate of 62.2%), Ingle et al. (2018) found PCs reportedly spent 16.96 hours per week on average (with a standard deviation of 10.59 hours) on program coordination activities. The vast majority of survey respondents held full-time faculty positions, namely in tenured (47.8%), tenure-track (12.0%), and non-tenure track (29.3%) roles, at public (81.5%) and/or doctoral granting (88.0%) institutions. Approximately 71% of survey respondents had held their PC position for three or more years. Findings from this study suggest that the role of the PC is often a significant, time-consuming, multi-year commitment (Ingle et al., 2018; see also Ingle et al., 2020; Marshall et al., 2021).

Authors of these book chapters offer a nuanced understanding of the significant influence of PCs on their respective programs and the time-consuming, potentially all-encompassing nature of program coordination responsibilities for individual PCs.

Karen D. Jones and Travis Lewis provide a visual framework of the educational leadership PC's role regarding partnerships between universities and K–12 school districts in "Connecting the Dots: Program Coordinator as

School-District-University Partnership Facilitator." The authors explain the partnership from the recruitment of students to the graduation of highly qualified leaders with ongoing feedback from districts for improvement of the higher education programs and the partnership. In this role, PCs work to bridge the gap between higher education leadership preparation programs and K–12 school districts' needs and navigate a unique position to ensure the needs of students, districts, and the university are met.

Jones and Lewis embrace continuous program improvement with their model. Program stakeholders such as the PC, program faculty, university administrators, students, and school district partners are the drivers. In essence, they "connect the dots." This chapter provides a new partnership model to the scant existing literature (Barnett et al., 2010; Korach et al., 2021; Reames & Kochan, 2021). PCs are encouraged to contemplate existing models and consider developing future models as they grow and improve their own programs.

In "Bridging the Gap Between Higher Education and K–12: The Role of Program Coordinators in Educational Leadership Programs," Isela Peña and Rebecca Schlosser examine the recertification requirements that increased the role of PC to include creating partnerships with K–12 school districts. The authors discuss the PC's role in university-district partnerships regarding partnership inception, collaborative efforts, relationship-building, role and responsibilities of the coordinator, and leadership commitments.

Ubiquitous is the PC as they navigate the nuances of state mandates and certification requirements. Accreditation as well as state, regional, and national standards influence educational leadership preparation programs in an ever-changing environment. Partnerships with K–12 school districts are one of the major shifts in PC responsibility. Oddly, it is a requirement of educational leadership preparation programs, but K–12 districts have no mandates or obligations to do this partnership work. It often becomes an added responsibility of the PC (Kochan et al. 2021; Reames & Kochan, 2021).

In "The Educational Leadership Program Coordinator: Partnerships and Recruiting," Ellen H. Reames, Angela C. Adair, and Alfred Parham explain the Auburn University Educational Leadership Administration of Elementary and Secondary (AES) education and the Administration and Supervision of Curriculum (ASC) preparation programs' recruiting and marketing plan accentuating the importance of building strong partnerships with K–12 school districts and other agencies closely aligned with preparing leaders for Alabama schools, industry, nonprofits, and military entities. Included in the chapter is a partnership model (Reames & Kochan, 2021) and a table for the organization of current and future recruiting strategies.

The authors had several goals for creating this chapter. There is an absence of literature regarding the role of the PC in the areas of partnership development and recruiting (Coleman & Reames, 2020; Reames, 2016). Second, literature surrounding the recruitment and retention of leadership students is nonexistent. Educational leadership faculty speak to recruiting, but it is suggested here that few have formal, detailed, recruiting plans and do not address how these are linked to college and university marketing strategies. Finally, partnership development in educational leadership preparation programs has been suggested since the early 2000s, but scant literature exists (Crow & Whitman, 2016). To date, there are only three relevant models specifically related to educational leadership programs (Reames & Kochan, 2021). In conclusion, as we move forward there is much research needed.

Program Coordination as Misunderstood

Defined by Merriam-Webster (n.d.) as "wrongly or imperfectly understood" or "not sympathetically appreciated," the adjective *misunderstood* can be readily applied to the role of the PC in one or both aspects. The role of the PC is not well understood in that it lacks a clear position description and generally has little, if any, formal authority (Hackmann & Wanat, 2008, 2016; Ingle et al., 2020). This ambiguity necessitates that PCs conceptualize and operationalize the role within the contexts of their own institutions (Hackmann & Wanat, 2008, 2016) and current partnerships (Coleman & Reames, 2020; Reames, 2016). Serving in this quasi-administrative role with limited authority to delegate responsibilities or tasks to program faculty and to address conflicts when they arise comes with some level of risk, particularly placing pre-tenure and non-tenure track faculty in a vulnerable position (Hackmann & Wanat, 2008, 2016). The significant time commitment required for program coordination further jeopardizes pre-tenure faculty who must balance what is usually considered service in the PC role with the research and teaching expectations for tenure (Ingle et al., 2018; Ingle et al., 2020). Although there seem to be fewer pre-tenure faculty serving as PCs than might be expected (Ingle et al., 2018), non-tenure faculty are increasingly assuming PC roles. Accordingly, ensuring faculty are adequately compensated for and supported in their work as a PC is increasingly important (Ingle et al., 2020). The authors of these book chapters highlight many of the ways the PC role and its associated risks and rewards are misunderstood.

Barbara Qualls and Stacy Hendricks examine the dual roles of two PCs in an educational leadership program in their chapter entitled "Two Lenses—One Focus: Examining Educational Leadership Coordinator Roles." The research framework is an examination of literature describing action research that utilizes self-study and critical friend methodology to foster the relationships that are necessary for leading educational leadership programs. The anecdotal narrative regarding the university where the authors' work is included to provide context for blending the available faculty to encompass the needs of two related but distinct degree programs. This context spans a wholesale university transformation including president change, workload policy redevelopment, and overhaul of college structure and policies.

Qualls and Hendricks point to risks and suggest that if a critical friend lens is used, the rewards can be vast. Their partnership with each other, their willingness to be critical friends to offer change to their master's and EdD programs brought great rewards to faculty, the university, and the students who came to their program for learning. In terms of partnerships, it was a great example of both internal and external partnerships (Kochan & Mullen, 2003; Reames & Kochan, 2021). Internally, the stakeholders within the university reaped rewards. Externally, the school districts and educational agencies touched by the university program and the students who went back to their school systems with new knowledge and skills all benefitted because of the risks these two PCs were willing to take as they supported their critical friend relationship.

William Kyle Ingle and Joanne M. Marshall's chapter entitled "Program Coordination at UCEA-Affiliated Universities in the Wake of COVID-19" discusses their research regarding how COVID-19 changed the scope of UCEA-affiliated university PCs' responsibilities. The study's findings revealed that professors spent more time on program coordination and less time on research than before the pandemic, revealed that minority PCs received less incentives than their White counterparts, and revealed the stressors that COVID-19 had on PCs' personal and professional lives, including the difficulties of transitioning to exclusively online instruction.

Ingle and Marshall bring to light another theme regarding risks, rewards, and misunderstanding. For quite some time, prior to COVID-19, it was apparent that the educational leadership PC role went unrewarded and misunderstood. As Ingle and Marshall point out, during COVID-19 the scope of PC work became more daunting. PCs were forced to spend even more time on coordination and less time on research than ever before. Recruiting and sustaining partnerships with the community became more difficult. Mental health issues for students, faculty, and PCs became more apparent. Moving completely to online forums compounded the stresses facing PCs. All of this increases the risks of PC turnover and a destabilization of program integrity thus complicating efforts to ensure quality programming.

In her chapter, "Successes, Challenges, and Hopes of an Educational Leadership Program Coordinator: Balancing the Self and Others,"

Barbara L. Pazey focuses on her role as the PC at a Tier 1 university as she attempted to reestablish and maintain unity and cohesion among members of the educational leadership program between 2019 and 2022, prior to, during, and following the COVID-19 pandemic and the events that occurred within that timeframe, including turnover amongst educational leadership faculty.

Pazey speaks to the role of a PC as she embraces the various backgrounds, perspectives, and generations of faculty members. These paradigms in higher education educational leadership preparation programs are often very different and can be misunderstood. The risks of being transparent in thought and action can be quite difficult for PCs as they navigate faculty, department heads, new deans, and university level administrators. Program changes due to attrition of tenure track and clinical faculty can complicate the misunderstanding. As Pazey suggests, the rewards of persevering can bring rewards for the PC, faculty, and the students they serve. The PC can know they were able to play an important role in developing a better learning partnership within the program. The PC is also rewarded by knowing that students have received the attention they need as they matriculate through their degree program.

Evolving Role of the Program Coordinator in Challenging Times

The role of the PC in higher education is continuously *evolving*, defined by Merriam-Webster (n.d.) as a verb meaning "to gradually become clearer and more detailed" (i.e., as in unfolding). Although most PCs have historically been tenured or a tenure track faculty (Ingle et al., 2018), PC positions are increasingly being filled by full-time, non-tenure track (e.g., clinical) faculty who often have extensive K–12 leadership experience. With reduced expectations for research, these non-tenure track faculty may have a more substantial teaching load with release time for program coordination. Considering shifting trends in higher education, particularly post-COVID, the role of the PC must be better understood, supported, and distributed (Marshall et al., 2021) in order to promote innovation and develop sustainable partnerships in educational leadership preparation. The authors of these book chapters discuss the evolving role of the PC, particularly in challenging times.

Wesley Henry, Ann E. Blankenship-Knox, Sarah Jouganatos, and Lori Rhodes collaborate in "We're Lucky to Have Each Other: Solo Leadership Faculty as Program Coordinators" as four principal preparation PCs who were the only tenure-track, full-time educational leadership faculty at their institutions as they engaged in program redesign to emphasize equity-focused leadership preparation. Findings explore the role of solo-faculty

PCs as agents of change and their abilities to accelerate change within their institutions. This chapter offers implications for solo-faculty PCs, for leadership preparation programs with small faculties, and for administrators seeking to better support addressing the challenges facing solo-faculty PCs.

Henry et al. bring to mind the importance of partnership between educational leadership programs and educational entities. Partnerships, rather than silos and collaboration between programs rather than competition, support innovation and improvement. Growing, changing, and evolving towards the future are ways to support the well-being of the individuals in charge of leadership preparation in our higher education institutions. In turn, this growth mindset allows faculty to be models for those K–12 practitioners seeking new knowledge and skills through preparation programs.

In their chapter entitled "The Role of the Clinical Professor: Program Coordination and Partnership Development," William A. Bergeron, Yvette Bynum, and Brenda Mendiola begin with the background and development of the clinical professor role and then focus on the advantages that lived experiences can have for the clinical professor as PC regarding mentoring, advising students, and developing partnerships with K–12 entities. Included in the chapter are several challenges faced by clinical professors who assume the role of PC with recommendations for professional development, mentoring, a change in terminology, rotating roles, and promoting collaboration.

What seems apparent is that the clinical role in educational leadership is growing and the inherent responsibilities of coordinating became a much larger focus of the clinical role. For example, partnership development with K–12 entities became a much larger focus with the redesign efforts suggested beginning in the early 2000s. Calls for reform of educational leadership put partnership development with K–12 schools and agencies squarely on the shoulders of higher education leadership preparation programs. Clinical professors, those in the field, are in a much better position to do partnership development work because many of them had administrative and teaching roles in K–12 school systems prior to becoming a clinical professor.

In her chapter, "Recruiting and Partnership Experiences of the Graduate Assistant to the Program Coordinator," Angela C. Adair discusses the role of the graduate assistant who is assigned to the PC for program support. From her viewpoint on the balcony, Adair speaks to the role of the PC, the mutually beneficial relationship between the graduate assistant and the PC, recruiting to build partnerships, building partnerships to improve recruiting, the benefits of partnerships, creating successful partnerships, and making the most of a graduate assistant as a resource for the educational leadership program. Included in the chapter is a table that provides an example of how the division of responsibilities between the PC and graduate assistant can ease the burden of responsibilities of the PC.

The chapter is instructive for the theme of evolving roles for several reasons. PCs should advocate for a graduate student assigned for program needs. The PC-graduate student relationship can become a mutually advantageous relationship for both. Graduate students become particularly skilled at the functions associated with the PC role, thus increasing their value as future faculty members in educational leadership programs. These graduate students become adept at scheduling, brokering initiatives with partners, recruiting, and scholarship. The collaborative partnership that is possible between the PC and the program graduate student allows for clarity of purpose and attention to detail far exceeding what one busy faculty member can do as the PC.

Future of the Program Coordinator Role

Volume two, *Innovative Partnership Practices in the Role of the Educational Leadership Program Coordinator,* will be an edited volume focusing on innovative partnership development practices of the educational leadership PC with local, state, and national educational agencies. It will include chapters that speak to facets of internal partnership development in higher education. It will also focus on external partnership development between educational leadership preparation programs and external agencies associated with leadership preparation. International educational leadership partnerships that have been established because of the creative endeavors of PCs will be addressed. PC partnerships in Egypt and Australia will inspire this section. Volume 2 will also engage in the exploration of various successful partnerships led by minority and indigenous PCs. *Innovative Partnership Practices in the Role of the Educational Leadership Program Coordinator* will conclude with an educational leadership partnership development model developed from a synthesis of the literature and the lessons learned regarding the PCs role in educational leadership preparation.

REFERENCES

Barnett, B. G., Hall, G. E., Berg, J. H., & Camarena, M. M. (2010). A typology of partnerships for promoting innovation. *Journal of School Leadership, 20*(1), 10–36. https://doi.org/10.1177/105268469900900602

Berdrow, I. (2010). King among kings: Understanding the role and responsibilities of the department chair in higher education. *Educational Management Administration and Leadership, 38*(4), 499–514. https://doi.org/10.1177/1741143210368146

Coleman, L. B., & Reames, E. (2020). The role of the educational leadership program coordinator (PC) in university-K–12 school district partnership development. *Journal of Research on Leadership Education, 15*(4), 241–260. https://doi.org/10.1177/1942775118803335

Crow, G. M., & Whiteman, R. S. (2016). Effective preparation program features: A literature review. *Journal of Research on Leadership Education, 11*(1), 120–148. https://doi.org/10.1177/1942775116634694

Hackmann, D. G., & McCarthy, M. M. (2011). *At a crossroads: The educational leadership professoriate in the 21st century. UCEA Leadership Series.* Information Age Publishing.

Hackmann, D. G., & Wanat, C. L. (2008). The role of the educational leadership program coordinator: A distributed leadership prospective. *International Journal of Educational Reform, 17*(1), 64–88. https://doi.org/10.1177/105678790801700105

Hackmann, D. G., & Wanat, C. L. (2016). Doing the work or sharing the work? The educational leadership program coordinator's role. *International Journal of Educational Reform, 25*(2), 100–124. https://doi.org/10.1177/105678791602500201

Kochan, F., Reames, E. H., Serafini, A., & Adair, A. C. (2021). Partnerships in educational leadership preparation and development: What works and what's next? In F. Kochan, E. H. Reames, & D. M. Griggs (Eds.), *Partnerships for leadership preparation and development: Facilitators, barriers, and models for change* (pp. 233–243). Information Age Publishing.

Kochan, F. K., & Mullen, C. A. (2003). An exploratory study of collaboration in higher education from women's perspectives. *Teaching Education, 14*(2), 153–167. https://doi.org/10.1080/1047621032000092959

Korach, S., Seidel, K., & del Carmen Salazar, M. (2012). Toward signature pedagogy for professional education: Collaborative partnerships in teacher and principal preparation. *Journal of Research on Leadership, 7*(2), 3–40.

Reames, E. H. (2016). From coordination to compliance: The program coordinator's changing role during redesign. *Planning and Changing, 47*(3/4), 263–277.

Reames, E. H., & Kochan, F. (2021). A model for future practice and research. In F. Kochan, E. H. Reames, & D. M. Griggs (Eds.), *Partnerships for leadership preparation and development: Facilitators, barriers, and models for change* (pp. 245–259). Information Age Publishing.

Ingle, W. K., Marshall, J. M., & Hackmann, D. G. (2020). The leaders of leadership preparation programs: A study of program coordinators at UCEA-member institutions. *Journal of Research on Leadership Education, 15*(2), 120–149. https://doi.org/10.1177/1942775118803334

Ingle, W. K., Worth, J. J., Marshall, J. M., & Hackmann, D. G. (2018). The incentives and costs of program coordinator in P–12 educational leadership programs. *Journal of Education Finance, 44*(2), 175–198. http://www.jstor.org/stable/45095013

Marshall, J. M., Ingle, W. K., & Hackmann, D. G. (2021). Roles and responsibilities of the educational leadership program coordinator in challenging times. *UCEA Review, 62*(1), 32–34. http://markfavazza.wpenginepowered.com/wp-content/uploads/2021/03/2021WinterReview_030121.pdf

Merriam-Webster. (n.d.). Evolving. In *Merriam-Webster.com dictionary*. Retrieval December 2, 2022, from https://merriam-webster.com
Merriam-Webster. (n.d.). Misunderstood. In *Merriam-Webster.com dictionary*. Retrieval December 2, 2022, from https://merriam-webster.com
Merriam-Webster. (n.d.). Ubiquitous. In *Merriam-Webster.com dictionary*. Retrieved December 2, 2022, from https://merriam-webster.com

SECTION I

CHAPTER 2

CONNECTING THE DOTS

Program Coordinator as School-District-University Partnership Facilitator

Karen D. Jones and Travis Lewis
East Carolina University

ABSTRACT

This chapter provides a visual framework of the role of Educational Leadership Program Coordinators (PCs) within the context of a school-district-university partnership. The example upon which this framework is based is the work of PCs within a College of Education at a large university in the southeastern United States. The Educational Leadership Department offers Masters of School Administration (MSA) and Doctor of Education (EdD) programs for K–12 leaders at the school and district levels. The programs serve a large, mainly rural area and partner with approximately 30 school districts and the individual school units therein.

The School-District-University Partnership Framework for Leadership Development outlined herein models the partnership between university leadership preparation programs, K–12 schools and school districts, and the PCs whose responsibilities include managing and fostering the partnership in service to the educator students training to become leaders. The chapter explains each aspect of the partnership from recruitment of students to the projects completed in districts to serve the needs of students, families, and staff to the graduation of highly qualified leaders with ongoing feedback from districts for improvement of the higher education programs and the partnership. PCs in this role work to bridge the gap between higher

---

Navigating the Ubiquitous, Misunderstood, and Evolving Role of the Educational Leadership Program Coordinator in Higher Education, pp. 17–32

education leadership preparation programs and K–12 school districts' needs. PCs navigate a unique position to ensure the needs of students, districts and the university are met. Structures and systems that support and hinder these partnerships are discussed.

INTRODUCTION

This chapter provides a visual framework of the role of Educational Leadership Program Coordinators (PCs) within the context of school-district-university partnerships. The role and duties of the PCs described herein are indicative of PCs at other institutions, as well. The university houses nine undergraduate colleges, a graduate school, and four professional schools. The university offers 16 doctoral degree programs, four professional degree programs, 76 master's degree programs, and 102 bachelor's degree programs. The programs discussed in this chapter are housed in the College of Education within the Department of Educational Leadership. The department offers a Master of School Administration (MSA) degree and an Educational Doctorate (EdD) with either a K–12 leadership focus or a higher education leadership concentration. The MSA degree also earns the graduate a K–12 Principal's License in the state. Students in the EdD program have the option of earning a K–12 Superintendent's License along with their degrees. This chapter focuses on the collaborations between local K–12 school districts and the university through the work of the PCs. Each program, the MSA and EdD, has a separate PC.

RESPONSIBILITIES OF THE PROGRAM COORDINATOR

The PCs in these programs are full-time tenured or tenure-track faculty who also have teaching, research, and service obligations. To help balance these standard faculty obligations with the additional responsibilities of program coordination, PCs are provided a stipend as well as a teaching course release each semester. The PCs are also provided with a budget to aid in marketing and outreach efforts to attract students to their programs. The following provides an overview of the primary responsibilities of the PC, which include the overseeing of admissions, advising, curriculum, development of new and existing programs, policies, student conduct and conflict, state and national accreditation, and partnerships.

The role of the PC is both fostered and hindered by their responsibilities in the department in addition to coordination. As active teaching faculty and researchers, the PCs are embedded in their respective programs. Given this, they maintain connections with faculty and students, providing PCs with a continued feel for the pulse of their program. Both PCs also chair EdD student dissertations and serve on additional dissertation committees, a rewarding but time-consuming task. These duties can also detract from the necessary PC responsibilities at various times in the academic year.

Admissions

Admission for each program begins with outreach to potential applicants. PCs solicit applicants through program graduates, partner school and district leaders, social media campaigns, program website promotion and updates, and conference attendance. PCs hold information sessions, often through videoconference, with interested candidates to provide an overview of the program structure and curriculum, admissions requirements, tuition costs, and other details relevant to candidates. Admissions itself involves a traditional online application that requires transcripts and reference letters along with an interview between the potential student and university faculty. The PCs work with graduate school admissions staff to establish admissions deadlines and ensure the online application meets the needs of each program, including what written response prompts are used. Soon after applications are received and the admissions deadline passes, PCs lead faculty involved in admissions decisions through a review of applications to identify applicants to interview. PCs work with graduate school admissions staff to notify applicants of denial to the program or of being selected for an interview. The PC then reaches out to applicants and program faculty to schedule interviews. Candidates for the MSA program engage in a 30-minute interview with two current program faculty. The interviews are virtual, and candidates are provided questions in advance so they can prepare. In the interim, the PC reviews and refines interview processes and interview questions with program faculty to provide insight into the appropriateness of applicants for admissions into their respective programs.

Once interviews are conducted, the PC reconvenes the faculty involved in admissions decisions to review interview results and make a determination regarding admission of interviewed applicants. Again, the PC works with graduate school admissions staff to notify applicants of the decision of the faculty. The PC may be asked of applicants denied admission for the rationale regarding the decision; conversely, the PC may be asked by faculty making admissions decisions to reach out to a student denied admission to encourage them to continue gaining school and leadership experience so that they may be a stronger candidate in the future.

Advising

Upon admission, the PC schedules and conducts orientation sessions with new students to prepare them for entry into the program. The PC serves as advisor for students currently in the program. Programmatic questions, personal concerns, and conflicts with faculty or peers are just a few of the more common advising issues that are presented to PCs by the students they advise. The EdD PC works with dissertation chairs to ensure student progress towards successful dissertation defense and degree completion. An EdD candidate has an option to earn a state superintendent's license along with the degree. The MSA PC tracks student success and course registration to ensure they are on track for both graduation and state principal licensure.

After successful admission to the program, the PC ensures retention through the course of study. During monthly program meetings, student concerns are discussed. If students are in danger of failing a course, the faculty discuss appropriate support and interventions to provide to these students to encourage success. At times, the PC may council an individual student to pause the program. There are times when a student may have multiple responsibilities from work, graduate school and family and need to take a break from school. There have been family tragedies or emergencies, or changes in job placement, that occur in the middle of the MSA or EdD. The PC counsels and advises students based on their individual circumstances and needs. It may be appropriate for the student to take a semester break from the program and return in good academic standing to continue studies when it better fits their schedule. The goal of the PC is for the student to have a successful course of study and graduate. Sometimes that path may require a pause so that the student can do their best work. The PC then works with the student for readmission to the program when appropriate.

Curriculum

The PCs also lead monthly curriculum meetings for their respective programs. These meetings include faculty who teach in the program along with the department chair. The purpose of the meetings is to discuss needed curriculum updates, consistency across courses with materials and assignments, and individual student concerns. The department and college have an equity focus, and PCs work with program faculty to support equity and diversity in course materials and texts through these monthly meetings to ensure that the leaders being produced are equipped to advocate for all students in their respective school or district. As such, PCs are crucially positioned to guide faculty through course and program redesigns (Hackman & Malin, 2016). Finally, the PCs are responsible for conducting annual program evaluations through the university to support and maintain accreditation.

Development of New and Existing Programs

There have been occasions when the PCs have worked to develop certificate programs to complement the traditional courses of study in the MSA or EdD. Creating these certificates involves course and curriculum review along with approval from appropriate university and state organizations. The PC works with faculty interested in developing these certificates to help them see their ideas brought to fruition.

The MSA and EdD both lead to state licensure for the principal or superintendent. It is an important part of the PC's role to ensure understanding of the licensure requirements and any changes at the state level that may impact the curriculum. For example, the state is in the process of revising the principal licensure process and standards. The MSA PC has participated in state level meetings to provide input on these changes and discuss with other PCs in the state how program curriculum may need to be adjusted to ensure compliance with updates. The PC serves as a liaison in this instance between the state licensing board and university faculty to coordinate dissemination of information and promote understanding of changes.

Policies

Both programs, the MSA and EdD, have handbooks and manuals for students on policies and procedures for the programs. These handbooks consolidate valuable information from multiple sources across the university that is relevant to graduate students in each program. The handbooks include information on items such as the code of conduct, academic integrity, attendance policies, and important deadlines. These handbooks and manuals also serve as advising resources with the program of study clearly outlined. The PCs work each year to update and revise the program manuals and handbooks.

Student Conduct and Conflict

Unfortunately, there are times the PC will work to manage conflict and intervene with suspected violations of the academic integrity policy. As the PC serves as the primary advisor for students in each program, they support students who may be struggling in different areas of the program. If a student has a conflict with an instructor or professor, they are encouraged to first discuss the concern with that instructor or professor. If the student feels they are not being heard or the matter has not resolved, they will bring the concern to the PC. The PC will listen to understand and help mediate, when appropriate, a mutually beneficial resolution for the student and faculty member.

There are occasions when a student violates the university's academic integrity policy through cheating, plagiarism, or another inappropriate action. Program faculty who suspect a violation provide evidence to the PC. The PC reviews the concern, contacts the student, and begins the process outlined by the university and administers any sanctions if necessary. It is important in such cases to ensure proper alignment with the university policies and procedures. These instances could result in a failing grade or removal from the program. The PC ensures the faculty and students are provided with the necessary information to navigate the process and maintain its integrity.

State and National Accreditations/Organizations

The PC works with university faculty to ensure the MSA and EdD programs maintain state and national accreditations. Data is gathered throughout the year for annual reports to the college and university. These reports reflect on goals and progress to ensure program quality. Also, every few years, larger reports are due to accreditation agencies. These reports consist of large amounts of data, both qualitative and quantitative, gathered from a variety of sources. The PCs also meet with representatives from the accrediting bodies to facilitate the processes and provide more detailed information than appears in the reports.

Partnerships

The PC is the point of contact for partnerships with schools and districts for the MSA and EdD programs. These partnerships are reciprocal in nature, as the schools and districts receive well-trained graduates from the programs for consideration as candidates for available education leadership positions; while the MSA and EdD programs continue to receive educator employees from the school-district partners ready to become students themselves again, thus sustaining the MSA and EdD programs. As called for by Reames (2016), this chapter further explores these partnerships between educational leadership programs within universities and K–12 school districts with emphasis on the role of the PC therein.

FRAMEWORK FOR LEADERSHIP DEVELOPMENT

To better understand the symbiotic relationship between university preparation programs and school districts to ensure a steady pipeline of quality leaders to guide K–12 schools, the following conceptual framework has been developed (see Figure 2.1). This section details the various key components of this framework and how each contributes to the larger system of the partnership with particular emphasis on the key role of the PC.

Figure 2.1

School-District-University Partnership Framework for Leadership Development

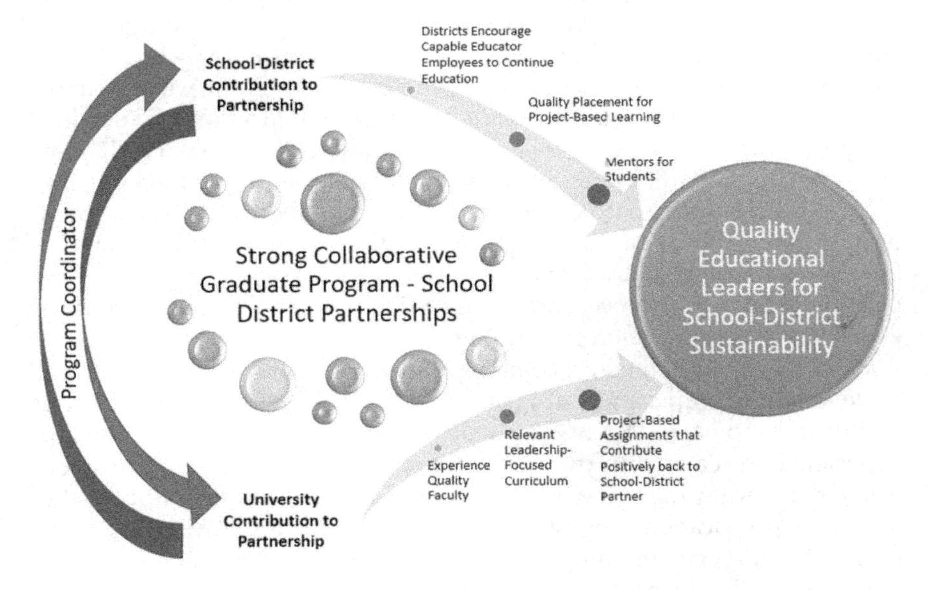

School-District Contribution Within the Framework for Leadership Development

For an effective partnership to be sustained, each partner must contribute to the relationship in their own respective manner. In a strong collaboration for educational leader development, K–12 schools and districts invest in the relationship by taking three key actions:

1. Encourage capable educator employees to continue their educations and become students themselves once again;

2. Provide quality placements for the employee-student to conduct project-based learning; and
3. Secure a mentor for the employee-student.

First, schools and districts must replenish the pipeline of potential leaders by scouring their pool of employees to identify those who demonstrate potential for continued leadership capacity, whether that be a teacher who seems capable of shifting into a school-based administrator, such as a principal or assistant principal, or a principal who seems capable of shifting into a district-level leadership role, such as a coordinator, director, or assistant/associate superintendent. As current school and district leadership ascertains which employees are well-suited for continued leadership growth and opportunity, they should encourage these employees to continue their educations by enrolling in the partner university's preparation program for educational leaders. Teachers and other staff interested in school-based leadership would enroll in a principal preparation program, while current school administrators would enroll in an advanced educational leadership program, such as a doctoral program in educational leadership (EdD) for example. Depending upon the resources available within each school district, enticement for these employees to continue their educations could include the possibility of a salary increase, tuition assistance, textbook reimbursement, assurance of securing a position commiserate to their intended training, a leave of absence, and/or time off for class meetings that conflict with current employment responsibilities.

Once the identified educator employee becomes a student again, quality leadership preparation programs work collaboratively with schools and districts to have students apply theory to practice and gain firsthand experience in leadership through project-based learning. Project-based learning is a win-win for the university-district-school partnership. For the university preparation program, project-based learning provides students with real-world activities and experiences that cannot be simulated in the classroom, aiding in exponential growth of leadership students. For schools and districts, project-based learning provides significant assistance towards advancing and completing improvement projects that may go unaddressed otherwise without the leadership and effort of the employee-student. Additionally, by collaborating with university programs and the employee students therein, schools and districts "have the opportunity to leverage the learning and momentum from the partnership to drive improvements in district-based principal development efforts" (Wang et al., 2022, p. 5).

Finally, as the employee-student transitions into an internship in conjunction with the university preparation program or into actual leadership job placement, the school or district should secure a high quality, experienced mentor who is thoroughly knowledgeable of the duties that the employee-student will be assuming in this new capacity. The mentor should be genuinely invested in the employee-student's growth and development and provided with the time and opportunity to coach them accordingly (Clayton et al., 2013).

University Preparation Program Contribution Within the Framework for Leadership Development

Just as schools and districts must contribute to sustaining the partnership, so too must university leadership preparation programs. In a strong collaboration for educational leader development, university leadership preparation programs invest in the relationship by taking three key actions:

1. Hire quality faculty with the requisite experience and skills to effectively train and support aspiring educational leaders;
2. Develop and utilize a relevant leadership-focused curriculum; and
3. Provide quality project-based assignments that contribute positively to the school-district partner.

In support of the partnership, university preparation programs should hire faculty whose primary strength is the ability to effectively develop aspiring educational leaders. This necessitates utilizing faculty who have served as practitioners and can provide guidance to students from firsthand experience as an educational leader themselves. The credibility of the university preparation program within the view of the school-district partnership is contingent upon this condition being met.

Upon hiring experienced, skilled faculty, university preparation programs must develop and utilize a curriculum that is relevant to aspiring educational leaders. Curriculum content that excludes the necessary skill development to prepare students to lead school or district staff in meeting today's challenges and opportunities will inevitably fail their partners in sustaining the pipeline of quality educational leaders.

With the right faculty and curriculum in place, university preparation programs should incorporate project-based assignments in educational leadership that challenge students to apply theory into practice. While school-district partners endeavor to provide a quality placement for such assignments, university partners should develop these assignments in a manner that nurtures the partnership by contributing positively back to the school or district placement. Project-based learning should benefit the student by providing them with hands-on experience, should benefit the school or district partner by providing them with assistance in addressing the project, and should benefit the university preparation program by providing an opportunity for student growth and application of learning that can otherwise only be simulated in the classroom.

The Program Coordinator's Contribution Within the Framework for Leadership Development

While the School-District-University Partnership Framework for Leadership Development clearly outlines the key contributions of each partner in collaboratively developing quality educational leaders, such a partnership would not be effective and sustainable without the critical role played by the PC. The PC contributes significantly to uniting the efforts of the partner organizations towards their common goal. By serving as the communication link between the university and the school-district, the PC helps ensure sustainability of the partnership by bridging the gap between these two organizations. The PC helps connect the proverbial dots for each partner so that their respective contributions to the development of educational leaders is as seamless as possible. The PC also serves as a key conduit of information to the educator employees in helping them navigate the program and the partnership embedded within the program. Without the leadership of the PC to guide and sustain the program and its partnerships, educator employees, university preparation programs, and schools would flounder in a loosely organized, inconsistent program of study riddled with conflicting information, a lack of common purpose, and ultimately poor leadership development.

Each of the specific contributions of the partners examined within the framework for leadership development will now be examined while considering the role of the program coordinator relative to the contribution.

SCHOOL-DISTRICT CONTRIBUTION TO PARTNERSHIP

Districts Encourage Capable Educator Employees to Continue Education

Visionary school and district leaders engage in succession planning to advance the organization and ensure continuity in purpose. Turnover in leadership is inevitable, whether due to advancement, resignation to pursue other professional opportunities, retirement, personal or health concerns, or ineffectiveness. However, effective school and district leaders understand that identifying and nurturing potential leaders is necessary to fill leadership voids as they arise. From within their own ranks are capable teachers and other school and district staff who have demonstrated the capacity to lead and share their common vision.

To this end, school districts within the service area of the university have partnered for decades with the MSA and EdD programs of the university to provide the leadership training and skill development for their educator employees who aspire to become school administrators and leaders. A common set of beliefs about school improvement and student success must be reaffirmed or recalibrated from time to time between district and school leadership and the faculty of the MSA and EdD programs to ensure that the most up-to-date research in school and district leadership practices are applied in both practice and in the teaching of these aspiring leaders. Program coordinators work to ensure this collective understanding by keeping lines of communication open, sharing constructive feedback with all partners, and providing opportunities for collaboration between program faculty and school-district leadership. As a result, school-district leadership entrusts program faculty with the preparation of their educator employees to become leaders themselves (Turnbull et al., 2021).

School-district leaders promote the university's MSA and EdD programs among their educator employees in several ways. In collaboration with PCs, they host program information sessions and distribute flyers or emails with key information and deadlines about the programs. Some school-district leaders request to establish a cohort of employee educators who will pursue and complete the program together. This includes hosting program faculty and the cohort of employee educators for in-person classes. School-district leaders who have the means may further entice program enrollment by providing funding for textbooks, tuition reimbursement, assurance of promotions, classroom coverage, or a substitute if needed for program class meetings or opportunities to engage in project-based learning.

Quality Placement for Project-Based Learning

School-district leaders understand that their university partners can provide educator employees with training in leadership skill development, exposure to research on school leadership, and experiences that simulate the work of school or district leaders; however, university program faculty are limited in their ability to provide real-world, hands-on opportunities for applying leadership skills in practice to their educator employees. School-district partners step in to collaborate with the MSA and EdD program to provide project-based learning opportunities to their educator employees. School or district sites for conducting project-based learning are identified by the school-district partner in consultation with the MSA and EdD program and with the employee educator. While often this may be the existing workplace of the employee educator, it is recommended that the employee educator garner experience in distinct kinds of settings and in distinct roles to broaden their leadership experience. For example, a middle school teacher may benefit from pursing a project-based learning opportunity in high school leadership, or a district student services director may diversify their background knowledge by addressing a district finance project with their chief financial officer (CFO). While the MSA or EdD program faculty can recommend the type of project-based learning that may best challenge the educator employee's growth, the school-district partner is ideally positioned to identify the based placement within their available settings for the educator employee to pursue the project and make the experience positive for all involved a true win-win.

Mentors for Students

While instruction in leadership skills and practices, combined with project-based learning, are critical to the development of aspiring education leaders, mentors are a necessary component to their success in honing their craft in practice (Herman et al., 2022). School-district partners support the educator employees enrolled in the MSA and EdD programs by assigning them mentors in the leadership positions to which the educator employees aspire. Often, internship experiences are the beginning of these mentor-mentee relationships for the educator employee and their internship placement supervisor. Internships help educator employees blend the theoretical and research-based content of their coursework with the practical day-to-day experiences of leadership. The mentor is the hands-on guide for the educator employee through the internship experience.

With the MSA and EdD programs, so that there are clear expectations established, the educator employee as the mentee, the workplace mentor within the school-district, and the university supervisor all sign a letter of agreement whereby their respective roles are clearly outlined and understood. While the mentor assigned is their official mentor, educator employees often develop unofficial mentors within their schools or districts. If this is a positive and supportive relationship, most school-district leaders welcome and encourage experienced leaders to demonstrate a vested interest in the development of new and aspiring leaders.

UNIVERSITY CONTRIBUTION TO PARTNERSHIP

Experienced Quality Faculty

Faculty in the MSA and EdD programs in this case are unique in that they all have practitioner experiences in K–12 leadership. They bring not only the research and theory about successful leadership in K–12 settings but also their own experiences and expertise in a variety of school and district settings. The full-time faculty's research has been published in numerous refereed journal articles, book chapters, and books and presented at national and international conferences in the field of educational leadership. The part-time faculty teaching in the programs have proven themselves as outstanding K–12 school and district leaders in their own right. This experienced, quality faculty builds a curriculum relevant to school leader practitioners.

Relevant Leadership-Focused Curriculum

The MSA and EdD programs are focused on developing scholarly practitioners. The goal is to develop leaders who use research to guide practical applications that build successful school experiences for students, staff, and families. The MSA program is offered in cohorts and consists of a set of courses that align closely with the state's principal licensure requirements. Course content includes strategic planning, problem-solving, instructional leadership, managerial leadership, organizational theory and development, and educational leadership skill development and application. MSA students are enrolled in either online only cohorts or hybrid cohorts that meet both in-person and online. The MSA principal licensure component requires a year-long administrative internship in addition to coursework.

The EdD program concentration of K–12 Administration allows students to be engaged in coursework relevant to their field and professional goals. The EdD program is also offered in cohorts that meet both online and in-person. The dissertation requirements of the EdD program are inspired by a program redesign which followed the principles of the Carnegie Project on the Education Doctorate (CPED). Students engage with stakeholders to examine a focus of practice in their schools or districts that deals with inequities in the educational systems. The students work to study and implement strategies to possibly improve the educational outcomes for students, teachers, and families.

Project-Based Assignments that Contribute Positively Back to School-District Partner

Service Leadership Projects (SLPs) are a highlight of the MSA program. These projects are part of the portfolio requirements submitted upon graduation for the candidate's state principal license. Students complete six SLPs during the two-year program, each with a different focus aligned to the state principal standards. Topics of the SLPs include: (1) positive impact on student learning and development, (2) teacher empowerment and leadership, (3) community involvement and management, (4) organizational management, (5) school culture and safety, and (6) school improvement. In each SLP, students collaborate with relevant stakeholders in their schools and districts to examine a need related to the project's topic. The student gathers data related to the area of need, confers with stakeholders, and reviews research for potential solutions. The student then implements the solution and measures its impact. In this way, MSA students do not simply read about the theories of engaging families and communities in K–12 schools, but they put research into action through implementing and facilitating community engagement activities.

These projects positively impact the school and community. By taking actions such as creating a Parent Teacher Organization (PTO) or implementing instructional rounds, MSA students are learning through actions that make an impact on others. These projects often lead to long-term changes in schools and communities (Lenz & Larmer, 2020). Often, the events or activities are replicated year after year, improving teaching, learning, and community support.

Students earning an EdD in K–12 Leadership also have an opportunity to earn a superintendent's license. This license also requires a portfolio of evidence, not a test score, for certification. EdD students pursuing the superintendent's license complete District Service Leadership Projects (DSLPs). These projects are similar to the MSA SLPs but occur at a district level rather than at the school level. Topics for the DSLPs are: (1) strategic leadership, (2) instructional leadership, (3) district culture, (4) human resources development, and (5) managerial leadership.

These projects are completed by MSA and EdD students and positively impact the relationship between the university and district partners. School leaders in regional partnership districts are eager to have students from the university programs in their districts. They know that students will do work and put into place activities and processes that will support students, staff, and families. As part of the admission to the program, students have school and district leaders sign letters of support that they understand the student is beginning the program and that the school and district will provide actionable space for the SLPs and DSLPs to be completed.

QUALITY EDUCATIONAL LEADERS FOR PARTNER SCHOOL DISTRICTS

School and district leaders have multiple responsibilities including school and student success. The difficult job of educational leadership has multiple facets and demands and can differ in different states and different regions. Creating a school-district-university partnership allows for a mutually beneficial situation by developing leaders who can meet specific needs (Gordon et al., 2016). This chapter outlined the process of creating one such partnership that produces successful school and district leaders. Within the context of the partnership, the invaluable role of the PC has been emphasized. The time commitment of PCs in support of programmatic responsibilities, including partnership support, is immense (Hackman & Wanat, 2016; Ingle et al., 2018). However, the PC's personal experience as a K–12 leader within school and district settings helps to efficiently facilitate partnership development and success (Coleman, 2016).

The PCs in the MSA and EdD programs cultivate and maintain these partnerships. This is an iterative, formative process that continually strives for improved communication, refined curriculum, and enhanced collaboration with the common goal of producing quality educational leaders. To this end, the university provides high quality instruction, faculty, and project-based assignments. The districts provide quality candidates, opportunities for site-based project learning, and mentors. This partnership, grown and refined by PCs in the MSA and EdD programs, requires feedback from all stakeholders. The PCs meet with district leaders to hear their suggestions for improvement and to explore what aspects of the partnership are going well. District leaders provide forecasting models for the university to help plan the number of school leaders they anticipate needing in coming years. The university can then target outreach and recruitment efforts in those regions.

The educational leadership department at the university convenes an advisory council throughout the year. This council consists of program faculty, school district leaders, students, and recent graduates. This council provides structured opportunities for feedback for both the university and school districts on the successes and areas of growth for the partnership in order to provide quality learning opportunities for students. This advisory council is the continuation of the university-district partnership even after students have graduated. The connection to building strong school leaders for the success of students, staff and families does not end with graduation.

REFERENCES

Clayton, J. K., Sanzo, K. L., & Myran, S. (2013). Understanding mentoring in leadership development: Perspectives of district administrators and aspiring leaders. *Journal of Research on Leadership Education*, *8*(1), 77–96. https://doi.org/10.1177/1942775112464959

Coleman, L. B. (2016). *University educational leadership program coordinators' perceptions of university-school-district partnership development* [Doctoral dissertation, Auburn University]. http://hdl.handle.net/10415/5187

Gordon, S. P., Oliver, J., & Solis, R. (2016). Successful innovations in educational leadership preparation. *International Journal of Educational Leadership Preparation, 11*(2). https://files.eric.ed.gov/fulltext/EJ1123995.pdf

Hackmann, D. G., & Malin, J. R. (2016). If you build it, will they come? Educational leadership program coordinators' perceptions of principal preparation redesign in Illinois. *International Journal of Educational Reform, 25*(4), 338–360. https://doi.org/10.1177/105678791602500401

Hackmann, D. G., & Wanat, C. L. (2016). Doing the work or sharing the work? The educational leadership program coordinator's role. *International Journal of Educational Reform, 25*(2), 100–124. https://doi.org/10.1177/105678791602500201

Herman, R., Wang, E. L., Woo, A., Gates, S. M., Berglund, T., Schweig, J., Andrew, M., & Todd, I. (2022). Redesigning university principal preparation programs: A systemic approach for change and sustainability. *Rand Principal Preparation Series, 3*(2). https://www.wallacefoundation.org/knowledge-center/Documents/redesigning-university-principal-preparation-programs-brief.pdf

Ingle, W. K., Worth, J. J., Marshall, J. M., & Hackman, D. G. (2018). The incentives and costs of program coordination in P-12 educational leadership programs. *Journal of Education Finance, 44*(2), 175–198. http://www.jstor.org/stable/45095013

Lenz, B., & Larmer, J. (2020). Project-based learning that makes a difference. *Educational Leadership, 77*(6), 66–70.

Reames, E. H. (2016). From coordination to compliance: The program coordinator's changing role during redesign. *Planning and Changing, 47*(3), 263–278. https://www.proquest.com/scholarly-journals/coordination-compliance-program-coordinator-s/docview/1917343789/se-2

Thessin, R. A., Clayton, J. K., & Jamison, K. (2020). Profiles of the administrative internship: The mentor/intern partnership in facilitating leadership experiences. *Journal of Research on Leadership Education, 15*(1), 28–55. https://doi.org/10.1177/1942775118770778

Turnbull, B., Worley, S., & Palmer, S. (2021). *Strong pipelines, strong principals: A guide for leveraging federal sources to fund principal pipelines*. Policy Studies Associates, Education Counsel, and the Wallace Foundation. https://www.wallacefoundation.org/knowledge-center/Documents/strong-pipelines-strong-principals.pdf

Wang, E. L., Gates, S. M., & Herman, R. (2022). District partnership with university principal preparation programs: A summary of findings for school district leaders. *Rand Principal Preparation Series, 3*(4). https://www.wallacefoundation.org/knowledge-center/Documents/district-partnerships-with-university-principal-preparation-programs.pdf

CHAPTER 3

BRIDGING THE GAP BETWEEN HIGHER EDUCATION AND K–12

The Role of Program Coordinators in Educational Leadership Programs

Isela Peña
University of Texas at El Paso

Rebecca Schlosser
Sul Ross State University–Alpine

ABSTRACT

In 2016, the Texas Education Agency (TEA) changed principal certification requiring a performance measure, the Performance Assessment for School Leaders (PASL), and requiring all Education Preparation Programs (EPPs) to reapply to offer the new *Principal as Instructional Leader Certificate.* When reapplying to offer the new certificate, it was mandatory for EPPs to include the TEA's framework of six pillar assignments. These re-certification requirements fueled EPPs to revise curriculum. Subsequently, the TEA offered a grant opportunity requiring EPP and K-12 partnerships to offer a year-long, full-time residency for principal candidates. This expanded the educational leadership preparation program coordinator's role to include developing K–12 partnerships. Against this backdrop, utilizing duoethnography, this chapter examines the program coordinator's role in university-district

Navigating the Ubiquitous, Misunderstood, and Evolving Role of the Educational Leadership Program Coordinator in Higher Education, pp. 33–59

partnerships looking at: partnership inception, collaborative efforts, relationship-building, role and responsibilities of the coordinator, and leadership commitments. Both coauthors served as program coordinators of Sul Ross State University's Educational Leadership Program and, as such, the chapter is situated in this context. We explore our shared experience to offer insight into this critical role in educational leadership programs.

Key Words: principal preparation, program coordinator, educational leadership, university/K–12 partnerships

The role of principal, perhaps more so today than at any other time, is critical to the new path being charted for public education as we come out of the collective COVID-19 crisis. Recognizing that principals are the second factor in determining educational outcomes of students (Grissom, et al., 2021), it is critical that they be properly trained, specifically to lead the charge of instructional leadership. Within principal preparation programs, we have seen a rise in university partnerships with K–12 institutions to create a more formal structure of full-time residencies, allowing for authentic mentoring. These total immersion residencies move away from completion of isolated tasks to a comprehensive approach that reflects the real-world demands of K–12 campus leaders. Within this ecosystem, the educational leadership program coordinator's role has expanded.

In this chapter, we aim to share our experience as program coordinators (PCs) in the Educational Leadership Program at Sul Ross State University (SRSU), a role we each played at separate times. We examine the educational leadership PC role in the university-district partnership development process. From partnership inception to implementation of collaborative efforts to nurturing relationships between the university and the K–12 partners, this chapter will look at the nuances of the educational leadership PC's official and unofficial function and leadership commitments within the larger context of the university structure and dynamic nature of leadership preparation requirements.

We utilized duoethnography to explore our shared experience, serving as PCs, to offer insight into this essential role in educational leadership programs. As a methodology, duoethnography allowed us to "turn the inquiry lens on ourselves" (Sawyer & Norris, 2015, p. 1) and explore and make meaning of our own experiences as educational leadership PCs, noting the similarities and differences. The role of PC served as the context for meaning making. In the spirit of duoethnography, the purpose of this chapter was not to generalize about the educational leadership PC experience or "to profess but rather to learn and change" (Sawyer & Norris, 2015, p. 2) through the conversation that ensued in writing this chapter. As we dialogued about our experience, we realized that we had been engaging in conversations about the educational leadership PC role since we began the university/K–12 partnership initiative. Throughout the duration of that time, we had been asking ourselves questions about the alignment of the university structure, systems, and curriculum to the new twenty-first century authentic residency experience. In doing so, we challenged our assumptions and beliefs (Sawyer & Norris, 2013) around educational leadership, pushing ourselves to reframe the day-to-day PC operations to a more systems approach (Senge, 2010).

We structured the chapter into sections around topics that we felt were most relevant to the role of the educational leadership PC. Organized by core ideas, each section begins with an overview of the topic, content that stemmed from our conversations, and within the context of the SRSU Educational Leadership Program. We have utilized boxes to frame these core ideas to highlight the general message within the relevant section. Each section is followed by our individual comments, structured as dialogue between the two of us, where we offer our key commentary on the specific topic. Hereinafter, we refer to the educational leadership program coordinator role as either educational leadership PC or the PC, utilizing the longer version where it makes the role clearer to the reader. This helps to distinguish between the K–12 coordinator role which, while not the focus of this chapter, is a key partner in this work. As a brief introduction, we provide a short profile of our professional backgrounds as related to the educational leadership PC role.

Researcher Profiles

Rebecca: I am a professor and director of principal preparation and outreach programs at Sul Ross State University in Alpine, Texas. SRSU is a Hispanic-serving, public university in West Texas near Big Bend National Park and the U.S.-Mexico border region of Texas. Prior to serving as the director, I was the program coordinator of the SRSU Educational Leadership Program from 2016–2019 and have worked in the SRSU program for 17 years.

Isela: I am an assistant professor at the University of Texas at El Paso (UTEP), a Hispanic-serving, R-1 public university located on the US-Mexico border. Prior to joining UTEP, I served as an assistant professor and program coordinator of the Sul Ross State University Educational Leadership Program from 2019–2021. I first met Dr. Schlosser when I was a masters student in the SRSU Educational Leadership Program. Since then, she has served as my mentor, my work colleague, and my friend. Our relationship is built on mutual trust and respect for what each of us bring to the table. This has facilitated the critical analysis of the program coordinator role.

SECTION 1—THE REDESIGN OF THE PRINCIPAL CERTIFICATION PROCESS IN TEXAS

> Core Idea
>
> State-mandated changes to the principal certification process in Texas, completed in 2019, added a performance measure to the principal practicum experience which fueled the need for university/K–12 partnerships.

The TEA Redesign

In 2014, the Texas Legislature revised the principal standards (Tex. Admin. Code §149.2001, 2014), which resulted in the TEA creating: (1) a more rigorous test with construct questions; (2) a rigorous performance measure with three campus improvement tasks; and (3) a new principal certification process that embedded the new principal standards into curricula requirements for all principal preparation program providers, commonly referred to as Educator Preparation Programs (EPPs) (TEA, n.d.). The new principal certification process to obtain the new *Texas Principal as Instructional Leader Certification* included not only success on the revised standardized test, the TExES 268, but also completion of a performance measure, the TExES 368 Performance Assessment for School Leaders (PASL).

> Core Idea
>
> The redesign of the principal certification process to include a performance measure prompted the TEA to initiate the principal residency grant to promote effective university and K–12 partnerships..

The Principal Residency Grant

After the redesign of the principal certification process, the TEA funded the Principal Residency Grant (PRG) with Title II monies to promote effective university/K–12 partnerships (TEA, 2021). A key component is a full-time, year-long residency, in which residents engage in authentic campus-based leadership experiences. Residents may not have significant classroom responsibilities during this period. The 2022–23 PRG is now beginning Cycle 6 and has become highly competitive. The grant is awarded to the K–12 school district but requires a TEA-approved EPP partner. Prior to starting, the K–12 principal mentors, K–12 coordinator, and educational leadership PC attend the TEA grant training to orient partners to grant responsibilities. The TEA orientation provides a framework to build systems to solidify the partnership.

> Core Idea
>
> The rigorous application process for the competitive, principal residency grant ensures that participants model exemplary residency programs.

The TEA's Role

The application for the TEA principal residency grant is a rigorous, two-phase process. First, EPPs are required to apply with the TEA to be an approved partner. Then, the K–12 districts complete a TEA application and interview. The applications emphasize: (1) effective collaboration of the EPP and K–12 partners; (2) authentic residency experience; (3) alignment to the TEA's *Effective Schools Framework* (Effective Schools Framework, n.d.) school improvement model; (4) recruitment and selection of highly qualified candidates; (5) residency design; (6) effective coursework; (7) residency completion, career advancement, performance outcomes; and, (8) ongoing monitoring with a focus on practice and continuous improvement to sustain the leadership pipeline (TEA, 2021). The educational leadership PC assists the K–12 coordinator in this grant-writing process. SRSU qualified as an approved EPP for the PRG Cycle 1, 2018–2019, and was awarded the grant with a K–12 district near El Paso, Texas. Since then, SRSU has expanded their K–12 partnerships to include grant and non-grant partners and has five partner districts. SRSU has partnered successfully for each PRG cycle.

> Core Idea
>
> Before awarding Texas EPPs the approval to offer the new *Principal as Instructional Leader Certificate*, the TEA required the EPPs to apply and provide evidence of rigorous curricula that met the new legislative standards.

Application to be an Approved EPP

When the TEA announced the new certification process and PRG, it also informed Texas EPPs that evidence of strict curricula requirements must be included with the application for the new *Princpal as Instructional Leader Certificate*. No EPP could continue without the TEA's approval of their curriculum. The TEA issued guidelines for the six pillar assignments aligned to the new principal standards and offered a workshop to orient educational leadership PCs to the new curricula requirements. The Texas Council for Professors of Educational Administration (TCPEA) also conducted a three-day work session in which EPP professors from around the state collaborated in writing the six pillar assignments.

Core Idea

The PASL Tasks have fueled the need for university and K–12 grant and non-grant partnerships.

The Three PASL Tasks and the Change Process for School Improvement

There are three tasks in the PASL. These tasks must be completed on a K–12 campus. The first task, *Problem Solving in the Field*, requires principal candidates to identify and resolve a significant academic problem on their campuses. The second task, *Supporting Continuous Professional Development*, requires principal candidates to plan and facilitate professional development on their campuses. The third task, *Creating a Collaborative Culture*, requires principal candidates to form a team of stakeholders and work with them to improve instruction, student achievement, and school culture. Without partnerships, university programs have long struggled in translating theoretical school improvement models into experiential knowledge. By requiring the PASL, the TEA made it essential that EPPs recruit and nurture K–12 partnerships to ensure principal candidates can successfully complete the PASL tasks (ETS, n.d.). The SRSU program updated to these 21st century standards by embedding the TEA's Effective Schools Framework (ESF) school improvement model into all coursework and designed the residency as an action research project.

Section 1 Discussion—PCs Spearheading the Change Process

Core Idea

University programs can get stuck teaching outdated curricula and educational leadership PCs often need motivation and vision to spearhead the change process.

Rebecca: Professors seldom change curriculum if their certification passing rates are in the acceptable range (Guerra & Pazey, 2016). Those rates typically dip when the standards and tests change without some curricula changes to realign. This redesign was different because the TEA evaluated curricula and failed some EPP's programs. For me, the TEA's vision and curricula mandate fueled a comprehensive overhaul of the SRSU program. When I attended the TCPEA workshop and collaborated on writing the pillars, it was inspirational and served as a springboard for the idea of the action research project. We know our curricula design is aligned to the TEA's vision because the TEA gave us a 4/4 evaluation score on the design, we have consistently been approved by the TEA for the PRG, and currently we have a 100% pass rate on the TExES 268 and 368 (PASL).

Isela: Stepping into the PC role after you had rewritten the curriculum and aligned the courses to the new principal certification requirements, I took for granted the challenge of such an undertaking. However, I recognized that I benefitted from your efforts in being able to step into a program that was already well-structured. I also witnessed how the students directly benefitted from this overhaul as evidenced by their growth in knowledge and skills from the beginning to the end of the program and, ultimately, in their ability to pass the new certification exams. It is important to note that the SRSU redesign did not end once the TEA approved our program as an EPP. We continued to work by revisiting the curriculum each semester, considering the experiences of the faculty teaching the courses, and reflecting on student feedback. We worked together to implement necessary changes, in some cases, in real-time. Our ability to be critical about our coursework and curriculum stemmed from the trust that existed between you and me, and our willingness to be honest about what was and was not working. In the numerous conversations we had about the curriculum, we anchored to the certification standards, exam requirements, and the experience of the students, which removed any unwillingness to implement changes. This continuous improvement cycle was not centered on us as individuals, but on the program.

SECTION 2—THE SRSU EDUCATIONAL LEADERSHIP PROGRAM

> Core Idea
>
> SRSU aligned its principal preparation program to the PASL Tasks by embedding an action research project to ensure its principal candidates could successfully complete the certification process.

The Action Research Project

From 2017 to 2019, the SRSU program was re-written to ensure that its principal candidates would be effective 21st century instructional school leaders and would be able to successfully complete the certification process. As a result, content courses and the year-long practicum focus on an action research project. Residents gather project artifacts throughout the program and showcase their portfolios at the end of the program. The action research projects provide real-world experiences in facilitating campus improvements.

The action research project requirements were carefully crafted to align to the PASL and the ESF campus improvement model. Candidates begin by learning how to access their campus data software system and gather, read, and analyze student achievement and other data to identify and prioritize major problems/challenges on their campus. Working with a principal mentor and university field supervisor, the candidate selects a high-priority student achievement problem to improve. As candidates progress through the program, they continue their action research by (1) forming a collaborative team of teachers who are integral to the academic problem selected, (2) facilitating the team's root cause analysis, (3) facilitating the team's targeted improvement plan, (4) facilitating the team's professional development on effective instructional strategies, and (5) providing continuous monitoring and retraining during implementation.

> Core Idea
>
> The student's portfolio defense not only serves as a summative assessment but also is an opportunity for the principal candidate to reflect upon the knowledge and skills mastered in the program.

The Portfolio Defense

In the final courses of the university program, candidates reflect on their action research findings; these are compiled in their program portfolios. Candidates defend their portfolios to a committee comprised of the K–12 coordinator, educational leadership PC, university instructors, field supervisors, and principal mentors. Without the partnership, the action research project would be impossible to complete. Candidates would not have access to the necessary data and would not have the authority to form teacher teams or conduct professional development. By creating K–12 partnerships, the educational leadership PC ensures candidates can successfully become certified and gain real-world experience.

> Core Idea
>
> There are always obstacles and barriers to change. Understanding the school culture is the guide to putting systems in place to address that resistance to change.

Obstacles and Barriers to Creating the University Program

The goal of the university/K–12 partnership is to create a collaborative culture to develop and sustain an effective principal pipeline of high-performing, twenty-first century campus instructional leaders. To effectuate this pipeline, the educational leadership PC must be prepared to confront the natural resistance to change. In writing about creating a collaborative culture for effective professional learning communities (PLCs), Dufour and Marzano (2011) have noted:

> There is growing recognition that the process represents a powerful strategy for improving student achievement but bringing it to life in the real world of schools remains difficult. Educators are asked to change long-standing assumptions, expectations, and habits regarding schooling. They are asked to relate to colleagues and students in new ways. They are called upon to abandon the tradition of pursuing the latest educational fad and instead are asked to sustain a commitment to a very different way of operating schools-forever. (p. 67)

There are some obstacles and barriers we repeatedly encountered in the last six years servings as PCs and working to continuously improve and sustain the educational leadership program at SRSU. These obstacles are catalogued hereafter.

- Size: large universities have several obstacles because of the difficulty in getting many professors' agreement on substantive curricula changes.
- Focus on research and writing not teaching: the cooperation of tenured professors to agree to make substantive curricula

changes is difficult because their time and attention are focused, not on teaching, but on researching and grant-writing.

- Academic freedom: because of the legal protection of academic freedom in universities, it is difficult for the educational leadership PC to enlist support to change curriculum in tenured professors' courses.
- Culture: while the K–12 curriculum is written by the Texas State Board of Education, in universities, the concept of academic freedom is so deeply engrained that the culture of teaching must be addressed.
- Lack of TEA guidance: in issuing its mandate for curricula change, the TEA did not provide (a) release tests, (b) PASL exemplars, (c) sufficient examples of the pillars, or (d) sufficient workshops. This guidance has since been provided but having it from the outset would have obviated some of the resistance to change.

Modern change process theory assumes resistance to change and provides helpful methods of approach including confronting the need for change, setting clear expectations, creating a safe environment for dialogue, and creating structures and systems to support the change and provide effective communication (Dufour et al., 2016). At SRSU, these obstacles were addressed in a concerted plan to facilitate the necessary curricula changes swiftly and effectively. Because SRSU is small, resistance to change was slight. The path selected was for the educational leadership PC to receive a stipend to write new courses. The old courses were retired, and professors were given new courses based on their expertise. Trainings and book reading sessions were conducted and a Blackboard Sandbox of new courses was made available to provide professors with an overview of the entire program. Curriculum and field supervisor monthly meetings were instituted to stimulate dialogue and collaboration. Professors are required to submit proposed curricula changes to the Curriculum Committee to avoid learning gaps. Applying professors are asked to agree to this process. There are other methods to overcome these obstacles that are based on the context and organizational capacity.

Candidates without the structure and support system of the university/K–12 partnerships struggle to complete the PASL. The only candidates that have not needed substantial partnership support in our program are those who are working as instructional coaches or probationary administrators. They can complete the work for the PASL because their jobs give them the authority needed. Candidates who remain classroom teachers while seeking the degree often do not have the necessary authority to obtain the data, form the PLC/data team, and implement improvement and professional development plans with teams of teachers. Reflecting on SRSU's effectiveness in developing K–12 partnerships, it cannot be over emphasized that having an aligned curriculum and well-trained faculty is the foundation for that success.

Section 2 Discussion—Importance of the Portfolio Defenses

Rebecca: The highlight of the program for me is the portfolio defense. While orientation, trainings, workshops, calendars, logs, reflections, and observation reports are all effective communications, the portfolio surpasses them in conveying the rigor and depth of the action research project. When stakeholders hear residents reflect on their transformative growth, it makes a tremendous impact and solidifies the partnership. With Stephen Covey's idea of "begin with the end in mind," we have new partners and university personnel attend the earliest showcase possible. The comments I have received from stakeholders support my conclusion that this event, more than any other, assists them in understanding the partnership's impact.

Isela: As I reflect on what you have shared, solidifying the partnership relationship requires the PC to manage the change process within all the parties involved—principal mentors, instructors, and other relevant district leaders—in preparing the principal candidates. With the changes to the principal preparation, the university faculty have had to adjust by revamping curriculum and other elements of their programs, but K–12 partners have had to adjust to an increased level of involvement in preparing future principals. The K–12 partners' participation at the portfolio defenses allows them to see the impact of their active participation in the principal candidates' journey in becoming an instructional leader. It is a culminating event where the principal candidates showcase their growth in terms of knowledge and skills and as we have talked about before, it can serve as an informal interview. The K–12 partners have an opportunity to hear about the candidate's growth, but more importantly, see the artifacts of the action research that the student implemented at the campus. However, all this cannot happen if the PC does not engage with the partners in developing the relationship, both through the grant and in non-grant funded partnerships. Managing the change process helps the PC create a more effective environment for relationships to flourish. Within this ecosystem of university/K-12 partnerships, the educational leadership PC is charged with establishing the culture not only within the program itself for students to thrive, but also within the external space where the interactions of the partners occur.

SECTION 3—THE EDUCATIONAL LEADERSHIP PROGRAM COORDINATOR ROLE AND RESPONSIBILITIES VIS-À-VIS K–12 PARTNERSHIPS

> Core Idea
>
> The educational leadership PC must have the vision, knowledge, skills, and commitment to guide K–12 partners in putting effective systems in place to create a sustainable principal pipeline.

The Characteristics of an Effective Educational Leadership PC

From recruitment to post-graduation career advancement, we have observed that the educational leadership PC must utilize a myriad of leadership characteristics: ambassador, communicator, diplomat, problem-solver, mediator, team builder, multitasker, and advocate. Other researchers confirm that many of these traits are essential to the role of PC (Coleman & Reames, 2020; Council of Chief State School Officers, 2018; Hackmann & Wanat, 2008). The PC must be approachable, available, and totally committed to the vision of building a sustainable principal pipeline for the K–12 partners by effectively recruiting and training quality principal candidates. Because the PC must juggle the calendars and event planning for multiple K–12 partners, the most essential managerial skills include sophisticated time-management and organizational skills.

> Core Idea
>
> SRSU actively recruits K–12 grant and non-grant partners to ensure its Educational Leadership Program excels in preparing principals as 21st century instructional leaders.

Recruiting Valuable K–12 Partners

The SRSU recruitment process for K–12 partners is a year-long process. There are two program rotations with cohorts beginning in summer and fall each year. Recruitment is conducted to fill both cohorts initially by email, phone, and video-conferencing communications with superintendents and central office personnel. Recruitment also targets several types of relationships including the existing relationships, new relationships, rural K–12 district partnerships, and districts with ongoing improvement initiatives.

Regardless of the type of relationship that is being pursued, the efforts begin with an initial meeting. It is a good idea to have a dean or department chair attend initial meetings with the educational leadership PC to show the K–12 district that the partnerships have university administrative support. The K–12 superintendent or an assistant superintendent (usually of curriculum) will likely attend. If a partnership is agreed upon, usually a K–12 coordinator is designated who will serve as the point of contact and work closely with the educational leadership PC.

The Goals of a Successful Initial Meeting

The initial meeting is the educational leadership PC's time to impress upon the K–12 district personnel why partnerships are beneficial and to outline the direct benefits to the district. These goals emphasizing the principal candidates' completion of the certification process. The PC must also impress upon the superintendent that without partnerships it is extremely difficult for candidates to get certified. This discussion is essential because most Texas K–12 administrators are currently unaware of the complexity of the new certification process and otherwise will likely not see the need for change. The PC must also stress the role played by the district, namely that the K–12 district improves candidate preparation resulting in better qualified administrators dedicated to the district. The cooperative effort will include workshops and training by K–12 personnel and university instructors to ensure that the leadership experience obtained meets the district's needs. K–12 campuses will likely see academic improvement because of the completion of the candidates' action research projects. Underscoring this important partnership outcome allows the PC to highlight an important return on the K–12 district's investment. To this end, discussions also occur around which campuses need improvement and which principals would excel as principal mentors to the selected principal candidates.

Shifting the Lens to a Teams-Approach: Building the Partnership

To accomplish these goals in the initial meeting, it is essential for the educational leadership PC to change the perceptions of the K–12 superintendent and district coordinator by shifting the lens from one that distinguishes the university program as simply a theoretical foundation for future administrators to a teams-approach that views the university as a vital partner in the ongoing training of residents who will be engaged in authentic administrative experiences. The partnership ensures that the residency experience will be a complete immersion in the role of campus principal. This systems or teams-approach, pioneered by Peter Senge (2010), reframes the relationship so that instructors are perceived as working within the K–12 district instead of outside of it (Dufour & Marzano, 2011; Fullan, 2020). In essence, the initial meeting should result in the superintendent's approval of the partnership and setting the partnership boundaries and conditions. Through experience, we have learned of additional beneficial conditions.

Conditions and Systems for Effective Partnerships

Conditions and systems allow partnerships to be effective and the education leadership PC must understand this, communicate it to K–12 partners, and assist those partners in putting the conditions and systems in place. At SRSU, we began our first K–12 district partnership relationships by referencing the requirements of the PRG and seeking to include the grant conditions in each of our K–12 non-partnership agreements. These conditions are memorialized in the university/K–12 memorandum of understanding (MOU). There are several conditions and systems that have become standard in the MOU. Some benefit the principal candidate throughout the program, and others incentivize highly-qualified teachers to apply to the program. The following five conditions are most important in ensuring the sustainability of the K–12 principal pipeline: (1) financial assistance, (2) release time, (3) orientations and trainings, (4) stipends for principal mentors, and 4) principal mentor attendance at PLCs/data team meetings.

Financial assistance is a critical component of successful university/K–12 partnerships. The financial assistance can come directly from a grant, such as the PRG and cover the students' full-tuition costs, plus other related incentives. These include paying for certification exams, related trainings, and required books. In the absence of resources, partners can make various financial commitments to support the principal candidates. For example, these may include K–12 partners paying for one of the trainings required of the principal candidates, purchasing the required books, or providing some tuition-assistance. The university partner can also mirror these financial commitments. For example, they too can identify funding sources to provide students with some tuition assistance or funding to pay for related training. These funding sources may exist outside of the educational leadership department, such as within the graduate school or student services department. Being creative and making the effort to work with other university departments to identify funding sources can prove beneficial. Without the incentive of financial assistance for the program from the K–12 district and university, quality candidates are less likely to step forward, especially in the poorer districts where they are most needed.

Outside of direct financial assistance, release time for principal candidates to engage in those authentic residency experiences is another essential condition for effective university/K–12 partnerships. The rigorous nature of the TExES 368 (PASL) necessitates release time for the principal candidates to complete their residency. Ideally, candidates would be fully immersed in the residency, released of any teaching and other related duties. The reality, however, is that in the absence of funding such as the PRG, K–12 districts may not be able to commit to 100% release time for their principal candidates. In those cases, we recommend releasing the principal candidate for a minimum of one class period. This may require campuses to offer a stipend for another teacher to take the course the principal candidate is not teaching, hire a substitute, or make another accommodation requiring a financial investment by the K–12 district. This investment is an indirect form of financial assistance provided to the principal candidate.

Orientations and trainings are another necessary condition for successful university/K–12 partnerships. To supplement the university program core content and meet the needs of individual districts, orientations and trainings have been developed. K–12 districts are not all at the same stage of the district/campus improvement process. It is the task of the educational leadership PC to assess the current state of the district's academic and personnel needs and address those in trainings with principal candidates and principal mentors. These discussions begin with the K–12 coordinator and educational leadership PC coordinators and expand once the relationship is well-established to include direct discussions with individual principal mentors. Orientations and trainings occur from inception to completion of the university program.

A critical actor in preparing principal candidates are the principal mentors. Direct financial support for these individuals includes stipends for serving as mentors throughout the principal candidates' residency. Given the ever-increasing complexity and demands of the principal's role and responsibilities, stipends encourage the principal's attention and are evidence of the superintendent's program support. Stipends also assists the educational leadership PC in motivating the principal mentor to attend orientations, workshops, and important events like the student's portfolio defense.

As principal candidates engage in fulfilling the requirements of the residency, they will conduct PLCs/data teams meetings. The required attendance and participation in these PLCs/data team meetings is also expected of the principal mentor. Not only does it signal to the teachers participating in the PLCs/data team meetings that the principal fully supports the principal candidate, but also highlights the importance of their collective effort. This often leads to teacher buy-in for the work and the principal candidate's role as the instructional facilitator of the PCLs/data teams. The principal mentors' attendance and participation allows them to coach the principal candidates in improving their instructional leadership skills and knowledge by providing them specific actional feedback. The expectations of principal mentors attending and participating in the principal candidate's team meetings are explicitly set in the SRSU Principal Mentor/Field Supervisor Training Manual and partnership MOU.

These conditions are virtually impossible for an educational leadership university program to achieve without K–12 partnerships. In the past, principals have mentored principal candidates to train them in basic managerial duties, mirroring the mentoring they received. This was done as a courtesy and as a way for the principal to give back to a system that provided them with a mentor. The university/K–12 partnerships greatly expand the traditional administrative internship. Without eliminating historical internship experiences, the university/K–12 partnership provides access to the strategic operations of the campus and experience in making executive leadership decisions. For some K–12 districts, especially the poorer, rural districts, some strategic operations and systems are created for the first time through the university/K–12 partnerships, such as functioning PLCs to focus on campus academic improvement. In those districts, the university functions not only as trainers for the principal candidates, but also for the campus administrators and K–12 coordinator through the technical assistance provided to develop and implement the strategic operations and systems.

Educational Leadership PC Role

The key positions within the university/K–12 partnership that will ensure its effectiveness and sustainability are the roles of educational leadership PC, K–12 coordinator, principal mentors, instructors, and field supervisors. While these roles are complex, there are some explicit expectations that should be delineated at the outset of the partnership to ensure effectiveness of the partnership. To formalize key expectations, we recommend they be explicitly stated in the educational leadership program and training manuals. We believe the roles are equally important and each deserves attention, but we focus on categorizing the role of the educational leadership PC below.

> Core Idea
>
> The educational leadership PC bears the largest workload and responsibility for the university/K–12 partnership. K–12 coordinators value a university partner that not only guides them but also shoulders the lion's share of the administrative workload.

Explicit expectations for the role of educational leadership PC include the following: knowledge of the program curriculum and university procedures, facilitating monthly meetings, three-way communication, orientation meetings and trainings, and providing technical assistance with writing the PRG.

Perhaps most important is the educational leadership PC's in-depth knowledge and understanding of the program curriculum. Because of the TExES 268 (PASL), the SRSU curriculum is sequential and provides principal candidates with a step-by-step guide to the improvement process. This work is the action research project which begins in the first class, *Educational Research I,* and is completed in the final courses, *Practicum III* and *Educational Research II*. In the practicum, candidates facilitate implementation of targeted improvement plans in their team classrooms, and in *Educational Research II,* they report student achievement growth results. The action research project is then presented to a team of stakeholders in the portfolio defense. It takes time for the PC to change candidates' perspective from seeing each course as separate and to understand instead that each course is a step in the sequential change process that scaffolds knowledge throughout the program until the action research project is showcased. It is essential that the PC understand the sequential and scaffolded nature of the program and be able to thoroughly communicate that information to all stakeholders: university administrators, principal candidates, K–12 coordinator, principal mentors, field supervisors and instructors.

To ensure that the curriculum and instruction are cogent and understandable, monthly curriculum meetings as well as monthly field supervisor meetings are conducted. The PC sets the meeting agendas and facilitates the meetings. This includes leading discussions regarding programmatic elements, sharing curriculum and program updates, and maintaining a running list of action items focused on improving the program. In this manner, needed changes are discussed, approved, and shared with all relevant instructors, field supervisors and principal mentors. These monthly meetings create consistency and continuity in how the program is being implemented, optimizing the experience of the principal candidates throughout the program.

Communication is equally as important as curricula in a university/K–12 partnership and the educational leadership PC and K–12 coordinator act as the gatekeepers for many channels of communication including: (a) principal candidate to PC, (b) principal candidate to K–12 coordinator to PC, (c) principal mentor to PC and principal mentor to K–12 coordinator to PC, (d) principal candidate to field supervisor to PC, and (e) all of the above lines of communication flowing in the opposite direction. Keeping these lines of communication flowing is critical to the success of each principal candidate and the key to establishing an ease of communication in the partnership relationship.

The PC at initial meetings with K–12 administrators, principal mentors, and principal candidates must emphasize their availability, ensure that all stakeholders have the PC's contact information, and feel comfortable communicating with the PC. This comfort comes when the PC has established and built rapport with stakeholders. The relationship is key to getting the K–12 partners to request assistance. It is essential that the PC responds to requests efficiently. If the K–12 coordinator needs help, regardless of the issue, that assistance must be provided. Most often received are requests about grant reports, tuition, registration, course rotation, training agendas, and events such as the portfolio defense and testing schedule. The PC schedules and conducts most meetings, orientations, trainings, and collects program data and portfolio rubrics.

The PC must have a wealth of program and course information to create collaborative workshops which cement partnerships and create opportunities for growth of K–12 coordinators, principal mentors, and field supervisors. We begin with a data analysis workshop, which is key because district data analysis software and trained personnel are not available to the university without this collaboration between the university and K–12 partners. Principal candidates are able in this workshop to get real-world experience on how to gather and interpret student achievement data. It is the PC that spearheads this and other workshops to ensure that the partnership thrives. Key to all these collaborations is the relationship of the educational leadership PC and K–12 coordinators.

Navigating university system, the K–12 coordinator and principal candidates need the assistance of the PC to unravel the intricacies of university procedures. Primary among these are admission, registration, scholarship, financial assistance, and graduation procedures. By assisting with these matters, the PC helps minimize potential frustrations the K–12 coordinator and principal candidates may encounter. Subsequently, this helps bolster the partner relationship.

At SRSU, the educational leadership PC provides the K–12 partner technical assistance for the completion and submission of the PRG. In most instances, the PC writes the PRG and guides the K–12 coordinator through the grant application and interview process. Once the grant is awarded, the PC assists and the K–12 coordinator throughout the recruitment and selection of principal candidate process.

Official and Unofficial Function of the Educational Leadership PC

From the foregoing it is obvious that the educational leadership PC must juggle many types of tasks to ensure the effectiveness of the program and the K–12 partnerships. These tasks are both official and unofficial. For example, while the PC's official function is to schedule and attend a pre-graduation celebration for candidates, K–12, and university administrators, it is also an unofficial function for the PC to greet, welcome, and distribute graduation gifts to graduates and to thank our partners for their continued participation and support. The PC is also front and center in organization of these types of events regardless of who is front and center in the memorial photograph.

Section 3 Discussion—Educational Leadership PC Role Requires a Strategic Hire and Intentional Support

Rebecca: In my experience, all the educational leadership PC skills discussed are essential. This is a complex leadership position. If the PC is not personable and diligent with communication, however, they will lose the K–12 partner. The K–12 coordinator will rely on the PC to bring important matters to her attention. It is the responsibility of the PC to provide information, materials, and guidance to ensure that partners know what steps to take with enough advance notice to ensure that any needed action on their part can be added to their busy calendar.

Isela: Working on this section, delineating the responsibilities of the PC, brings home the difficulty of performing the role in the absence of institutional structures and policies in place that support the role. I do think that for those who have not done this type of work, it is easy to take for granted the scope of the work; much of it occurs behind the scenes. As a PC, I did the work out of a sense of responsibility to the students, our partners, and to our internal team (you and the adjunct professors). Because SRSU program is online, it was very easy to work around the clock to attempt to get everything done. With the onset of COVID in the spring

2020, boundaries between the work and other aspects of my life became nonexistent. The mentoring you provided was critical to doing the work effectively, but also to remaining sane in the process. However, this mentoring was informal and stemmed from our pre-existing relationship. There was a lack of formal mentoring and training. Programs are fortunate when the individual who steps into this role comes with prior leadership experience, particularly in a K–12 setting, and some knowledge of principal preparation. But the university has an obligation to train and help this person develop and strengthen those skills. Also, the burnout from performing this role creates the potential for a high turnover in the role which does not help the program. In addition to serving in this capacity, the PC also teaches and mentors students, and in some cases, is required to actively research and publish.

Rebecca: One of the terrible lessons learned during the pandemic is that a crisis is an incredible obstacle to change. Not only did superintendents and principals leave the profession in droves during the pandemic but K–12 administrators and teachers were also too overwhelmed to take on any additional responsibilities. Some of our university/K–12 partnerships survived the pandemic but those were districts that had a well-established relationship with the university before this partnership. In those districts, the number of principal candidates did decline but the partnership survived. The added strain of these losses added to our feelings of being overwhelmed. The K–12 priority was safety and understandably school improvement had to take a backseat. The good news is that with the COVID crisis receding, numbers of candidates are now increasing as well as increasing numbers of K–12 partners.

SECTION IV—ORGANIZATIONAL MANAGEMENT WITHIN THE LARGER CONTEXT OF THE UNIVERSITY STRUCTURE

> Core Idea
>
> With an understanding of the university's organization culture, the educational leadership PC serves as a liaison for the K–12 partners, sharing information around university processes and procedures. This provides an environment for the partners to engage in joint problem-solving, thereby avoiding misunderstandings and solidifying the partnership.

It is not sufficient for the educational leadership PC to build relationships with the K–12 administrators. It is also the task of the PC to ease the burden of the bureaucratic complexity of admission, registration, payment, acquisition of textbooks, graduation, and other university procedures to ensure that these occur as smoothly and with as little red-tape as possible. There are several keys to successful communication about the partnerships with the university. The PC must conduct informational meetings with key university personnel to ensure the success of the K–12 relationship. These meetings serve to ensure the PC secures the full cooperation of the department chair and dean of their college. The PC must also conduct meetings with the registrar, admissions clerk, and bursar's office to communicate the anticipated creation of the K–12 partnerships. As a best practice, these university information meetings should occur before formalizing agreements with potential K–12 partners to ensure key university stakeholders are aware of the partnership. Along with conducting these meetings, the PC must have knowledge of strategic and relevant university procedures and contact information for the key personnel in those departments. This allows the PC to have information that can be readily provided to the K–12 coordinator in advance.

Regularly written reports are another means for the PC to communicate with the university the status of the partnerships. The PC writes a regular report to the provost and dean about the progress of all grant and non-grant partnerships. These reports highlight recruitment efforts, progress of principal candidates, and grant information. These elements are often connected to how principal preparation programs are formally and informally evaluated by the university. Formally documenting the progress can support requests for expanding program resources, including additional staff. The information included in these written reports may also serve as points to be highlighted by the PC in future partnership recruitment efforts.

In addition to reporting on the status of the partnerships, the PC shares relevant news with university and district stakeholders. The PC writes and shares reports of newsworthy events of its principal candidates pre- and post-graduation on its department website and university or department social media. By highlighting these career advancements, certification results, grant awards, new partnerships, and accolades received by our graduates and principal candidates, we celebrate with the entire university and educate them about the work being done through these partnerships.

One of the most rewarding experiences of serving as the PC is planning events for the university, K–12 partners, and principal candidates to celebrate together. In the SRSU Educational Leadership Program, the PC ensures that the department chair, dean of the college, university provost and/or president are invited to the pre-graduation ceremony and that one of them participates in awarding certificates to outstanding principal candidates. The dean disseminates the graduation gifts to the principal candidates and K–12 administrators. We also invite the department chair and dean to the initial meeting with the superintendent to discuss the possibility of a partnership and invite them to serve on the selection committee for principal candidates. By including these university administrators throughout the process, it maintains them apprised of the successes of the partnership and includes them as relevant stakeholders. Perhaps more consequential to the success of the principal preparation program and its candidates, it also conveys the importance of the partnership to our K–12 stakeholders.

Section 4 Discussion—Educational Leadership PC Helping Navigate University System Complexities

Isela: Navigating the bureaucratic complexity of the university is one of the areas where K–12 partners and students can experience negative experiences. This has the potential to dissuade partnerships and more broadly, give your program a bad reputation which can impact enrollment. The oversight by the PC over these areas can minimize the challenges and frustration that K–12 partners and students may encounter. Problem-solving through any issues necessitates a strong understanding of the internal university policies and structures, and key relationships with the individuals in the different university departments. As I mentioned before, with the possibility of high-turnover, the learning curve of a newly hired person is steep and increases the stress associated the responsibilities of the PC. It is also necessary to have a basic understanding of the policies and timelines of the K–12 districts to be able to anticipate challenges that may surface. All this coordination requires the set of skills we have discussed in previous sections. If the bridging of the gap between the university and K–12 world is done effectively, it creates the space for those moments of collective celebration. If it is not, it can lead to long-term, disastrous consequences.

Rebecca: I agree that university processes can be problematic, and it was the knowledge that the K–12 coordinator could reach you that stalled many potential crises. On the other hand, the pre-graduation celebration creates tremendous goodwill among stakeholders. I am so delightful to see the graduates' happy faces and hard-earned confidence. The celebration also serves to emphasize to stakeholders how much the district has benefitted from the work of these candidates.

SECTION 5—PROGRAMMATIC SYSTEMS AND METRICS THAT HELP ENSURE SUCCESS OF THE PARTNERSHIP RELATIONSHIP

Core Idea

From the initial meeting to the pre-graduation ceremony, the educational leadership PC must be diligent in ensuring that all the systems for programmatic success are in place and functioning effectively.

Some of the most important systems that have been put into place to nurture and sustain the university/K–12 partnerships have been discussed earlier in this chapter. It is important to contextualize the actions of the PC as part of a systemic effort and not solely as isolated, disjointed efforts. We briefly list the key systems below:

- Implementing a system of orientation meetings, trainings, and workshops conducted by the K–12 and university administrators as a joint collaborative effort
- Planning and hosting celebrations at the outset and conclusion of each partnership cohort that includes both university and K–12 administrators and board members
- Utilizing three-way communication between the field supervisors, principal mentors, and principal candidates throughout the residency using real-time calendars, logs, reflections, and observation reports
- Engaging in continuous communication between the PC, instructors and field supervisors using monthly curriculum and field supervisor meetings
- Reviewing of portfolio work at the end of each course by the instructor or field supervisor to ensure that principal candidate understands the sequential nature and scaffolding of knowledge about the ongoing change process model throughout the program
- Tracking career advancement using surveys for three years after graduation to ensure that the goal of placing highly qualified, 21st century instructional leaders into administrative positions within the K–12 partner district is achieved

- Conducting program satisfaction surveys to gather feedback from principal candidates and principal mentors
- Disseminating program satisfaction survey data to both K–12 and university administrators
- Facilitating the process whereby the program curriculum and field supervisor committees discuss and act upon program satisfaction survey data to continuously improve the educational leadership program

The systems and metrics put in place provide for the use of the continuous improvement cycle allowing for the program's effective functioning at all times. It is an integral role of the educational leadership PC to ensure that these systems and metrics are in place at both the university and K–12 levels to ensure the success and sustainability of the university/K–12 partnerships.

Section 5 Discussion—Curriculum Committees as a System for Continuous Improvement

Isela: Thinking about the programmatic systems and metrics, this work is so important to ensuring the program runs smoothly and that there is a feedback loop from the students and mentors to continuously improve the courses and overall experience of everyone involved. But much of this work is also invisible PC work that again, can be taken for granted, ironically, if performed well. The need for ongoing touchpoints throughout the program not only serves to keep everyone informed, but also engages the partners in a cycle of continuous improvement.

Rebecca: Your idea to conduct monthly program curriculum committee meetings, I think has been the most instrumental element to impact the program because it allows for continuous improvement of the program. This comfortable, safe space for discussion allows instructors and field supervisors to work through programmatic issues. The PC facilitates the meetings, allows a consensus to be reached, and ensures the changes are made. The last step in this process is to review the changes in the Blackboard Sandbox course at the next committee meeting. This process empowers the committee members and motivates them to continuously strive to improve the program.

Isela: The goal of those curriculum meetings was twofold. Yes, it was about improving curriculum, but it was also about building relationships within our internal team. It was also about creating systems that would endure beyond the time I served as educational leadership PC.

SECTION 6—WHY DOES THE PARTNERSHIP RELATIONSHIP MATTER?

The are many reasons why the university/K–12 partnerships are important. Overall, the partnership provides principal candidates with a deeper and more rigorous authentic residency experience that better prepares them to assume the role of a K–12 campus instructional leader. We share some of the specific takeaways below.

The university/K–12 partnership provides an effective, sustainable principal pipeline ensuring that rising star teachers remain in the K–12 district that has helped train them and provided both financial and non-monetary support. The partnership creates access through the university to additional resources and training to ensure principal candidates are highly effective campus, 21st century instructional leaders, well-versed in their districts' leadership philosophy and expectations of their campus leaders and, as such, ready to lead from day one. The partnership also serves as an affordable avenue for advancement, through reduced tuition, K–12 tuition assistance, and scholarship opportunities for rising star teachers from historically underserved districts.

Through the partnership, collaborative cohort experience for principal candidates is created, easing navigating the complexities of any university master's program. For example, principal candidates are allowed access to K–12 district data systems which facilitate gaining real-world experience by setting campus improvement priorities with real-time data. Principal candidates, and in some cases, principal mentors gain experiential knowledge and learn to create PLCs/data teams of teachers and to work collaboratively to improve campus culture and student achievement.

The learning and growth are not limited to individuals within the K–12 system. University instructors and field supervisors gain greater knowledge of the current K–12 systems in place, and ever-changing roles of the K–12 campus instructional leader. This helps to bridge the divide between leadership theory and practice. Beneficial to both partners and principal candidates is the environment created by the partnership that gives the principal candidate access and authority to complete activities necessary to ensure completion of the PASL tasks. The K–12 districts and the university share in the success of the principal candidate.

By influencing principal candidates and advancing them into the position of a campus instructional leader, the partnership ensures that the entire culture of the campus will be positively impacted with time. New and transformational systems like data-driven improvement plans, PLCs/ data teams, coaching, and continuous practice and monitoring of instruction become the norm on these campuses. The success of a highly effective partnership ensures the sustainability of the relationship and generates new cohorts of principal candidates, building upon the work of previous cohorts in deepening the partnership relationship.

In sharing our collective experience serving as PCs in an educational leadership program, we hope this gives other programs an opportunity to critically reflect on their own journeys, taking what makes sense given their university and K–12 partners' capacities and needs, in the larger context of their respective communities.

REFERENCES

Coleman, L. B., & Reames, E. (2020). The role of the educational leadership program coordinator (PC) in university-K–12 school district partnership development. *Journal of Research on Educational Leadership, 15*(4), 241–260. https://doi.org/10.1177/1942775118803335

Council for Chief State School Officers Network for Transforming Educator Preparation. (2018). *Council of Chief State School Officers Next Steps from NTEP State report: Working better together: A continuum rubric for self-assessing & strengthening partnerships.* Council of Chief State School Officers. https://www.ccsso.org/sites/default/files/2018-02/Working%20Better%20Together.pdf

Dufour, R, Dufour, R., Eaker, R., Many, T.W., & Mattos, M. (2016). *Learning by doing: A handbook for professional learning communities at work* (3rd ed.). Solution Tree.

Dufour, R., & Marzano, R. (2011). *Leaders learning: How district, school, and classroom leaders improve student achievement*. Solution Tree.

Effective Schools Framework. (n.d.). *Texas effective schools framework*. https://texasesf.org/

ETS. (n.d.). *Task requirements for the ETS performance assessment for school leaders (PASL).* ets.org/ppa/test-takers/school-leaders/requirements

Fullan, M. (2020). *Leading in a culture of change* (2nd ed.). Jossey-Bass.

Grissom J. A., Egalite A. J., Lindsay C. A. (2021). *How principals affect students and schools: A systematic synthesis of two decades of research*. Wallace Foundation. https://www.wallacefoundation.org/knowledge-center/Documents/How-Principals-Affect-Students-and-Schools.pdf

Guerra, P. L., & Pazey, B.L. (2016). Transforming educational leadership preparation: Starting with ourselves. *The Qualitative Report, 21*(10), 1751–1784. https://doi.org/10.46743/2160-3715/2016-2440

Hackmann, D. G., & Wanat, C. L. (2008). The role of the educational leadership program coordinator: A distributed leadership perspective. *International Journal of Educational Reform, 17*(1), 64–88. https://doi.org/10.1177/105678790801700105

Sawyer, R., & Norris, J. (2015). Duoethnography: A retrospective 10 years after. *International Review of Qualitative Research, 8*(1), 1–4. https://doi.org/10.1525/irqr.2015.8.1.1

Sawyer, R. D., & Norris, J. (2013). *Duoethnography: Understanding qualitative research*. Oxford University Press.

Senge, P. M. (2010). *The fifth discipline: The art of practice of the learning organization*. Crown.

Tex. Admin. Code §149.2001 (2014). https://tinyurl.com/2p9e9dux

Texas Education Agency. (2021). *Letter of interest grant opportunity for recruiting and preparing principals via residency*. https://tea.texas.gov/sites/default/files/letter-of-interest-grant-opportunity-for-recruiting-and-preparing-principals-via-residency.pdf

Texas Education Agency. (2021, August 20). *2022–2023 Principal Residency Cycle 5 Webinar* [Video]. YouTube. https://www.youtube.com/watch?v=LP8PBIk6XWg&ab_channel=Ms.E.Love

Texas Education Agency. (n.d.). *Principal certification redesign*. https://tea.texas.gov/texas-educators/educator-initiatives-and-performance/principal-certification-redesign

CHAPTER 4

THE EDUCATIONAL LEADERSHIP PROGRAM COORDINATOR

Partnerships and Recruiting

Ellen H. Reames, Angela C. Adair, and Alfred Parham
Auburn University

The Auburn University Educational Leadership Administration of Elementary and Secondary (AES) education and the Administration and Supervision of Curriculum (ASC) preparation programs' recruiting and marketing plan is closely tied to the to the missions and visions of the program, the College of Education, and Auburn University. These mission statements accentuate the importance of developing strong partnerships with K–12 school districts and other agencies closely aligned with preparing leaders for Alabama schools, industry, nonprofits, and military entities. Data indicate that applicants for the program are referred to us by multiple sources. These sources include alumni, current students, advisory council partners, community stakeholders, school system visits by our Program Coordinator (PC), information booths at state and regional conferences, the internet via ZOOM and social media, and college and program websites. The personal relationships which have been established by the PC are important sources for our recruiting efforts. These relationships have been influenced by the strong partnerships we have built over many years.

The role of the Auburn University's Educational Leadership PC is closely tied to many areas of partnership development, but none seem as important as the recruiting and marketing of its leadership programs.

Navigating the Ubiquitous, Misunderstood, and Evolving Role of the Educational Leadership Program Coordinator in Higher Education, pp. 61–78

Without the recruitment of students, there are no programs. There are also no programs without K–12 partners and other educational entities who recommend the educational leadership programs to their teachers, administrators, and employees. They work with the educational leadership program to encourage their practitioners to join the educational leadership faculty in study of current best practices and theory.

PARTNERSHIPS ARE THE FOUNDATION OF RECRUITING

In the early 2000s, educational administration preparation programs across the country were criticized for lacking recruitment efforts in K–12 school environments and for not being collaborative with these K–12 entities (Levine, 2005). Within these calls for change was the recommendation that university educational leadership programs create and engage in partnership arrangements with other entities, particularly with primary and secondary schools and systems. The call for partnerships was a task assigned to the higher education institutions as they developed new educational leadership preparation programs (Reames, 2010). There were no models and, even in 2022, there appear to be only three models that are directly linked to educational leadership preparation programs (Barnett et al, 2010; Korach et al., 2012; Reames & Kochan, 2021).

The rationale behind the partnership concept is that differences in the context and perspectives of those involved will enhance and strengthen university programs and the preparation and further development of educational leaders (Barnett et al., 2010; Browne-Ferrigno & Sanzo, 2011; Reames & Kochan, 2015; Reames & Kochan, 2021). Those advocating such relationships stress that including voices from the field in conversations about educational leadership preparation and development is vital in ensuring a better understanding of the needs of the field, assisting in maintaining a proper balance between theory and practice, enhancing opportunities for effective field-based experiences, and keeping educational leadership programs grounded in the local community context (Reames & Kochan, 2015; Reames & Kochan, 2021). Partnerships can strengthen schools and foster K–12 school improvement. These same partnerships can also strengthen and even transform educational leadership preparation programs (Coleman & Reames, 2020; Kochan & Reames, 2013; Kochan et al., 2021; Reames, 2010).

MODELS FOR PARTNERSHIP DEVELOPMENT IN EDUCATIONAL LEADERSHIP PREPARATION PROGRAMS

The Auburn University Educational Leadership Preparation Program has developed recruiting and marketing efforts over the years along with a model of partnership development as seen in Figure 4.1 (Reames & Kochan, 2021). We see our partnerships with external and internal stakeholders as learning partnerships based on communities of practice (Kochan & Mullen, 2003; Wenger, 1998). At the heart of learning partnerships as communities of practice are relational factors, organizational structures, and operational processes. The PC as chief recruiter and marketer for the educational leadership program inhabits all of these areas. The PC is personnel in operational processes. The PC is part of all organizational structures because they oversee many of these, and they are critical in developing the relational factors described in the model. Elements of each of these are emphasized as we describe the role of the PC in this chapter.

THE ROLE OF THE PROGRAM COORDINATOR IN PARTNERSHIP DEVELOPMENT AND RECRUITING

One of the outcomes from the important redesign efforts from the early 2000s was that someone at the university educational leadership program

Figure 4.1

Learning Partnerships as Communities of Practice

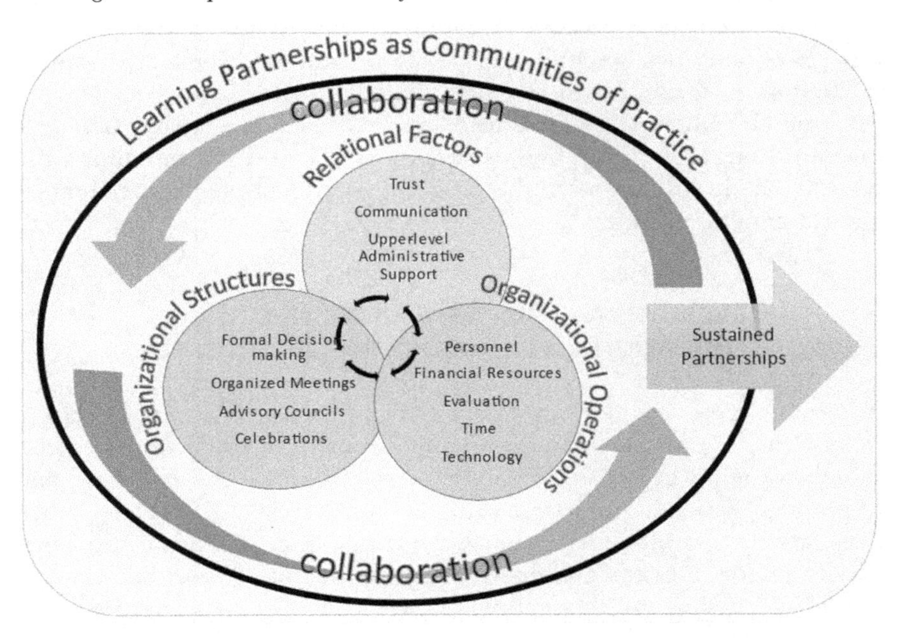

Source: Reames and Kochan (2021).

had to coordinate all important changes in program curriculum, instructional delivery models, development of partnerships in the university communities, and encourage recruits for the programs. While faculty have always been involved in this, there is growing consensus in the literature that the PC has been a driving force behind all of these efforts (Coleman & Reames, 2020; Hackman & Malin, 2016; Ingle et al., 2020; Milstein & Krueger, 1997; Reames, 2010, 2016).

This chapter includes the recruiting and marketing efforts the PC advanced by considering what the research suggests should be done and what was learned from our own research and experiences. PCs have developed into more important roles over the years, especially for educational leadership preparation programs (Coleman & Reames, 2020; Kochan et al., 2021; Reames, 2016; Reames & Kochan, 2021). Accreditation agencies such as the Southern Association of Colleges and Schools Commission on Colleges (SACSCOC) and the Council for Higher Education Accreditation (CHEA) created the role of program coordinators in their Principles of Accreditation (*The Principles of Accreditation: Foundations for Quality Enhancement*, 3.4.11). This role was created so that all university program areas would have a knowledgeable faculty member overseeing their areas of expertise. Over time, the few of us that do research on the role of the PC in educational leadership are revealing that the PC role is very different for educational leadership preparation programs than other programs throughout the university structures (Coleman & Reames, 2020; Ingle et al., 2022; Reames, 2016). The PC for educational leadership preparation is more joined to outside agencies such as state departments of education, accrediting bodies such as CAEP and partnerships with educational entities than are the program coordinators for other higher education fields of study.

RECRUITING FROM THE PERSPECTIVE OF THE EDUCATIONAL LEADERSHIP PREPARATION PC

According to the 2020 Ruffalo Noel Levitz | 2020 Marketing and Recruitment Practices for Graduate Students Report, the following five best practices should be considered for the establishment and improvement of graduate recruiting practices (Ruffalo Noel Levitz, 2020). These practices are making immediate contact with potential recruits, optimizing programs for online searchers, making use of marketing dollars with digital advertising and retargeting, emphasizing outcomes and flexibility with recruitment, and creating a dedicated, focused, and robust graduate recruitment program.

Immediate Contact is Critical

Prospective graduate students are on an accelerated timeframe to research, apply, and enroll at a program of study, yet many respondents in the Ruffalo Noel Levitz (2020) study said that programs often took days or even weeks to respond to inquiries. Because of this research, the PC does not waste time. Most contact occurs within 24 hours of the inquiry. Engaging and building a relationship with the applicant is an important first step. The PC immediately follows up telephone conversations with recruiting flyers and program application packets to assist the candidate with a seamless and friendly admissions process. The PC is there to guide the student throughout the application process.

Optimalization of Programs for Online Searchers

Graduate students are program-driven and their online searches for a program of study can often be the difference between a potential inquiry and a lost opportunity. Currently, the AES/ASC programs connected to the Auburn University Search engines are optimized for online searchers, especially for those using cell phones. It is vital to regularly update online information so that prospective candidates are quickly directed to the AES/ASC programs in which they are interested and are directed to the PC's email for further questions or concerns. This also allows the PC the information needed to personally contact prospective students and explain why Auburn University's Education Leadership Program is superior to others in the state. For example, the PC makes a distinction between Auburn University's R1 Carnegie classification and the status of other higher education institutions within the state of Alabama. The PC also explains why this makes a difference in a student's education in graduate school and what it could mean for a student's future career. That future includes their present occupations, usually as K–12 school district professionals as well as careers that will become available to them as a result of earning an advanced degree at Auburn University.

Marketing Budget for Digital Advertising and Retargeting

It is the intent of the AES/ASC PC to offer various digital resources for the information prospective students want in their hands when making their matriculation decisions. We offer updated website pages, information and application packets, handbooks, and recruiting flyers for all AES/ASC programs. A future goal is to develop program highlight videos that are posted on our website and Facebook page.

Emphasize Outcomes and Flexibility With Recruitment

Today's graduate students want to make sure their investments will pay off, so the AES/ASC program takes the following actions to demonstrate career and educational outcomes. We offer course delivery through online/face-to-face executive format hybrid models by which students attend classes on campus approximately three weekends per semester and work online for most of their coursework. The PC is instructive here because they can find clusters of interest in various geographic locations. The PC then offers that degree programs be taken to the students in their local context. For more than 10 years, the Auburn Educational Leadership Program has offered degree programs at sites other than the main campus. Partnerships with K–12 districts have yielded successful master's level and PhD opportunities in the Alabama Wiregrass regions of Greenville, Eufaula, and Dothan. This platform offers us a way to partner with districts and take a quality educational leadership program to many areas in the state. These areas often lack effective educational leadership preparation because they are not near a university. Rural areas want to grow their own leaders specifically for their local context. These formats have allowed the AES/ASC programs to gain connections with school systems and communities that otherwise would not have developed. It is the PC that coordinates these efforts.

The PC maintains professional contact with program alumni to assist prospective graduates with employment opportunities. Auburn University's alumni are an extremely important recruiting tool. Strategically using adjunct scholars that support our program operations, instruction, and recruitment efforts is a vital part of the PC's role. This is critical to our program goals of blending theory with practice, a hallmark of Auburn's AES/ASC program for decades. Partner adjuncts provide current practical knowledge necessary for preparing school leaders and provide a source of recruitment for students to the AES/ASC programs. Additionally, as they teach our students, they recognize those that might be assets for their own districts and often suggest to students that they should apply for positions within the adjunct's district.

A Dedicated, Focused, and Robust Graduate Recruitment Program

As competition increases for graduate students, institutions must approach graduate recruitment similar to that of undergraduate recruitment. Hiring an experienced marketing director to coordinate efforts at the university, college, and department levels is the most important part of this task (Ruffalo Noel Levitz, 2020). The Auburn University's Educational Leadership PC actively involves clinical positions, program staff, and stakeholders to facilitate the planning and communications for our graduate market. Because of the changing landscape of public education and the added pressures of COVID-19, recent statistics show much higher attrition rates for teachers and administrators (Levin & Bradley, 2019 [No reference]). Current rates of leaving or retiring from teaching suggest that during the past three years, over 50% of teachers have considered leaving the profession (Jotkoff, 2022). Furthermore, there has been a twenty percent increase in administrative retirements from 2019 to the present. These added pressures suggest that school leaders and those in other educational leader positions are choosing to leave the profession thus creating massive shortages in teaching and administrative ranks (Béteille et al., 2012; Parker, 2019). Furthermore, national statistics also point to a shrinking market of those seeking teaching or educational leadership related occupations (Bottery et al., 2018). All of this suggests that university leadership preparation programs are competing against each other in a shrinking market.

OTHER RECCOMMENDED BEST PRACTICE

Advisory Council

The Auburn University Educational Leadership Advisory Council has been instrumental in recruiting and is an example of how strong partnerships with the advisory council's members can encourage the recruiting of candidates to our program. Since 2007, this advisory council has been led by the PC who has worked side-by-side with faculty to develop, implement, and evaluate the educational leadership programs. Future plans include restructuring the advisory council to include more than superintendents from the current 15+ partner districts. The PC has reorganized the advisory council and has launched a three-phase advisory council. Group 1 will be superintendents, central office personnel, industry, nonprofit, military, and CLAS (Council for Leaders in Alabama Schools) and ALSDE (Alabama State Department of Education) representatives; Group 2 will include principals and assistant principals of partner districts; and Group 3 will consist of other stakeholders and alumni. The PC views the restructuring as a way to broaden our contacts across educational entities and believes it will lead to stronger commitments and sustainability of our program.

Recently, the PC held discussions with the College of Education's Clinical Experiences Committee to combine forces and use this committee as a more succinct Group 1 advisory council. This allows the AES/ASC program to combine forces with PCs from other preparation programs such as the special education programs to support teacher education.

Because the Clinical Experiences committee would consist of superintendents and other central office personnel from K–12 districts and teacher education faculty in the COE, the PC will market the Clinical Experiences committee as Group 1. The PC will focus on Group 2, principals and assistant principals, and Group 3, AES/ASC program alumni, as an internal program activity.

Partnership With the Graduate School and Graduate Program Officer

The PC regularly meets with the GPO within our department to make the admissions process seamless and remains in close contact with recruits from their initial interest in the program until the recruit becomes a student in the program. The PC's connection with students is critical and continues throughout the program. In addition to collaborating with the EFLT Graduate Program Officer (GPO) and the Graduate School, the PC currently attempts to strengthen our relationship with other programs within EFLT and the College of Education to mutually support increasing enrollments.

The PC also works with the dean, associate dean, and senior staff at the Auburn Graduate School. Auburn graduate students fall under the umbrella of the Graduate School and the relationships between the educational leadership PC and these administrative personnel are critical to the health of our program. The Graduate School, like the PC, is student-focused and supports the needs of AES/ASC students from the time they are recruited until they graduate from the program. Even after graduation, the Graduate School, like the PC, maintains contact with graduate students who matriculate through our programs of study.

Digital Communications: Internet and Email

Research shows that a graduate program's website is its most valuable recruitment tool (Ruffalo Noel Levitz, 2020). The AES/ASC PC communicates with COE administrators and staff to update our online profiles. The PC takes a more active role to make sure that we are better represented on other Auburn University digital platforms in addition to the COE website. PCs should include their office and personal cell phone numbers at the bottom of their email signature blocks to encourage contact from prospective students. The Auburn University Educational Leadership Program has a Facebook recruiting page and a presence on Twitter, Instagram, and

LinkedIn. The PC frequent updates and encourages students and alumni to do the same. We also have a student-generated newsletter which is distributed electronically to our stakeholders and alumni.

Brochures and Print/Digital Publications

The PC actively updates print material for the AES/ASC programs. There is a university-approved program brochure which briefly introduces all masters-, educational specialist-, and doctoral-level programs. This program brochure is available both in print and digitally and is shared by our partners and featured in the CLAS Weekly Update. The PC has also developed internal recruiting brochures, program curriculum plan sheets, handbooks, admission packets, and business cards. For example, admissions packets give step-by-step instructions to applicants on how to navigate the Apply Yourself (AY) system, and the PC is available by telephone, email and text to assist. Business cards include all contact information for the PC.

Graduate School Fairs, Conferences, and Consortia

As part of a centralized outreach and recruiting effort, COE undergraduate and graduate studies send representatives to numerous information fairs. The PC attends these and is prepared to distribute print material and contact information for recruits. Additionally, the PC frequently participates in several consortia and attends conferences that permit identification and recruitment of a diverse pool of students. This is an area for improvement within our recruitment program. While we do not control who participates in the university-level events, the PC likes to be included and informed of their existence.

Educational leadership has support from the EFLT department and COE to provide an informational table at important state conferences such as the Council for Leaders of Alabama Schools (CLAS) conference, the Alabama State Department of Education (ALSDE) sponsored MEGA Conference, and the School Superintendent Association of Alabama (SSA) conference. These three statewide events are the most important and a continued presence is critical to recruiting across Alabama.

Collaboration with School Partners and Advisory Council

Our university is in a rural area in which most school systems are small. It is necessary to have partnerships with multiple K–12 school systems because of this rural context. In 2008, the AES Advisory Council included eight K–12 school districts. The Auburn AES Advisory Council was formed to share in redesigning, planning, implementing, and evaluating the AES master's program. The Advisory Council has grown to 15 core members and 23 contributory partners. Superintendents, central office staff, school-level administrators, ALSDE personnel, Auburn AES faculty, the EFLT department head, and the Auburn College of Education dean are included. Maintaining these relationships is critical to the continued success of our recruiting efforts. The PC stays closely connected to these entities and attends organizational events on a regular basis. The PC recognizes the need for the dean to be involved in reaching out to these organizations. Superintendents, heads of private schools, military base command personnel, and non-profit executives need attention from senior college and university level administrators. The PC facilitates those collaborative actions.

Innovative Higher Education Collaborative Efforts

The Auburn University/University of Alabama/CLAS Aspiring Leader Conferences are held throughout the year to provide professional development for those wishing to become school administrators. Conference topics include mock administrative interviews, the administrative application process, becoming a mentor or mentee, and other current trends in school leadership. This conference is a vital networking event and a unique recruiting tool. The PC is deeply involved in the planning and execution of these conferences.

The Auburn AES/ASC programs also partner with other teacher preparation graduate programs to provide opportunities for students from teaching areas to receive administrative certification. For example, students who are enrolled in a PhD program for special education can use their electives to receive the reduced-hour option (RHO) certification in instructional leadership. This is an example of interdepartmental recruiting which is a responsibility of the educational leadership PC.

Auburn University considers outreach a major focus of our land grant and R1 status. As part of our outreach mission, the PC is tasked with reaching out to various educational entities to provide professional development for leaders and practitioners. The PC often sends emails, flyers, and personal messages to these partners, inviting them to participate in the ongoing professional development initiatives of the AES/ASC programs. The PC arranges for these outreach opportunities to occur on campus, online, and in the local community setting (see Table 4.1).

Table 4.1

Current and Future Recruiting Strategies

Recruiting Theme	Current Recruiting Strategies	Future Recruiting Innovations
Let Social Media Tell the Story	• Facebook AU Ed Lead Recruiting Page • Twitter • Instagram • LinkedIn • Share on social media those graduates who are promoted and highlight success for graduates in their current district positions • Monthly facilitated informational meetings via ZOOM	• Dedicated cell phone for text message contact with PC • Paid social media adds • Video/written graduate testimonials: YouTube • Record general information video and post it to Facebook page • Gather data about placement rates • Highlight successes • Share Praxis pass rate
AES/ASC Program Search Resources	• Showcase rankings such as R1 Carnegie status • Print brochures & handouts • Virtual open house • Face-to-face and virtual information sessions • Faculty/Graduate Student Events	• Magazines, newspapers, websites • Expand communication about the virtual open house • Live chats • Open House
Response to Inquiries	• Respond to inquiries within 24–48 hours • Personal touch is a must	• Offer contact with a current graduate student to share meaningful information • Purchase recruiting lists
Partnerships	• K-12 Partners • Advisory Council • U.S Military • Alabama State Department of Education • U.S Military • CLAS • In-state higher education institutions	• Advisory Council as Clinical Experiences Committee • Group 2–Principal/Assistant Principal • Group 3–Alumni
Course Format	• Semester offerings: Hybrid/Online, Cohort model, weekend classes, evening classes, satellite campuses, rolling admissions	• Mini-mesters (8-week course) • Offer more than one start date • Meet with undergraduate students about the possibilities for their future (before they earn their master's degree in a program that doesn't require three years of experience

(Table continued on next page)

Table 4.1 (Continued)

Current and Future Recruiting Strategies

Recruiting Theme	Current Recruiting Strategies	Future Recruiting Innovations
Personal Touch Recruiting	• Former and current students, adjunct faculty, emeriti faculty, alumni network, superintendents, professional associations • Site visits to teachers and principals • Professional Development Workshops provided by program faculty	• Partner PD Days • Expand outreach sessions provided by program faculty
Demographic Trends	• Target diverse candidate pool	• Continue to define inclusion and diversity
Practitioner Fairs/ Conferences	• Council for Leaders of Alabama Schools (CLAS) • CLAS publication advertising; research stories • MEGA	• Packets prepared for in-person meetings including TPI meetings • Further develop partnership with CLAS—advertise in their publications/events
Beyond Alabama	• Market online/hybrid program format beyond state lines	
Continuous Updating of Print Documents	• Program flyers—one page: Masters/RHO; EdS to PhD Fast-Track; PhD Informational handouts • Degree program handbooks • Plan sheets for all programs • Application packets	
Have Graduates Spread the Word (The best recruiters are alumni and students)	• Graduates/current students write an email to their districts about their experiences: template created • Offer contact information of students willing to recruit • Encourage "grow your own" leader programs in school districts and organizations • Have ASC PhD students add RHO to their plans of study • Encourage excellent students from Masters/ RHO to EdS and PhD • Encourage former graduate students to spread the word that aspiring leaders can now get their Master's/RHO is online	• Superintendents and military officers can use program to grow leadership in their organizations • Meet with partners' teachers and explain the path to principalship • Form Group 3 alumni working group
Create Formal Recruiting and Marketing Plan for Program	• Program recruiting plan marketing director to formalize graduate program marketing • Marketing Budget	

RESEARCH AND BENCHMARKING

The AES/ASC program continuously uses the best practices and research available to improve our recruitment and marketing strategies. In addition to collaborating with other universities, professional associations, and stakeholders, we initially utilize the Ruffalo Noel Levitz national, Web-based poll to help inform our practices (Ruffalo Noel Levitz, 2020). The PC's plans are to incorporate some of the practices espoused by the Council for Accreditation of Educator Preparation (CAEP) standards for Initial Standard 3, Candidate Recruitment, Progression, and Support (CAEP, 2020).

Using Benchmarks From Accrediting Agencies

The AES/ASC program aligns recruiting and marketing efforts with components of accrediting agencies such as the Council for Accreditation of Educator Preparation (CAEP). CAEP (2020) suggests that advanced graduate programs such as the AES/ASC recruit high-quality candidates from a broad range of backgrounds and diverse populations. The PC supports this charge with visits to various stakeholders. The PC looks at regional and national trends in leadership and assists partner school districts and organizations that are experiencing hard-to-staff schools. The PC's goal is to provide evidence that our program is progressing towards a candidate pool which reflects diversity in education related fields.

Monitoring and Supporting Candidate Progression

The PC also creates and monitors transition points from admission through completion to indicate candidates' developing content knowledge, critical dispositions, professional responsibilities, and the ability to integrate technology effectively in practice. If the student needs support, many times it is the PC who arranges for interventions. The PC understands the importance of foundational academic knowledge for the graduates of the AES/ASC programs and works to ensure that competencies are met using multiple measures. In essence, the PC ensures auditing for success.

Market Analysis

The AES/ASC recruiting market generally consists of the State of Alabama and more specifically the counties and school districts located within the program's established partnerships. This has changed significantly since the introduction of distance and hybrid program formats. Most of Alabama's counties are considered rural counties. The Auburn's Educational Leadership Advisory Council Core Partners all are rural with only a few small city (urban) systems. This makes Auburn's immediate recruiting area different than many of the other educational leadership programs in higher education institutions throughout the state. Auburn is an R1 (research-intensive) institution that does not have a major metropolitan city in its immediate area. The University of Alabama has Tuscaloosa City School System and the many city systems that make up the Birmingham area. The University of Alabama at Birmingham sits in the most populated area of the state. This context is important because it means our recruiting efforts must pay specific attention to our rural/small city system complex. While the University of Alabama can rely heavily on recruiting in Tuscaloosa and Birmingham, Auburn does not have that luxury. The PC is charged with visiting many rural areas around the surrounding Auburn University area and recruiting far beyond the close at hand borders. Technology allows for meetings and recruiting sessions to be done digitally, but there is still nothing that is more important than personal, face-to-face contact (see Figure 4.2). The Auburn Educational Leadership Program embraced this identity many years ago. We recruit in our immediate area, but we also recruit in remote areas across the state and are proud to sell the "Auburn Brand" in any location.

The program faculty recognize Auburn University as an international provider of educational preparation, and we seek to recruit students from all parts of the world and the United States of America. We have recruited students from states including Washington, Maryland, Connecticut, South Carolina, Georgia, Florida, and Mississippi, as well as from international countries including China, Egypt, Saudi Arabia, and Viet Nam.

Benchmarks and Goals for Enrollment

One area of targeted growth was with master's and education specialist-level certification students. Research suggests that targets for growth in graduate student enrollment should be aimed at certification-level programs. The PC is responsible for meeting the growth goals that are set by program faculty. The PC evaluates the overall health of AES/ASC program enrollments but also monitors various degree and certification programs within the educational leadership program. The AES/ASC PhD programs have always been strong but, according to research in educational leadership and other graduate programs, revenue streams should not be solely based on PhD recruitment. For example, how many master's level students have enrolled during a calendar year? The PC has found that focusing on

Figure 4.2

Alabama's Rural Counties

the entry level degree programs is more beneficial to the overall health of the AES/ASC programs as students who grow to love and respect the entry level degree programs at Auburn often continue their educations through completion of their doctoral degrees at Auburn.

The PC also works closely with the department head and program faculty to establish a yearly recruiting budget. The PC travels to state conferences, individual school districts, and military institutions to recruit and build partnerships. It is being in the field with practitioners that is of vital importance, and the PC is the linchpin for this activity. One of the most important tasks for the PC is to foster internal relationships within the COE and university. This includes recognition by college and departmental administrators for the challenging work that is being done, but it also includes a budget which will support the efforts to market an exemplary program.

CLOSING THOUGHTS

Creating a recruiting and marketing plan around university-district partnerships and using the PC as the linchpin for these activities has proven to be successful and all parties have benefitted. The findings presented in this chapter align with the findings of Ingle et al. (2020) describing recruiting and retention of graduate students as the most prevalent responsibility of PCs. Interwoven in the Ingel et al. work is the importance of partnership development by the PC and the functions related to partnerships, such as representing the leadership community within the university and with external entities important to the sustainability of the program. The Auburn University Educational Leadership AES/ASC programs have stayed current with best practices and trends in leadership preparation. The PC has used the organizational structures, operational processes, and relational factors of the partnership model to carry out these efforts by focusing on the development of the role of the PC.

1. Auburn University Institutional Research/Demographics IR | Demographics (auburn.edu)
2. Auburn University, University Council of Educational Leadership (UCEA) Exemplary Educational Leadership Preparation Program (EELP) Application.
3. Best Practices in Graduate Student Recruitment | Hanover Research
4. Council for the Accreditation of Educator Preparation (caepnet.org)
5. CONFERENCE | SRCEA
6. Graduate Student Recruitment Report | Graduate Student Marketing | RNL (ruffalonl.com)

REFERENCES

Barnett, B. G., Hall, G. E., Berg, J. H., & Camarena, M. M. (2010). A typology of partnerships for promoting innovation. *Journal of School Leadership, 20*(1), 10–36. https://doi.org/10.1177/105268461002000103

Béteille, T., Kalogrides, D., & Loeb, S. (2012). Stepping stones: Principal career paths and school outcomes. *Social Science Research, 41*, 904–919. https://doi.org/10.1016/j.ssresearch.2012.03.003

Bottery, M., Ping-Man, W., & Ngai, G. (2018). *Sustainable school leadership: Portraits of individuality*. Bloomsbury.

Browne-Ferrigno, T., & Sanzo, K. L. (2011). Introduction to special issue on university-district partnerships. *Journal of School Leadership, 21*(5), 650–658. https://doi.org/10.1177/105268461102100501

CAEP. (2020). *Council for the accreditation of educator preparation*. http://caepnet.org/

Coleman, L. B., & Reames, E. (2020). The role of the educational leadership program coordinator (PC) in university-K–12 school district partnership development. *Journal of Research on Leadership Education, 15*(4), 241–260. https://doi.org/10.1177/1942775118803335

Hackmann, D. G., & Malin, J. R. (2016). If you build it, will they come? Educational leadership program coordinators' perceptions of principal preparation redesign in Illinois. *International Journal of Educational Reform, 25*(4), 338–360. https://doi.org/10.1177/105678791602500401

Ingle, W. K., Marshall, J. M., & Hackmann, D. G. (2020). The leaders of leadership preparation programs: A study of program coordinators at UCEA-member institutions. *Journal of Research on Leadership Education, 15*(2), 120–149. https://doi.org/10.1177/1942775118803334

Jotkoff, E. (2022). *NEA survey: Massive staff shortages in schools leading to educator burnout; alarming number of educators indicating they plan to leave profession* [Press release]. *NEA*. Retrieved February 27, 2022, from https://www.nea.org/about-nea/media-center/press-releases/nea-survey-massive-staff-shortages-schools-leading-educator

Kochan, F., & Reames, E. H. (2013). Experiencing educational leadership preparation program redesign in Alabama: One university's perspective. *Journal of Research on Leadership Education, 8*(2), 152–167. https://doi.org/10.1177/1942775113491946

Kochan, F., Reames, E. H., Serafini, A., & Adair, A. C. (2021). Partnerships in educational leadership preparation and development: What works and what's next? In F. Kochan, E. H. Reames, & D. M. Griggs (Eds.), *Partnerships for leadership preparation and development: Facilitators, barriers, and models for change* (pp. 233–243). Information Age Publishing.

Kochan, F., & Mullen, C. A. (2003). An exploratory study of collaboration in higher education from women's perspectives. *Teaching Education, 14*(2), 153–167. https://doi.org/10.1080/1047621032000092959

Korach, S., Sidel, K., & Salazar, M. D. C. (2012). Toward signature pedagogy for professional education: Collaborative partnerships in teacher and principal preparation. *International Journal of Educational Leadership Preparation, 7*(1), 1–11.

Levine, A. (2005). *Educating school leaders*. Education Schools Project.

Milstein, M. M., & Krueger, J. A. (1997). Improving educational administration preparation programs: What we have learned over the past decade. *Peabody Journal of Education, 72*(2), 100–116.

Parker, C. (2019). *Principal retention: Why leaders stay* [Doctoral dissertation, Abilene Christian University]. Abilene, Texas.

Reames, E. H. (2010). Shifting paradigms: Redesigning a principal preparation program's curriculum. *Journal of Research on Leadership Education, 5*(12), 436–459. https://doi.org/10.1177/194277511000501205

Reames, E. H. (2016). From coordination to compliance: The program coordinator's changing role during redesign. *Planning and Changing, 47*(3/4), 263–277.

Reames, E. H., & Kochan, F. (2015). Examining the status of partnerships in university educational leadership doctoral programs. *International Journal of Educational Research, 24(3)*, 233–247. https://doi.org/10.1177/105678791502400303

Reames, E. H., & Kochan, F. (2021). A model for future practice and research. In F. Kochan, E. H. Reames, & D. M. Griggs (Eds.), *Partnerships for leadership preparation and development: Facilitators, barriers, and models for change* (pp. 245–259). Information Age Publishing.

Ruffalo Noel Levitz. (2020). *Resource Library. 2020 Marketing and Recruitment Practices for Graduate Students Report*. Retrieved October 31, 2022, from https://www.ruffalonl.com/papers-research-higher-education-fundraising/2020-marketing-and-recruitment-practices-for-graduate-students-report/

Wenger, E. (1999). *Communities of practice: Learning, meaning, and identity*. Cambridge University Press.

SECTION II

CHAPTER 5

TWO LENSES—ONE FOCUS

Examining Educational Leadership Program Coordinator Roles

Barbara Qualls and Stacy Hendricks
Austin State University

ABSTRACT

The term "coordinator" may better be termed "herder of cats" because it often represents an organizational role with much responsibility, little authority, and reluctant participants. It sounds lower than director and implies the shuffling of disparate entities to create order. For program coordinators in higher education, the position likely includes a residual teaching load so that the overall function has one foot in the faculty breakroom and the other in the front office. We will examine the dual roles of two coordinators in educational leadership programs who share faculty across two degrees and certifications. To effectively provide oversight for an educational leadership program, developing and nurturing relationships is vital. Accordingly, this study explores literature that implements self-study and critical friend methodology as its framework. The anecdotal narrative regarding the university where the authors work is included to provide context for our story in blending the available faculty to encompass the needs of two related but distinct degree programs. This context spans a wholesale university transformation including president change, workload policy redevelopment, and overhaul of college structure and policies. While specific literature is sparse about the academic role and responsibilities of program coordinator PCs, informa-

Navigating the Ubiquitous, Misunderstood, and Evolving Role of the Educational Leadership Program Coordinator in Higher Education, pp. 81–95

tion about the noncognitive, intuitive, and interpersonal characteristics and behaviors necessary for functioning and thriving in the role may not exist at all. Two quite different individuals can manage two robust programs, share faculty and other resources, and remain friends. But it takes work.

Keywords: self-study, critical friend, action research, program coordinator, educational leadership

Our Story: Becoming an Educational Leadership Preparation Program Coordinator

Every program coordinator (PC) likely has some version of the same story about how they became a PC. It is equally likely that no one held "program coordinator" as the terminal dream job when launching an academic career. What is likely is that most PCs moved into that position as a result of someone else getting a promotion, retiring, or the genesis of a new program. That almost-accidental path is how both authors of this chapter became PCs. The university where these authors work houses two educational leadership programs, one an MEd program and the other an EdD program. Each author is the PC for one of those programs, but the faculty members who deliver the instruction for both programs are shared. In addition, one PC is also a full-time instructor, and the other PC is an associate dean with extensive administrative responsibilities. One factor that helps this complex arrangement work is that both PCs were originally in the same program and had the same role. It was not necessary to build a common language or the contextual structure for communication because that common language, the understanding of the functions of the programs, and the areas in need of improvement were already understood and had been part of the collegial conversation between the two PCs for several years.

The MEd and EdD programs were originally quite separate with little communication and little cross-over. One criticism of the "old" structure was that the two programs functioned as separate silos. The simultaneous retirement and promotion of several EdD faculty members left a significant gap and occurred while many EdD candidates were in various stages of program completion. Due to the retirement of faculty related to the EdD program, the associate dean whose academic home was in educational leadership was appointed interim program coordinator for the EdD program, an interim title that has lasted for over three years. While a sudden departure of virtually all the EdD faculty would normally be seen as an unfortunate situation, there were two conditions in play that softened the impact of that loss. One condition was that the EdD program was ripe for change, having had little structural overhaul in over a decade, and several leaders in the college and university were pleased with the opportunity to effectuate changes. The other condition that helped soften the impact of the loss of faculty was that the university and college were undergoing massive change, too. A new president joined the university during the same summer that the educational leadership program changes took place, and the educational leadership programs moved from one department and building to a new department and building as part of a significant reorganization of the college. The new president replaced a revered icon who had passed away while in office and brought a wave of new ideas and expectations. The new "home" for the educational leadership programs meant new offices, a new department chair, new colleagues, and even a new name for the reconstructed department. In the middle of those tectonic shifts, the changing PC roles seemed almost tame.

Having the faculty from both the MEd program and the EdD program teach in both programs was a change that the college leadership had long intended to make. Because no new faculty were added amid the changes, the practical outcome was that formerly MEd faculty took on teaching responsibility in the EdD program, and more adjuncts were recruited to teach in both degree programs. One serious challenge was finding sufficient faculty for taking on the completion of serving as dissertation chairs and committee members for those students who had begun their degrees with the original faculty and structure. The new EdD coordinator had to spend a great deal of time simply filling teaching vacancies with the best faculty members available, resulting in a mix of full-time educational leadership faculty, visiting and adjunct faculty, and other experienced research faculty from across the university.

At the same time that stop-gap measures were taken, significant improvement planning was also taking place. These included a complete overhaul of the degree itself, concentration areas, new courses, wholesale updating of some existing courses, a recruiting plan, and plans for moving the entire degree to online delivery. The responsibility for this very large-scale change fell in large part to the newly appointed interim PC although all faculty members were included. Approval from the state higher education board and the commissioner was also necessary because the changes were fundamental and far exceeded minimal tweaking. After the new structure was in place, all the courses had to be written, examined, and approved for online delivery. All faculty members participated in that process, and several discipline experts outside the programs were recruited to write special courses. After two years of concentrated work, most of the courses are complete or near completion. The improved EdD program began reaping the benefits of such a concentrated effort even during a period of extreme change.

In addition to the EdD programmatic changes, the MEd program added a new concentration for those students who wished to prepare for a leadership career as an athletic director. The new athletic director concentration was written as a proposal and approved, and new courses were added to the curriculum offerings. While the MEd programmatic changes were not as detailed and extensive as those in the EdD program, the curriculum processes were similar in nature. Of course, all the normal extra duties that occur in university life continued throughout the changes. These extra duties included audits, accreditation reviews, and the incorporation of a new state-wide certification process. There were also internal changes with some faculty turnover; however, university-wide turmoil and budget insecurities limited the replacement of all the faculty lost. The new president encountered strong resistance to his leadership style and was given a vote of no confidence by all the different groups on campus—faculty, deans, chairs, and staff. His departure was negotiated with the governing board after less than three years.

Overshadowing many of those changes was the profound and worldwide phenomenon that continues now, the COVID-19 pandemic. While the EdD program was developing intentional online courses, the entire university shifted to varying types of distance-learning platforms. Students learned to redefine their expectations for in-person, hybrid, streaming, and online course delivery and faculty learned new instructional strategies. In some ways, the turmoil created by the pandemic's closure of the university simultaneously served as a foil for the programmatic changes already underway. The change was happening at all levels of life—work, teaching, learning, communicating, and economics. In close-range retrospect, it is possible that the somewhat self-imposed changes that happened within the educational leadership program were made more palatable by the overwhelming changes happening universally. The PCs for the two programs strategically planned and implemented much of this change. The EdD program experienced the greatest redevelopment but, because of the blending of the faculty of both degree programs, everyone shared in that shift. While much change has been achieved, there remain unfinished components. The university changes are still at the forefront; budgetary insecurities still exist, and post-COVID-19 student enrollment is stagnant. Still, the dizzying pace of change during the preceding few years may have abated enough to allow the PCs the time for effective reflection concerning how the roles, responsibilities, expectations, resources, and other components of program coordinator life have evolved and to reaffirm some control over the direction of that evolutionary process.

The Importance of Friends and Critical Friends

Developing and nurturing relationships is vital for a PC. Self-study allows one to develop and analyze his/her practices and experiences through reflective practices. "Critical friends and collaborative interactions are central to self-study" (Alan et al., 2021, p. 319). Specifically, the dialogue and the collaborative interactions between the "friend" and "self" are so important. A self-study with critical friendship as an instrumental component within the self-study provides many strengths for all involved in the process.

It is difficult to determine whether "critical" or "friend" is the dominant concept in discussing what makes a critical friend in the context that the term is used in academia. Both terms are crucial. The concept of critical friends is used most frequently in the United Kingdom and entered general usage from a self-characterization by Peter Kilfoyle, a British MP who resigned his position when he could no longer support the policy agenda of then Prime Minister Tony Blair, saying that he wished to retreat to the back benches but remain a "critical friend" of the government (Swaffield & McBeath, 2005). A similar term used in politics is "loyal opposition"—indicating both a level of allegiance (loyal/friend) but also tension (opposition/critical). A critical friend is a collaborator, but also much more. A PC in educational leadership is partly a teacher and partly an administrator. In combing out that tangle of dual roles, listening to and hearing the voices of many others is essential. Those others include other teaching faculty and other administration officials. The PC has a foot in two camps—teacher and administrator, executor and executive, planner, and implementer. In addition, PCs are both mentors and mentees. The multilevel duality of the position of PC is a natural fit for self-study research, a major feature of which is collaborating with others (Lighthall, 2004). In education, collaboration and partnerships are valued. For PCs, collaboration and partnership are practiced laterally (with others of similar roles and ranks) and in both directions by sometimes being a mentor and sometimes being a mentee. The capacity to change roles swiftly and convincingly is a skill that must be developed by PCs. For example, in the course of just one day, a PC may lead a meeting of faculty members from their academic program, move immediately to teach a class, then join a group of other PCs at the request of a dean or provost. In those three spaces, the PC would have acted as a collaborator, a leader, and in a subordinate role within a few hours. Participating appropriately in each space can be a challenge.

For the authors, the constant role change and need for tailored participation in groups added another layer of complexity. One author is both an associate dean and PC. Depending on the context of the situation, the duality of her role specifically with faculty members changes from parallel to dominant/subordinate. She also balances role changes with the department chair in the academic unit that houses educational leadership. Whether she is wearing the "associate dean hat" or the "PC hat" determines her level and type of participation. Without the grounding of critical friendship, where mutual respect and concern for the well-being of the other are present, the fluidity of constant role-shifting would prove unworkable. Some examples of how we practice critical friendship are the following: care is taken to make program planning sessions inclusive, frequent catch-up conversations take place in a variety of modalities, and common terminology is intentionally chosen when creating program documents. While it is important to look for areas of commonality, it is also important to retain sufficient independence for each program so that the students who are in each program can build their separate communities and not be considered simply an appendage of the other.

Critical friendship can be the defining component of successful self-study. To change participatory roles fluidly as is needed for PCs, a thorough and honest understanding of one's strengths and weaknesses is necessary. The development of that honest understanding is achieved by self-study in the company of a critical friend. The authors practice critical friendship through the intentional use of several repetitive language tropes. For example, one coordinator/author ends most ideas or proposals with "What do you think?" and the other coordinator/author ends most telephone conversations with "We'll talk later." Both phrases serve to invite the other person to continue the conversation, avoiding polarizing take-it-or-leave-it stances. Of course, when a decision is needed, both coordinators recognize the importance of closure. Often, when neither persuasion nor compromise prevails, the "winner" is the coordinator who holds the most responsibility for the outcome or has the stronger attachment to their argument's position.

While seemingly contradictory in nature, self-study, as a research exercise, is most effective when it is practiced with others. As noted earlier, critical friendship is an important part of self-study. Without the sounding board aspect of critical friendship, self-study would lack the clarity that is achieved when you must share an idea, wish, or concept with another—and accept the judgment of that other. The acceptance part is what elevates critical friendship above simple criticism. As anyone who grades or adjudicates written essays knows, it is very easy to find errors, but it is much harder to focus on perceived errors and convince the writer that a suggested alteration is better. An effective critical friend can make the work of another better without usurping the ownership of the original writer. Among education professionals, self-study with critical friendship enriches the work and practice of both parties (Berry & Russell, 2014). Critical friendship promotes skills and fluidity in communication because it requires reasoned defense of assumptions and reality checks. Critical friendships are mutually beneficial (Baskerville & Goldblatt, 2009).

Incorporating Critical Friends in Research and Practice

Although an equal partnership may be desirable, balanced power in a two-member relationship is rarely equal. At best, the power pendulum swings with one member having more power more often than the other. Just as self-study is an important factor in critical friendships, so is mentoring. Some of the proven methods for critical friendships in educator training and preparation programs include student support groups, PCs paired with less experienced faculty (or adjunct instructors), equal partners in collaborative research or work, transference, and retention of training, and collaborative support strategies.

Student support groups are effective platforms for critical friend theory. Fletcher et al. (2016) employed two layers of critical friendship with three participants in the initiation of pedagogical innovation. Two of the participants operated as a dyad, incorporating self-study, critical conversations, and interactivity during a period where the two participants were engaged in the same pedagogical innovation in their separate classrooms. The third participant acted as a "meta-critical friend" triangulation point, providing support and critique for both the others. The researchers found several faults with the design during the first year of implementation. Namely, the participants had not established sufficient goals or defined expectations. Instead of critical friendships and collaborative self-study, they found that each participant had taken on a role more nearly resembling that of a coach. Through the efforts of the meta-critical friend, they self-corrected. During the second year, they engaged in better planning and provided intentionally contentious feedback to help each other push the boundaries of their initial levels of comfort. In this two-year study, the participants were all of the same academic rank, and all took their turns being a meta-critical friend. At the end of the study, all three reported greater confidence, better communication skills, and wider perspectives concerning their pedagogical innovation (Fletcher et al. 2016).

Another model for practicing critical friendship is with a clearly defined static role of mentor and mentee. Baker and Bitto (2021) established a critical friend dyad with the PC and an adjunct instructor as the two participants. They explored the barriers in a critical friendship when the two participants are separated by hierarchical rank and experience and sought ways to use self-study to foster a reciprocal mentorship relationship that would help both grow in their practice. One finding was that the critical friend method is messy and exposes vulnerability. They selected weekly telephone conversations as their primary communication tool after the adjunct participant had finished teaching. In their early individual reports, both researchers wrote about feeling frustrated, confused, excluded, and unappreciated. Addressing these negative observations, the researchers developed collaborative norms that defined a safe environment for critical conversations. Baker and Bitto experienced the same error in planning that the Fletcher group encountered—a lack of preplanning for communication style, time frame, verbal cues, and other protocols that allow the *critical* part of critical friends methodology to function. The reflective protocol they developed gave shape, assessment, and measurement to their critical friend conversations. Specifically, the Baker and Bitto reflective protocol articulated an intention, questions to ask in the reflective conversations, and a description of the actions that each participant took as a result of the answers to the questions. The end product was a rubric chart that not only worked for the researchers but is also a model for others using critical friendships for self-study.

Another model for using the critical friends approach is with two participants of equal hierarchical rank and power. Martin and Dismuke (2015) recognized that some of the traditional values found in higher education, such as individual achievement, academic freedom, and scholarship are not conducive to a collaboration of the sort that is encouraged in K–12 public schools (co-teaching, professional learning communities). During their study, both researchers were teaching the same course but with different sections. The agreed protocol was that of two equals, even though their relationship had been hierarchical in the past. As in other studies, Martin and Dismuke determined that structured conversations with mutually generated questions would provide the best product and sufficient data. In addition, they engaged in extensive reflective writing, simultaneously creating a transcript for trend analysis. The four major findings were descriptors of the ways that their collaboration evolved. The first was that the initial structured conversations became more fluid, especially in the number of their interactions. As equal partners, the second factor they found was that they shifted between the roles of mentor/mentee and each served as a critical friend to the other, thereby challenging and growing. The third factor found was the evolution of a collective vision which included individual practices, and the fourth was support for risk-taking. Collaborative professional practices that were adopted by public schools two decades ago are slowly emerging in higher education (Martin & Dismuke, 2015).

Stolle et al. (2019) employed a self-study model similar to others, using written communication, recorded and transcribed telephone conversations, and memos related to critical friend responses. One major difference in their model was that, in addition to the two primary researchers, they invited two other participants external to their study to serve as critical friends to both researchers. The decision to use external critical friends was due to the influence of the layering approach in Fletcher et al. (2016). Martin and Dismuke's (2015) research produced two tools for other researchers in critical friends theory, the Critical Friend Definition Continuum and the Critical Friend Guide for Quality Assurance. The Definition Continuum demonstrates the ranges of eight constructs: Close Friend/Stranger, Insider/Outsider, Expert/Non-Expert, Fully Involved/Loosely Involved, Reciprocal in Nature/One Way, Multiple Critical Friends/Single Critical Friend, Productive/Not Productive, and Defined Expectations/No Defined Expectations. They stated unequivocally that the eight terms on the Definition Continuum are not values but are merely descriptors of eight of the components of the relationship among critical friend researchers and practitioners. The Guide for Quality Assurance is a set of questions to ask and answer at the start of a study, throughout the implementation of the study, and at the end of the study. The last question for the end of the study is "Did the critical friends offer alternate perspectives, lead you to new insights, or help to reframe your thinking?" (Martin & Dismuke, 2015). If the critical friends theory has been used effectively, that answer is a positive endorsement of the critical friends process of self-study.

Another model for the use of critical friends theory is with larger groups than dyads or dyads plus external critical friends. Unlike public schools, there is no structured preparation program designed to provide training for the role of PC. Ladyshewsky and Flavell (2011) found that concentrated, prolonged, and well-planned leadership development programs, when accompanied by group identification and communication, resulted in long-term behavioral changes. Furthermore, the self-study with shared peer reflections revealed strong retention of the learned changes in leadership behavior for the PCs who participated in the study (Ladyshewsky & Flavell, 2011).

A final model for the permanent transfer of skills through critical friends-types of self-study involved measuring the extent of retained leadership skills at one month, six months, and one year after the training (Cromwell & Kolb, 2004). The four work-environment factors studied were support from the organization, support from a supervisor, peer support, and participation in a peer support network. The results indicate that all forms of support are useful, but primarily at the point most distant from the training. While a peer support network is not necessarily critical friend theory behavior, it could signify a similar positive effect. The researchers recommended that universities explore the viability of long-term peer support groups for midlevel administrators because it was a strong indicator of retention of the desired behaviors and is at no cost and with little risk.

What do critical friends theory and self-study mean for PCs in higher education? It provides a research-validated map for efficient and effective use of time and provides a foundation for true collaboration that is not likely to emerge organically among the rich broth of personnel types at many universities: scholars, adjunct instructors, non-tenured instructors, part-time teacher/administrators, online instructors, remote instructors, and many others. Opportunities for the informal growth of social friendships that may evolve into scholarly friendships are not as prevalent with the many delivery options available. For the authors of this chapter, the variation among our shared faculty is such that there is not even an identifiable trend. Gender, prior experience, research interests, and time in higher education are just some of the areas where our descriptors would track along a continuum. For that reason, critical friends models for shared decision-making, course construction, and other tasks that currently are performed in silos are filled with potential for the two coordinators/authors to expand our critical friend relationship to blend the faculty mindsets more effectively.

Critical Friends in Action Research and Evolution of the Program Coordinator Role

Research on leadership is by nature action-oriented. Even though theories and worldviews impact how leadership is performed, ultimately it is in performance where leadership can be observed. Collinson and Collinson (2009) posed an interesting departure from traditional research on leadership and leadership behavior. Their specific area of focus was on further education (FE) in the United Kingdom. This level of schooling is similar to community colleges in the United States (p. 366). Leadership was examined as evolving from "heroic"—leaders who have a clear sense of direction, are good strategic planners, are inspirational, and are self-confident. That vision of leadership has come under some criticism for being unrealistic and not recognizing the impact of context on leadership behavior. The "post-heroic" leader shares decision-making and planning and eschews "heroic" top-down leadership, favoring what Collinson and Collinson call blended leadership. Another factor in the conversation about heroic and post-heroic leadership is followership, which is a logical extension of leadership—without followers, a leader cannot lead. Their research design centered on interviews with a large number of educational professionals who held varying levels of leadership and instructional roles throughout the FE programs in the United Kingdom. Specifically, the interviews sought to determine what types of leadership were desired and what characteristics a perceived effective leader might hold or exhibit. While there were small groups on the extreme ends of preference for directive and decisive leaders to hands-off and silent leaders, the majority preferred a combination of exhibited behaviors and skills. For example, "blended leadership" is where both delegation and direction are valued, and both proximity and distance are valued. The emergent profile of a perceived effective leader points to a large task for educational leader preparation programs—to define, itemize, teach, and assess such a dichotomous leadership style. This model is found in much popular literature on leadership and appears to be the ideal. Collinson and Collinson conclude with a prediction that leaders in higher education may be well-suited for developing blended leadership because they are already familiar with the balancing act of blending scholarship, teaching, and service. Certainly, an effective leader who practices blended leadership would do well to consider the use of self-study and critical friend methodology.

Mena and Russell (2017) conducted a meta-analysis of the 65 studies presented at a 2014 conference on the concept of self-study in educator preparation, specifically to determine whether self-study research effectively incorporates five important components of self-study: self-initiated inquiry that is fixed, improvement-aimed, collaborative, diverse in research methodology, and credible (Mena & Russell, 2017). The analysis showed that most of the studies presented at the conference were from faculty teaching programs with case studies and analyses as the primary instructional method and that most were conducted in collaborative settings. While the overall review concluded that most of the presented studies met the minimum bar of incorporation of the major components of self-study, not all of them provided adequately for multiple research methods, collaboration, and credibility. For PCs in education leadership programs, the cautionary tale would be to critically examine program curricula related to self-study.

Two New Zealand researchers recorded their planning, communication, and actions during a self-study utilizing critical friend methods and discovered a process for learning how to be a critical friend (Baskerville & Goldblatt, 2009). Their study utilized field notes and transcriptions of conversations and interviews and reflections. The result was a model that fosters the development of critical friendship, moving through identified phases. The researchers were not acquainted before embarking on the project, so the development of the necessary trust was authentic. They named the first phase *Professional Indifference* where they found shared values and shared commitment to the specific project at hand, which was studying teacher in-service effectiveness.

As commonalities were identified and some values shared, the friendship moved to developing respect for the opinions of the other, labeled *Tentative Trust*. As the work progressed, a genuine interest in the work and success of the other developed, which they named the *Reliance* phase. The Reliance phase was followed by *Conviction* and culminated with *Unguarded*

Conversations. They were quick to point out that these labels were attached in hindsight, upon completion of the 18-month project. One product was a critical reflection worksheet that provided the probing questions needed for critical friendship. Examples are "In what ways were you a critical friend today?" and "How did others stimulate your thinking?" These questions and others of a similar nature encourage the *critical* part of the concept, opening areas that the other participant may not have noticed. They also developed a worksheet for the transcriptions of conversations that elicit reflective responses to the partner's affirmative statements. The actual worksheet resembles a Twitter thread but with two columns, one for the actual words spoken in the interview or meeting, like a play script, and the second column for the reflective observation of the partner (Baskerville & Goldblatt, 2008).

Action research is not always the first choice for serious academicians, but the work done on critical friend methodology and the efficacy of self-study should make it more attractive. One group of PCs in Hong Kong produced a new model for the role of the critical friend (Kember et al., 1997) with the assignment of several different functions to team members. Although the members had unique functions within the team, all seven of them acted as mutual critical friends, one with the other. The roles within their support group for the action research project included experts in design as well as rapport builder and matchmaker. The matchmaker was responsible for bringing together two compatible critical friends. After the project one member summarized the group's experience with this observation:

> Having been an associate coordinator for more than a year, I am now fully aware of the importance and difficulties of building a non-threatening and mutual respect relationship with the teams. Yet I have to admit that I was a bit naïve when I first took up the job, which was in part due to the unfamiliar working environment and in part the ambiguity of my role. (Kember et al., 1997, p. 479)

The concluding statement of their paper was the recognition of the value of critical friendships both in action research and in developing competence in the role of the PC.

A decade after the Kember study, an educational leadership professor in Arizona voiced similar findings in her discovery of the value of external conversations with a critical friend outside the contextual setting of her research. Qualitative studies, especially when done alone, may easily overwhelm the researcher, which is what Foulger (2010) found. When she recruited an external critical friend who was familiar with the experiences of the researcher but not steeped in the setting, their critical friendship conversations provided a level of clarity and objectivity that might not have occurred had the researcher continued alone (Foulger, 2010).

Conclusion

PCs in educational leadership departments can easily fall victim to any of the difficulties reported by the cited researchers who examined various aspects of critical friend theory and methodology. Remember that most practitioners preferred blended leadership from their PCs, as opposed to the directive approach, and that there are several vetted tools for conducting action research and self-study utilizing critical friends. Further, critical friends may be equal partners, mutual support groups, or mentors/mentees.

The role of the PC is a hybrid one—part teacher, part leader—and is often ambiguous. Critical friends have a variety of roles depending on the situation. For instance, the critical friend may be a facilitator, collaborator, researcher, supporter, critic, or confidant (Alan et al., 2021; Mat Noor & Shafee, 2000). Having a critical friend to go through systematic self-study with may be the answer for both a research agenda as well as for program and professional development. In the self-study, the critical friend would serve as a facilitator or guide and challenge the researcher to think differently by asking provocative questions. Then, after a complete assessment of the work, the "friend" would provide a critique of the work (Alan et al., 2021). Alan et al. (2021) describe many basic attributes that critical friends possess. The skills and attributes include: (a) providing challenging questions, (b) being a respectful careful observer, (c) context awareness, (d) responsibility commitment, (e) analytical skills, (f) being perceptively detail-oriented, (g) listening skills, and (h) provide constructive criticism (p. 329).

Self-study with critical friendship is an interactive process between the friend and researcher. While it may seem easy, as friendships usually are, the critical friendship arrangement is often complex and complicated at times. While the authors of this chapter have not conducted formal critical friend research, our relationship which has been intentionally developed over several years has provided structure for addressing the very tumultuous events that our university, college, and programs have faced. Through these difficult times, the authors have helped each other by asking difficult but critical questions. In other words, the authors have become the "critical friend" that assists the other PC to recognize issues and change the lenses to see the possible solutions in a different light. Through collaborative efforts with one focus, the authors can provide better educational leadership programs for the students.

REFERENCES

Alan, B., Sariyev, H., & Odabasi, H. F. (2021). Critical friendship in self-study. *Journal of Qualitative Research in Education, 25*, 316–334. https://doi.org/10.14689/enad.25.14

Baker, C., & Bitto, L. (2021). Fostering a critical friendship between a program coordinator and an online adjunct to achieve reciprocal mentoring. *Studying Teacher Education, 17*(2), 188–207. https://doi.org/10.1080/17425964.2021.1903413

Baskerville, D., & Goldblatt, H. (2009). Learning to be a critical friend: from professional indifference through challenge to unguarded conversations. *Cambridge Journal of Education, 39*(2), 205–221. https://doi.org/10.1080/03057640902902260

Berry, M., & Russell, T. (2014). Critical friends, collaborators and community in self-study. *Studying Teacher Education, 10*(3), 195–196. https://doi.org/10.1080/17425964.2014.958283

Collinson, D., & Collinson, M. (2009). 'Blended leadership': Employee perspectives on effective leadership in the UK. *Leadership, 5*(3), 365–380. https://doi.org/10.1177/1742715009337766

Cromwell, S., & Kolb, J. (2004). An examination of work-environment support factors affecting the transfer of supervisory skills training to the workplace. *Human Resource Development Quarterly, 15*(4), 449–471. https://doi.org/10.1002/hrdq.1115

Fletcher, T., Chróinín, D. N., & O'Sullivan, M. (2016). A layered approach to critical friendship as a means to support pedagogical innovation in pre-service teacher education. *Studying Teacher Education, 12*(3), 302–319. https://doi.org/10.1080/17425964.2016.1228049

Foulger, T. (2010). An unexpected discovery about the critical friend in action research inquiries. *Action Research, 8*(2), 135–152. https://doi.org/10.1177/1476750309351354

Kember, D., Ha, T., Lam, B., Lee, A., NG, S., Yan, L., & Yum, J. C. K. (1997). The diverse role of the critical friend in supporting educational action research projects. *Educational Action Research, 5*(3), 463–481. https://doi.org/10.1080/09650799700200036

Ladyshewsky, R., & Flavell, H. (2011). Transfer of training in an academic leadership development program for program coordinators. *Educational Management, 40*(1), 127–147. https://doi.org/10.1177/1741143211420615

Lighthall, F. (2004). Fundamental features and approaches of the S-Step Enterprise. In J. J. Loughran, M. L. Hamilton, V. K. LaBoskey, & T. Russell (Eds.), *International handbook of self-study of teaching and teacher education practices* (pp. 193–246). Kluwer.

Mat Noor, M. S. A., & Shafee, A. (2020, July). The role of critical friends in action research: A framework for design and implementation. *Practitioner Research, 3*, 1–33. https://doi.org/10.32890/pr2021.3.1

Martin, S., & Dismuke, S. (2015). Maneuvering together to develop new practices: examining our collaborative processes. *Studying Teacher Education, 11*(1), 3–15. https://doi.org/10.1080/17425964.2014.1001356

Mena, J., & Russell, T. (2017). Collaboration, multiple methods, trustworthiness: Issues arising from the 2014 international conference on self-study of teacher education practices. *Studying Teacher Education, 13*(1), 105–122. https://doi.org/10.1080/17425964.2017.1287694

Stolle, E., Frambaugh-Kritzer, C., Freese, A., & Persson, A. (2019). Investigating critical friendship: peeling back the layers. *Studying Teacher Education, 15*(1), 19–30. https://doi.org/10.1080/17425964.2019.1580010

Swaffield, S., & MacBeath, J. (2005). School self-evaluation and the role of a critical friend. *Cambridge Journal of Education, 35*(2), 239–252. https://doi.org/10.1080/03057640500147037

CHAPTER 6

PROGRAM COORDINATION AT UCEA-AFFILIATED UNIVERSITIES IN THE WAKE OF COVID-19

William Kyle Ingle
University of Louisville

Joanne M. Marshall
Iowa State University

ABSTRACT

We surveyed program coordinators at UCEA-member institutions in the spring of 2022 to understand how COVID-19 has shaped their work and their responsibilities. Among our findings, 79.1% of respondents reported that their research responsibilities received less attention due to program coordination responsibilities. Interestingly, the average number of responsibilities decreased from approximately 18 in 2017 to 17 in 2022 and the percentage of respondents reporting at least 11–15 hours weekly on program coordination decreased from 60.8% in 2017 to 47.7% in 2022. Our respondents reported decreases in the number of incentives and supports in comparison to 2017 prior to the pandemic. Furthermore, we found a significant difference between White and non-White program coordinators ($p > .05$), such that minority program coordinators reported receiving significantly fewer incentives than their White counterparts did. Analysis of open-ended responses revealed that respondents highlighted the challenges associ-

Navigating the Ubiquitous, Misunderstood, and Evolving Role of the Educational Leadership Program Coordinator in Higher Education, pp. 97–133

ated with transitioning to online instruction, challenges in recruitment, the increase in demands of scholar-practitioners in their professional lives, and the rise in mental health needs among students and faculty alike. The stresses wrought by the pandemic may contribute to program coordinator turnover and complicate efforts to ensure quality educational leadership preparation and sustainable cultures that foster transformative change around diversity, equity, and inclusion.

Keywords: Program Coordination, Educational Leadership Programs,

Higher Education, Faculty

Since its emergence in late 2019, the COVID-19 pandemic has disrupted everyday life, commerce, and education in communities around the world. In response, individuals, communities, and governments adopted measures to mitigate infections, hospitalizations, and deaths. These measures included social distancing, self-quarantining, widespread testing, stay-at-home measures, and vaccines. The United States reached a grim milestone of one million reported COVID-19 deaths in May 2022 (Donovan, 2022). Elected officials and educational leaders in K–12 and higher education bore the responsibility for safeguarding the health, safety, and well-being of students and staff members. Their options included reopening schools and universities, closing them, or adopting online instruction. Educational institutions—both K–12 and postsecondary—struggled to provide instruction and adapt to ever-changing conditions (e.g., Piotrowski & King, 2020; Van Lancker & Parolin, 2020).

Leaders of educational institutions also struggled to provide socioemotional support to students, faculty, and staff (Johnson, 2022; Reich & Mahta, 2021; Trinidad, 2021; Woo & Steiner, 2022). Some researchers were already concerned about teacher stress leading to attrition *before* COVID-19, and predicted that COVID's stresses would lead to more employee turnover and shortages (Cooper & Hickey, 2022; Zamarro et al., 2022), though others disputed that prediction, noting that shortages vary widely by district and content area (Diliberti & Schwartz, 2022; Schwartz & Diliberti, 2022a). Principals' job dissatisfaction is also high because of the pandemic and political pressures (National Association of Secondary School Principals, 2021; Schwartz & Diliberti, 2022b), though it is not clear whether that will lead to them actually leaving their jobs (Kaufman et al., 2022).

Plagued with uncertainties associated with infections, budgets, and enrollments, institutions of higher learning struggled to adapt to an ever-changing educational landscape. COVID-19 related budgetary shortfalls forced higher education leaders to consider a wide range of actions, including furloughing employees, cutting services, cutting expenses, eliminating programs altogether, and even rethinking the viability of future operations (Piotrowski & King, 2020). Staff members at institutions of higher learning struggled with stresses associated with the pandemic, disruptions in operations, a lack of social interaction, and necessary changes in communication due to the pandemic (Filho et al., 2021). Students in higher education also adapted to challenges wrought by the pandemic. Piotrowski and King (2020) noted that students thrust into online instruction due to the pandemic had wide-ranging prior experience with this mode of instruction and wide variation in access to the technology needed to participate. Furthermore, the pandemic affected the provision of services and learning experiences adversely. These included the delay, cancellation, or adaptation of student internships and field experiences due to placement sites being unable to accommodate them, as well as limited physical access to university libraries and services. Students with full-time employment also faced the possibility of unemployment caused by the pandemic or working in high-risk health environments.

In the case of graduate students in K–12 educational leadership programs—who tend to be practicing teachers, counselors, or educational leaders—changes in instructional delivery not only occurred in the graduate degree programs and certificates they were pursuing, but also in the school districts that employed them. Teachers and educational leaders had to adapt instruction and operations to address logistical challenges associated with providing internet access, technology, and resources to ensure an equitable online learning environment for students (Fagell, 2020; Kaden, 2020). There were other factors to consider, such as students' access to food (Van Lancker & Parolin, 2020) and mental health needs (Hoffman & Miller, 2020; Torres-Pagán & Terepka, 2020). K–12 students and their parents had to adapt to the changes in instructional delivery by developing new learning strategies and coping skills to combat social isolation and loneliness (Brooks et al., 2020), not to mention disruptions to daily schedules and financial stresses wrought on household budgets by the pandemic (Kaden, 2020; Phelps & Sperry, 2020), particularly for women (Barroso & Horowitz, 2021; Craig, 2020).

Program coordinators of K–12 educational leadership preparation programs witnessed and addressed these challenges present in both higher education and in K–12. The program coordinator is a quasi-administrative role within universities, which balances program coordination responsibilities alongside other faculty responsibilities, including teaching, advising, research, and service. Initially developed in 2016 and first implemented in the spring of 2017, we reissued the Program Coordination Survey[1] (PCS) to program coordinators at member institutions of the University Council for Educational Administration (UCEA) in the spring of 2022 to understand how COVID-19 had shaped their work and their responsibilities. The

PCS asked program coordinators to provide demographic information, estimates about the time commitments associated with program coordination, the extent to which program coordination conflicted with other faculty roles, incentives provided by their institution for assuming program coordination responsibilities, and open-ended items on how the COVID-19 pandemic affected their work as a program coordinator.

In this study, we addressed the following research questions:

- What are the characteristics of program coordinators at UCEA-member institutions during the COVID-19 pandemic in terms of gender, race, faculty rank, experiences, and the number of programs for which they are responsible?
- How much time do program coordinators commit to program coordination during the pandemic?
- What roles do program coordinators report as falling under their responsibilities during the pandemic?
- What supports and incentives do program coordinators report as being provided for their assumption of these duties during the pandemic?
- What do program coordinators perceive as the greatest rewards and challenges of serving as a program coordinator during the COVID-19 pandemic?
- How do the responses in 2022 compare to those provided in 2017 prior to the COVID-19 pandemic?
- Has the COVID-19 pandemic affected the work of program coordinators? If so, how?

EDUCATIONAL LEADERSHIP DURING THE PANDEMIC

Given the disruptive nature of the COVID-19 pandemic, it should come as no surprise that scholars are interested in how a major public health crisis has affected the work of educational leaders (e.g., Johnson, 2022; Piotrowski & King, 2020; Reich & Mahta, 2021; Trinidad, 2021; Van Lancker & Parolin, 2020; Woo & Steiner, 2022). These studies are relatively recent, and the research will continue to unfold as researchers explore COVID-19's impact on higher education and K–12 education in both broad and institutional contexts. Researchers in P–12 educational leadership have noted that crisis leadership has not had a sustained focus within the field, characterizing the extant research as focused on a sudden specific crisis or on specific phases of a crisis (Mutch, 2018; Striepe & Cunningham, 2022). For example, Hemmer and Eliff (2020) explored how seven superintendents responded to Hurricane Harvey striking their Texas school districts in 2017. Hemmer and Eliff organized their findings into four distinct episodes: (1) the superintendents' work prior to the arrival of the hurricane (e.g., review of procedures and the illusion of truly being prepared); (2) Hurricane Harvey's landfall (e.g., taking stock, waiting, and wondering); (3) no calm immediately after the storm (e.g., pressures to re-open, rebuilding, repairing); (4) after the hurricane: new challenges/norms (e.g., challenges of bureaucracy, regulations, and insurance claims). Hemmer and Eliff found that crises exert pressure on superintendents to strategize and act in the moment, leveraging positive opportunities and managing threats and challenges. Studying leaders in crisis provides an opportunity to gain a deeper understanding of leaders in crisis, their reflexive practice, prior experiences that aided them through the crisis, and adaptation and innovations made in the moments of crisis. Challenges posed by the hurricane pushed superintendents to collaborate more closely in the face of shared challenges.

Researchers define a crisis as a situation, event, or series of events that present a risk to the reputation of an organization, the safety and well-being of its employees and customers, and/or results in substantial damage to physical property or institutional financial well-being (Bataille & Cordova, 2014; Blumenstyk, 2014; Gigliotti, 2020; Kruse et al., 2020). Characterized by their complexity and susceptibility to externalities, higher educational institutions are particularly vulnerable to crises at multiple levels, including the program-, department-, college-, institution-, and system-levels (Brennan & Stern, 2017; Kruse et al., 2020). As Gigliotti (2021) notes:

> The current historical moment presents an interesting set of paradoxes for leaders across the higher education landscape, including the desire for information during a time of remarkable uncertainty, the hunger for connection during a period of social distancing, and the need for swift and agile leadership within organizations and environments that tend to privilege careful and deliberative decision-making. (p. 433)

The research on crisis leadership in higher education has tended to focus on formal administrative positions, such as university presidents (e.g., Brennan & Stern, 2017), college deans (e.g., Shaw, 2018), and department chairs (Gigliotti, 2021; Kruse et al., 2020) rather than program coordinators or program directors. Kruse et al. (2020) focused on three department chairs, utilizing a qualitative design; specifically, they used dialogic inquiry, to reflect on their experiences and responses to the demands wrought by the pandemic. They noted that the pandemic, subsequent budget woes, and the preexistence of systemic racism emerged as interwoven crisis events, creating challenges for higher education institutions. Kruse et al. found that department chairs "and by extension other educational leaders"

(p. 12) who engage in shared inquiry and models of support that focus on empathy and compassion in times of crisis may be more effective than traditional mentoring and coaching models that tend to focus on problem resolution. They and others (e.g., Alford & Head, 2017) noted that crises cause long lasting disruptions on budgets practices, research productivity, faculty evaluation, student learning experiences, and K–12 school/university partnerships that must be systemically explored. Kruse et al. also recommended that department chairs consider the ways in which institutional policy, practice, and departmental missions might be reconsidered and restructured in the wake of crises. Lastly, they acknowledge an ongoing disconnect between the scope and difficulty of department chairs' work and the ways in which that work is recognized and supported by their supervisors and employees.

Marshall et al. (2020) critically examined how higher educational leaders managed the initial phase of the COVID-crisis in Barbados and Canada, identifying the leadership strategies used to address the challenges posed in the early phase of the pandemic. While Marshall et al. do not specify what types of higher educational leaders participated, they identified four critical leadership skills and behaviors needed during the pandemic: providing clear direction, communicating effectively, working collaboratively, and engaging in adaptive leadership. Marshall et al. found that educational leaders acted carefully, decisively, and efficiently despite the ambiguous nature of the early stages of the pandemic. Second, they found that educational leaders communicated effectively with their stakeholders, thus providing reassurance and comfort during a particularly anxious time. Third, educational leaders worked collaboratively with stakeholders, involving them in decision-making. Last, the pandemic required educational leaders to become adaptive leaders, responding to ever-changing conditions and unpredictability.

Utilizing a survey research design, Gigliotti (2021) explored the impact of COVID-19 on department chairs, but in the context of Big 10-affiliated universities in the United States. He noted that, "in normal circumstances, the role of the academic department chair is both complex and ambiguous" (p. 429), but the convergence of crises, including the COVID-19 pandemic, economic concerns, racial unrest, partisan polarization, and climate change, exacerbated the challenges of department leadership in institutions of higher education. These crises heightened the complexity of the work, accentuated the liminality of the department chair role, and intensified the challenges of academic department leadership, requiring department chairs to continually pivot among supporting the needs of senior administrators, colleagues, and students within their departments. This kind of middle manager role is similar to that of the program coordinator but with more formal authority.

In sum, the research on higher educational leadership in crises has tended to focus on formal leadership positions, such as presidents, deans, and department chairs rather than program coordinators who occupy informal, quasi-administrative roles. We know of no other study to date that focuses on the role of program coordinators during crises, whether that of the COVID-19 pandemic or another.

METHODS AND ANALYSIS

We utilized a mixed methods research design, employing a concurrent embedded design (Creswell, 2013) in which we collected quantitative and qualitative data simultaneously to address a different question than the primary method or to seek information at a different or deeper level. We delimited our study to program coordinators at member institutions of the UCEA, due to its being a leading professional organization that fosters quality educational leadership preparation and research. The organization agreed to assist in the proliferation of the survey and encouraged program coordinators at member institutions to respond.

In 2022, UCEA consisted of 113 member institutions. However, the number of program coordinators at each UCEA institution varies within their respective departments, as program coordinators may coordinate single or multiple programs (Ingle et al., 2020). We began by reviewing member institution profiles at UCEA's website, which includes information about each member institution, their educational leadership faculty, their emails, and their roles (e.g., faculty, plenary session representatives, department chairs, program coordinators). We also visited each member institution's program websites to triangulate information at UCEA's website, assuming that some member institution profiles may not be up to date. We identified 200 potential program coordinators across all UCEA member institutions. We extended email invitations to complete the survey. In some instances, faculty members responded to our email invitation, informing us they were no longer serving in the role and providing us with updated contacts. Follow-up emails were sent approximately two weeks after our initial invitation. In total, we received 86 complete responses, representing a response rate of 43%.

The PCS was initially piloted and administered to program coordinators in the 2016–2017 academic year (Ingle et al., 2018, 2020) and reissued in the spring of 2022. In addition to demographic information, the self-report questionnaire asked program coordinators to provide responses estimating the time commitments associated with program coordination, the extent to which program coordination conflicted with other faculty roles and identifying incentives institutions provided for assuming program coordination responsibilities. The survey concluded with five open-ended items. These items asked program coordinators about their administrative experiences prior to taking on program coordination; what they perceived as the greatest rewards of serving as a program coordinator; what they perceived as the greatest challenges of serving as a program coordinator; how the COVID-19 pandemic affected their work as a program coordinator; and if they would be interested in participating in an individual interview that explores more deeply how the COVID-19 pandemic has affected their work. The last question was to identify willing participants for qualitative study of program coordination during the pandemic.

Our analytical strategies consisted of simple descriptive analyses and independent *t*-tests, comparing means of male/female, White/non-White, public/private, and tenure-track/other program coordinators (e.g., tenured, non-tenure track) in terms of the number of responsibilities and incentives provided. For the open-ended qualitative items, we coded the responses in order to identify central constructs that existed across respondents, drawing upon theories of role conflict, role ambiguity, role commitment, and crisis leadership.

QUANTITATIVE ANALYSIS

We organize our discussion of findings by research question. We provide both simple descriptive analysis and independent samples *t*-tests between male and female program coordinators, program coordinators at public versus private institutions, White and non-White program coordinators, and tenured and non-tenured program coordinators in terms of average numbers of responsibilities and incentives offered. Throughout, we compare our present findings to those from our previous studies of UCEA program coordinators prior to the pandemic.

Characteristics of Program Coordinators

Of the 200 program coordinators invited to participate, we obtained 86 useable responses, representing a 43% response rate. This represents a decrease in response rate in comparison to our administration of the survey in 2017, which yielded a 62.2% rate (Ingle et al., 2020). In terms of the characteristics of our convenience sample, more female program coordinators (51; 59.3%) than males (33; 38.4%) completed our survey (Table 6.1). Similar to our previous study, an overwhelming majority (80.2%) of the respondents were White and worked at public state universities (86%).

Table 6.1

Descriptive Analysis

Variable		N = 86	%
Gender			
	Male	33	38.4
	Female	51	59.3
	Nonbinary	2	2.3
Race			
	White, non-Hispanic	69	80.2
	Hispanic	7	8.1
	Black or African American	7	8.1
	Native American	1	1.2
	Asian/Pacific Islander	1	1.2
	Multiracial	1	1.2
Faculty Status			
	Full-Time Tenured	46	53.5
	Full-Time Tenure-Track	11	12.8
	Full-Time Non-Tenure-track	28	32.6
	Other	1	1.2
Experience			
	Years of Service–2 Years or Less	26	30.2
	Years of Service–3 to 5 Years	34	39.5
	Years of Service–6 or More Years	26	30.2
	Has Prior Administrative Experience	62	72.1
	No Prior Administrative Experience	24	27.9
Number of Programs Coordinated			
	1 Program	32	37.2
	2 Programs	22	25.6
	3 Programs	11	12.8
	4 Programs	8	9.3
	5 Programs	8	9.3
	6 Programs	5	5.8

(Table continued on next page)

Table 6.1 (Continued)

Descriptive Analysis

Variable		N = 86	%
Institutional Type			
	Private University	12	14.0
	Public University	74	86.0
	R1: Doctoral University-Highest Research Activity	52	60.5
	R2: Doctoral University-Higher Research Activity	22	25.6
	R3: Doctoral University-Moderate Research Activity	6	7.0
	Master's College/University-Larger Program	1	1.2
	Master's College/University-Medium Program	1	1.2
	Unsure/Do Not Know	4	4.7
Institutional Provision of Training			
	Yes	7	8.1
	No	79	91.9
Selection Process			
	Elected by Faculty	9	10.5
	Nominated by Faculty & Appointed by Department Chair	4	4.7
	Appointed by Chair	42	48.8
	Volunteered	17	19.8
	Hired Specifically for the Position	7	8.1
	Coordination Rotates among Program Faculty	4	4.7
	Other (e.g., Developed and coordinated, No one else available)	3	3.4

In 2022, a majority of respondents (53.5%) were full-time tenured faculty members. Full-time non-tenure-track faculty members (e.g., clinical faculty members) were the second largest faculty status reported (32.6%). Consistent with our sample from 2017, only 12% of respondents in 2022 were full-time tenure-track faculty members. This suggests that UCEA member institutions are largely protecting pre-tenured faculty members from program coordination responsibilities to aid them in developing their research agendas and increasing the likelihood of earning tenure. In terms of years of service as program coordinators, 30% of our sample had two years or less in the role. Almost 40% has three to five years of experience and 30% had six or more years in the role. In 2017, 82.6% had prior school administrative experience. In 2022, this number was down to 72%. We asked respondents to identify how many programs for which they were responsible. In our sample, 37% coordinated a single program (e.g., master's in educational leadership) while 25.6% reported coordinating two programs. The remainder reported coordinating 3 or more programs. Consistent in both the 2017 and 2022 samples, a minority of respondents indicated that their institution provided any formal training for program coordinators.

Also consistent across the 2017 and 2022 samples were trends in the path to program coordination, with an appointment by their department chair reported as the predominant means by which respondents became program coordinators (48.8%). Only 10.5% reported being elected by their faculty. Nearly 20% volunteered.

Time Commitments of Program Coordination

When asked to estimate how many hours weekly were spent on program coordination during the academic year, responses varied widely. We aggregated the responses into ordinal range variables (Table 6.2). Nearly 21% of respondents in 2022 indicated they spent 1–5 hours per week on program coordination as compared to 12% in 2017. Twenty-seven percent of respondents in 2022 indicated they spent 6–10 hours per week on program coordination, whereas in 2017, that percentage was 25%, and 20.9% reported 11–15 hours weekly compared to 24% in 2017. Approximately 11% of our respondents in 2022 reported spending 31 or more hours a week on program coordination compared to 7.6.% in 2017.

Program coordinators were asked about the extent to which other responsibilities (research, teaching, other service, home/family life) received less attention as a result of assuming program coordination responsibilities. These Likert scale items had options ranging from "Never" to "Always." In 2017, 78.2% indicated research responsibilities received less attention (sometimes, often, or always) due to their assuming program coordination responsibilities. In 2022, 79.1% indicated research responsibilities received less attention (sometimes, often, or always) due to their assuming program coordination responsibilities (see Table 6.3). In 2017, 69.6% of respondents indicated teaching responsibilities received less attention (sometimes,

Table 6.2

Reported Number of Hours Per Week Spent on Program Coordination

Hours per Week	*N*	%
1–5 Hours Per Week	18	20.9
6–10 Hours Per Week	23	26.7
11–15 Hours Per Week	18	20.9
16–20 Hours Per Week	7	8.1
21–25 Hours Per Week	3	3.5
26–30 Hours Per Week	4	4.7
31–40 Hours Per Week	6	7.0
41–45 Hours Per Week	2	2.3
46–50 Hours Per Week	0	0
51–60 Hours Per Week	1	1.2
Missing Data	4	4.6
TOTAL	86	100%

often, or always) due to their assuming program coordination responsibilities. In 2022, that number decreased to 60.5. In 2017, 80.4% indicated other service responsibilities received less attention (sometimes, often, or always) due to their assuming program coordination responsibilities. That number slightly increased to 81.4% in 2022. In 2017, 80.5% of respondents indicated family responsibilities received less attention (sometimes, often, or always) due to their assuming program coordination responsibilities. That number increased to 87.1% in 2022.

We undertook analysis using the Mann-Whitney U test to compare differences between two independent groups when the dependent variable is either ordinal or continuous but not normally distributed (Corder & Foreman, 2014). Specifically, we analyzed difference between male and female program coordinators, program coordinators at public versus private institutions, White and non-White program coordinators, and tenured and non-tenured program coordinators in terms of the extent to which other responsibilities (research, teaching, other service, home/family life) received less attention as a result of assuming program coordination responsibilities. As in 2017, there were no significant differences ($p > .05$) in 2022 (see Table 6.3).

Table 6.3

Extent to Which Other Responsibilities Receive Less Attention Due to Program Coordination

Responsibilities	Never *N* (%)	Sometimes *N* (%)	Often *N* (%)	Always *N* (%)	Missing Data *N* (%)
Research	12 (14.0)	16 (18.6)	30 (34.9)	22 (25.6)	6 (7.0)
Teaching	31 (36.0)	40 (46.5)	9 (10.5)	3 (3.5)	3 (3.5)
Other Service	14 (16.3)	50 (58.1)	17 (19.8)	3 (3.5)	2 (2.3)
Family	10 (11.6)	42 (48.8)	23 (26.7)	10 (11.6)	1 (1.2)

Roles and Responsibilities

We asked respondents to indicate all program coordination duties at their institution. We ordered the responses by frequencies from the largest to smallest (Table 6.4). Consistent across the respondents in 2017 and in 2022, 90% or more of the respondents reported having responsibility for recruitment, addressing student issues, retention, and coordination of admissions. Three roles were reported by 80–89% of respondents: facilitating reviews and revisions of program curriculum, addressing faculty concerns, and representing program(s) on departmental committees. All the discrete roles and responsibilities had at least 23% of the respondents indicate these were under their purview. Respondents also had open-ended "other" responsibilities that could be marked and identified. Other responsibilities ranged from schedule development, coordination of qualifying exams, management of personnel, oversight of certification processes, "other duties as assigned," advisement of graduate students, graduation preparation, offering professional development, pursuing program grants, service on all capstone committees, and writing reference letters. One notable addition in 2022 that was not present in 2017 was "social media activities," such as posting program information and the accomplishments of program faculty, students, and alumni on platforms such as Facebook and Twitter. While social media platforms such as these existed in 2017, none of the program coordinators who responded to the survey then reported this as a responsibility.

In terms of descriptive statistics, our data revealed a mean of 17.28 responsibilities assumed by program coordinators in 2022 (Table 6.5). This is a slight decrease from 2017 prior to the pandemic, when the mean was 18.13 (Ingle et al., 2020). While female program coordinators had slightly

Table 6.4

Responsibilities of Program Coordinators by Reported Frequencies

Responsibilities	*N*	%
Recruit students	84	97.7
Address student issues	81	94.2
Retention of students	81	94.2
Coordinate admissions processes	78	90.7
Facilitate reviews and revisions of program curriculum	76	88.4
Address program faculty concerns	73	84.9
Represent program(s) on departmental committees	70	81.4
Coordinate program assessments	66	76.7
Recruit adjunct faculty	66	76.7
Maintain relationships and visibility with local school district(s)	65	75.6
Select adjunct faculty	65	75.6
Troubleshoot for adjunct faculty	59	68.6
Train adjunct faculty	57	66.3
Complete state accreditation reports	56	65.1
Collect data on program alumni	52	60.5
Represent program(s) on college committees	47	54.7
Maintain relationships and visibility with state professional organizations	45	52.3
Maintain relationships and visibility with local professional organizations	43	50.0
Complete national accreditation reports	41	47.7
Mentor junior faculty	41	47.7
Maintain relationships and visibility with national professional organizations	40	46.5
Represent program(s) on university committees	35	40.7
Maintain relationships and visibility with regional professional organizations	33	38.4
Review teaching evaluations	32	37.2
Complete regional accreditation reports	25	29.1
Develop program budgets	24	27.9
Locate off-campus teaching sites	20	23.3
Other—Schedule development	4	4.7
Other—Coordinate qualifying exams	3	3.5
Other—Manage personnel (e.g., supervise graduate assistants, chair searches)	3	3.5

(Table continued on next page)

Table 6.4 (Continued)

Responsibilities of Program Coordinators by Reported Frequencies

Responsibilities	*N*	%
Other—Oversee certification processes	3	3.5
Other—Social media activities	3	3.5
Other—"Other duties as assigned"	2	2.3
Other—Advise students	1	1.2
Other—Graduation preparation	1	1.2
Other—Lead faculty meetings	1	1.2
Other—Offer professional development	1	1.2
Other—Program innovation/grants	1	1.2
Other—Service on all capstone committees	1	1.2
Other—Write reference letters for graduates	1	1.2

higher means than males and program coordinators at public institutions had slightly higher means than their counterparts at private institutions, the result of independent samples t-tests revealed the average number of responsibilities did not differ significantly ($p > .05$) between male and female program coordinators, program coordinators at public versus private institutions, White and non-White program coordinators, or tenured and non-tenured program coordinators. This was also the case in 2017.

Supports and Incentives for Program Coordination

In terms of incentives, respondents identified reductions in course teaching loads, stipends, supplemental professional development funds (for conference travel), graduate assistants, and clerical support staff. In 2017, 66.3% indicated they received at least one course reduction in teaching load per academic year as an incentive for assuming program coordination responsibilities. That average dropped to 50.1%, with 29% reporting a one-course reduction, 19.8% reporting a two-course reduction, and 1.2% reporting a four-course reduction (Table 6.6). Half of respondents reported no teaching reductions. In 2017, that percentage was 33.7%.

In 2017, 38% of respondents indicated receiving a stipend for program coordination. In 2022, that number decreased to 32.6%. Stipends ranged from less than $1,000 per academic year to as much as $13,999, although most were less than $6,000. In 2017, a majority of respondents (73.8%) indicated they did not receive supplemental funds for professional devel-

Table 6.5

Average Number of Responsibilities Identified by Respondents

Respondents	*N*	Min.	Max	Mean	Std. Deviation	*t*-test
All Respondents	86	6	28	17.28	5.608	N/A
Male[a]	33	6	28	16.15	5.489	.154
Female	51	8	28	17.96	5.720	.154
White, non-Hispanic	69	6	28	17.32	5.725	.896
Non-White[b]	17	9	28	17.12	5.266	.896
At Private Institutions	12	9	28	16.83	7.272	.769
At Public Institutions	74	6	27	17.35	5.349	.769
Full-Time Tenured	46	6	28	16.65	5.650	.227
Full-Time Tenure-Track	11	6	28	15.36	6.392	.227
Full-Time Non-Tenure-track[c]	28	9	27	19.00	5.033	.227
Other	1	19	19	19.00	N/A	.227

[a] We excluded nonbinary respondents from this analysis. [b] We aggregated racial identity categories into two categories (White, non-Hispanic and non-White). [c] We ran an independent *t*-test comparing tenure-track to all other faculty statuses also. There was no statistical difference.

Table 6.6

Incentives Provided to Program Directors at UCEA-Member Institutions

Incentives		*N* (86)	%
Reductions in Teaching			
	1 per academic year	25	29.1
	2 per academic year	17	19.8
	3 per academic year	0	0.0
	4 per academic year	1	1.2
	None	43	50.0
Stipend			
	Less than $1,000	2	2.3
	$1,000 – $1,999	2	2.3
	$2,000 – $2,999	2	2.3
	$3,000 – $3,999	4	4.7

(Table continued on next page)

Table 6.6 (Continued)

Incentives Provided to Program Directors at UCEA-Member Institutions

Incentives		*N* (86)	%
Stipend			
	$4,000 – $4,999	4	4.7
	$5,000 – $5,999	8	9.3
	$6,000 – $6,999	0	0.0
	$7,000 – $7,999	1	1.2
	$8,000 – $8,999	0	0.0
	$9,000 – $9,999	0	0.0
	$10,000 – $10,999	2	2.3
	$11,000 – $11,999	0	0.0
	$12,000 – $12,999	3	3.5
	$13,000 v $13,999	0	0.0
	$14,000 v $14,999	0	0.0
	$15,000 or more	0	0.0
	None	58	67.4
Supplemental Professional Development Funds			
	$500	1	1.2
	$1,000	2	2.4
	$1,500	1	1.2
	$2,000	2	2.4
	$3,000	2	2.4
	Unspecified	3	3.5
	None	75	89.5
Graduate Assistants			
	1 per academic year	18	20.9
	2 per academic year	1	1.2
	None	67	77.9
Clerical Support Staff			
	Yes	17	19.8
	No	69	80.2

opment. In 2022, that number increased to 89.5%. In total, 11 (12.8%) respondents received supplemental professional development funds. These ranged from $500 to $3,000. Three did not specify in their responses.

In 2017, a majority of respondents (70.6%) received no graduate assistant to support their work, over and above those funded by grants and/or routinely assigned to faculty. In 2022, that number increased to 78%. For those faculty members assigned a graduate assistant for assuming program coordination responsibilities, a majority received one per academic year. One respondent reported receiving two per academic year. In 2017, 70.7% of respondents reported no clerical support staff to provide assistance with program coordination responsibilities. In 2022, that number increased to 80.2%

We undertook an analysis of the average number of incentives reported by all survey respondents (Table 6.7), seeking to determine whether there were differences in means based on gender, race, institutional type, and tenure status. The average number of incentives was only slightly higher among male respondents in comparison to female respondents. A similar trend was found in comparing public and private institutions. In 2017, the mean number of incentives for program coordination was higher for tenure-track program coordinators (2.55) in comparison to tenured program coordinators (1.84). In our 2022 sample, the mean number of incentives provided was lowest among pre-tenure respondents in comparison to full-time tenured and full-time non-tenure track respondents. However, the result of independent samples *t*-tests revealed the average number of incentives provided did not differ significantly ($p > .05$). Nor did the result of independent samples *t*-tests differ significantly for male and female program coordinators or program coordinators at public versus private institutions. Notably, the result of independent samples *t*-tests revealed the average number of incentives was significantly lower ($p > .05$) for non-White program coordinators in comparison to White program coordinators.

QUALITATIVE ANALYSIS

We now turn to our analysis of responses to qualitative questions seeking to determine the greatest challenges and rewards of serving as a program coordinator as well as how the pandemic has affected their work as a program coordinator. We analyzed these responses using open coding to identify categories (Strauss & Corbin, 1990) and to develop emerging themes in multiple passes through the data (Anfara et al., 2002), checking each other's work. Open-ended responses were broken down into multiple codes. For example, in answer to the "rewards" question, a respondent

Table 6.7

Average Number of Incentives for Program Coordination by Respondents

Respondents	*N*	Min.	Max	Mean	Std. Deviation	*t*-test
All Respondents	86	0	5	1.41	1.259	N/A
Male[a]	33	0	5	1.48	1.349	.393
Female	51	0	4	1.37	1.232	.393
White, non-Hispanic	69	0	5	1.55	1.334	–3.295*
Non-White[b]	17	0	2	.82	.636	–3.265*
At Private Institutions	12	0	3	1.08	1.084	–.959
At Public Institutions	74	0	5	1.46	1.284	–.959
Full-Time Tenured	46	0	5	1.37	1.372	.633
Full-Time Tenure-Track	11	0	3	1.18	.982	633
Full-Time Non-Tenure-Track[c]	28	0	4	1.57	1.200	633
Other	1	1	1	1.00	N/A	633

[a] We excluded nonbinary respondents from this analysis. [b] We aggregated racial identity categories into two categories (White, non-Hispanic and non-White). [c] We ran an independent *t*-test comparing tenure-track to all other faculty statuses also. There was no statistical difference. *Significant at .05

stated, "[I] love the deep relationships with students, professors, and district personnel and the very real improvements we see in our schools as a result of our work." We coded this response in our first analysis as five different codes: Working with students, collaboration, graduates' successes, relationships, and making a difference. The second analysis looked for frequency among codes, as well as ways to group together, or categorize, similar codes. A third analysis looked for ways in which codes were unique or disconfirmed other categories (Maxwell, 2005). Themes emerged from these three iterations of analysis.

Rewards

Program coordinators' open-ended responses mentioned a range of aspects they found rewarding about the role (see Table 6.8). Indeed, a number of the themes present in the 2022 open-ended responses were similar to those found in the 2017 survey responses. The most mentioned reward was working with students. Respondents mentioned students 36 times. For example, one respondent said:

> I really enjoy supporting students in their work as K–12 leaders. I see this work as an extension of the university's land-grant mission and the mission of the college. When I left my role as a practitioner in the field to become a faculty member, I didn't want to lose this connection to the K–12 classroom. I believe the program coordinator role enables me to maintain that connection through my students.

The second most recurring code to emerge was the reward of working to ensure program quality. One respondent stated, "I have been able to help further develop the program in ways to be more responsive to student needs—both academically and personally." Twenty respondents indicated that one of the rewards of program coordination was leading, and for many of them this was an extension of their prior leadership experiences from K–12. One, for example, talked about "being a part of the decision-making about the programs, having voice, and making a difference." Another stated, "I like having a sense of 'control' in terms of scheduling, planning, and I enjoy the engagement with others at the university and in the field."

Table 6.8

Rewards

Code	Example	Frequency
Students	"Being able to support our students through the program and into their leadership careers."	36
Program Quality	"I can set the program's direction and continuously improve."	28
Leading	"I enjoy overseeing the program."	20
Collaboration	"Collaborating with the program faculty on program initiatives."	14
Graduate Success	"Hearing about how beneficial the program was from graduates representing the program to district partners."	8
Faculty Support & Development	"Share in the growth of faculty."	7
Relationships	"Love the deep relationships with students, professors, and district personnel and the very real improvements we see in our schools as a result of our work."	6

(Table continued on next page)

Table 6.8 (Continued)

Rewards

Code	Example	Frequency
Making a Difference	"The capacity to make a difference in the delivery of our services to our students."	5
Helping/Nurturing	"Helping students navigate their program"	5
No Rewards	"There are no rewards. It has cost me promotion to professor."	4
Program Advocacy	"Being able to advocate for our program and our students."	4
Equity	"I love watching our students develop in their thinking, action, and sense of self as scholar-practitioners committed to equity and social justice reforms. "	3
Program and Curricular Development	"Planning new programs"	3
Shaping School and District Leadership	"Having an influence on how schools are led."	3
Troubleshooting	"Working on curricular issues and handling student problems."	2
Appreciation	"Others are appreciative of my work and support."	2
Meeting Enrollment Goals	"Increasing our admissions numbers the last two years."	1
Giving Back	"Opportunity to give back to students."	1

The latter provides evidence of what 14 program coordinators saw as a reward of program coordination—the opportunity to collaborate with a variety of stakeholders, including fellow faculty members, school leaders, district leaders, and state leaders. For example, one respondent discussed the opportunity to collaborate with and support fellow faculty members, stating, "I can mold faculty/adjuncts to create the kind of program collaboration needed and share in the growth of faculty." Another reported that "building relationships with the local districts and partnering with districts to grow their own school leaders" were rewards of program coordination. Five respondents saw the success of their programs, the quality of their graduates, and the positive outcomes that they facilitate in schools as rewards of program coordination. For example, one respondent said:

> One of the greatest rewards for serving as program coordinator is that I get to personally know all of the students in the programs. Since I advise them as to what classes to take, teach them, and interact with them through the program, it is exciting to see the teachers to blossom into school wide leaders.

This emphasis on relationships, whether with students or with colleagues, was another theme that surfaced regularly as a reward. Language about "helping" and "nurturing" students and faculty colleagues also emerged, which we identified as both collaboration and relationships, as well as an echo of the student-centered, service orientation towards the program already mentioned above.

One difference between respondents in 2017 and in 2022 is that four of them stated that there were no rewards for serving as a program coordinator. One explained:

> Honestly, not much at all. It is largely a position with little to no incentives. During the COVID-19 pandemic, my job responsibilities and stresses have increased. I receive little to no incentives in terms of course releases or additional pay. My research projects are adversely impacted by the position and [I] am constantly addressing program-related issues that are abruptly handed down from my college.

Another stated, "There are no rewards. It has cost me promotion to professor." These two quotations highlight the opportunity costs incurred for assuming program coordination responsibilities that come at the expense of other faculty responsibilities—in this case, research productivity.

Given our field's emphasis on preparing leaders who can serve all students, and the previously noted racial stresses concurrent with COVID-19, we note that three respondents directly mentioned preparing equitable leaders as a reward. One said a reward was providing "leadership to advance our mission to identify, prepare and support school and school district leaders to be agents of the change equity demands and our nation's students deserve."

Despite the challenges of program coordination, a majority of the respondents reported rewards of the job that reflected a strong orientation toward service to students, the profession, the program(s), the department, and the institution. These rewards are common to other studies on faculty satisfaction (Converso et al., 2018). Program coordination also served as a way to apply prior administrative experiences and leadership skills in program coordination. For those respondents who reported a lack of rewards, these serve as a reminder that the important work of program coordination and its multitude of responsibilities need incentivization to attract individuals willing to take up the role.

Challenges

In our prior research (Ingle et al., 2020), program coordinators in 2017 identified the lack of time associated with program coordination responsibilities and how these responsibilities adversely affect their ability to do other faculty responsibilities, such as research. The lack of structural (e.g., course releases) and emotional (e.g., lack of understanding from colleagues) supports were also reported as challenges in 2017. Similar trends emerged in our present study. As was the case in 2017, respondents in 2022 mentioned the lack of time the most frequently as a challenge. For example, one respondent stated, "It is the biggest time suck I have ever experienced professionally. It is very hard to find time to do anything else." One just repeated, "Time, time, time." Another captures the impact that program coordination has on other faculty responsibilities, stating:

> The program coordinator role is a full-time job. I joined the faculty when the program was only a few years old and have spent considerable time developing program materials, recruiting and supporting students, and building relationships with regional institutions and local school districts. Curriculum development and continuous program improvement also take considerable time. The program has grown considerably over the past few years. As a tenure-track faculty member, my research is a priority that, unfortunately, often gets finished in the evenings and on the weekends.

Table 6.9

Challenges

Code	Example	Frequency
Time	"In order for me to do an outstanding job as program coordinator, other functions such as writing, collaborating with peers, developing my teaching, and serving are limited as there are only so many hours in the day."	43
Lack of Supports	"Getting others engaged in program development" "There are not any course releases or scholarly releases." "Lack of training for the role."	30
Faculty Issues	"Competing interests of faculty when determining course assignments."	11

(Table continued on next page)

Table 6.9 (Continued)

Challenges

Code	Example	Frequency
Program Complexity	"It's a big job and much more involved (because of licensure regulations and report) & multiple cohorts than other programs in the college, yet everyone thinks they are the same."	10
Misunderstanding	"The responsibilities for a program coordinator, especially in a program that is so heavily guided by state/national accreditation standards, is often underestimated at my university. I suspect that because of such oversight, I am not able to receive any type of reduction in courseload to maintain the program. This has caused a significant reduction in my research productivity."	8
Short-staffed	"We have the largest graduate program in the college and in the university. However, we only have a small number of faculty."	7
Bureaucracy	"The length of time it takes for changes to be made."	7
Licensure & Regulations	"Managing and reporting program data to various stakeholders, e.g., accreditation teams, the [state] professional standards board, institutional program improvement."	6
Compensation	"We finally have a draft of expectations and a course release (prior to this year, I did not receive any course releases, stipend or extra GA time)"	6
Role Ambiguity	"Uncertainty about parameters"	5
Student Issues	"Supporting students who may be struggling academically or in their home/work lives."	4
Limited resources/ budget	"Lack of resources such as a graduate assistant, money for recruiting and advertising."	4
Recruitment Pressures	"The constant pressure to recruit enough students to maintain the programs."	3
Adjunct Oversight	"Selecting and training adjuncts."	2

Program coordinators identified supports they lacked, ranging from a lack of program coordinator training, lack of incentives (e.g., course releases, stipends), and getting other program faculty to engage in program-wide responsibilities. Some responses were not specific, such as one program coordinator who simply stated, "I don't have time and have very little support." Others were specific in what they were not receiving, such as a program coordinator who stated:

> There is no training, but colleagues have been helpful answering questions. There is no certification officer to support the coordination. There is no course release to do the additional administrative duties assigned (this is beyond "service").

Two respondents noted specifically the lack of support for pre-tenure faculty serving in the role of program coordinator and the risks of such responsibilities to a positive tenure decision. One stated:

> I am a pre-tenure single parent trying to continue an active research agenda during a global pandemic with a child who is too young to be vaccinated. I am angry and in despair that my department elected me, in my absence, to this position. It is insane. I hate that I was put in this position.

Another, a program coordinator at the rank of professor, described his institution's propensity to "exploit faculty, particularly junior or associate professors that are attempting to achieve tenure and/or promotion and their research scholarship suffers because of the myriad of job responsibilities."

Program coordinators also discussed the challenges that fellow faculty and students may pose, such as students complaining about unresponsive professors and having to confront professors with these complaints. Other faculty issues were associated with scheduling difficulties. Program coordinators discussed the complexities of their specific programs, which include working with state licensing agencies, school-, and district partners. These complexities, paired with a lack of supports, made program coordination even more difficult. As one program coordinator explained:

> The biggest challenges are the amount of work. It is literally a full-time job juggling all of the responsibilities. The biggest frustration is that the university has created no way to address the fact that I am a 9-month employee but a [program coordinator] role is a 12-month job. This often creates situations where the university benefits from my labor without having to compensate me.

This complexity of educational leadership program coordination and the way it differs from other faculty responsibilities or other program coordination in the university surfaced many times, and we coded it as "misunderstanding" of the role by others, particularly supervisors. Similar to the response above, where the coordinator noted the difference between 9-month employment and 12-month work, another respondent noted:

> The responsibilities for a program coordinator, especially in a program that is so heavily guided by state/national accreditation standards, is often underestimated at my university. I suspect that because of such oversight, I am not able to receive any type of reduction in course load to maintain the program. This has caused a significant reduction in my research productivity.

This lack of compensation was another common theme, mentioned six times, and is a specific lack of support.

Seven program coordinators discussed the challenges of being short-staffed and the difficulties of meeting program and student needs. One stated, "Our program faculty are very collaborative, but the majority of the small group serve in school or university admin roles, so we are spread thinly." Six program coordinators complained about the bureaucracy associated with working in higher education, such as one who mentioned an "unresponsive Provost's office—i.e., to creating MOUs with districts in a timely fashion." Five discussed the ambiguous nature of the role. For example, one program coordinator said, "[There are] no clear expectations." A smaller number of program coordinators reported the challenges of meeting recruitment targets and selecting/training adjuncts.

Similar to our previous work, the challenges of program coordination are both structural (e.g., lack of course releases, lack of compensation, being short-staffed) and emotional (e.g., misunderstanding from colleagues and supervisors, cutting into personal time). Often, they are both, as the lack of structural support makes program coordinators feel additional pressure. For example, people mentioned both a lack of budget for recruiting students and pressure to recruit students. That kind of conflict between resources available to meet requirements, or a perceived lack of equity among faculty members, or the misunderstanding of supervisors, leads to stress, burnout, and job dissatisfaction (Barkhuizen et al., 2014; Gerich & Weber, 2019; O'Meara et al., 2019).

The Impact of COVID-19

We also asked respondents a yes or no question: "Has the COVID-19 Pandemic affected your work as a program coordinator?" Of our 86 respondents, 66 respondents (77%) indicated that the COVID-19 pandemic had affected their work as a program coordinator. If they marked yes, respondents were asked to discuss how the pandemic has affected their work. Our analysis revealed a number of codes and themes (see Table 6.10). Not surprisingly, adapting to the stresses wrought by the pandemic were most common. A small number of program coordinators (3) discussed the stresses on themselves personally as the boundaries between home life and work life blurred due to the pandemic. One program coordinator noted, "I cannot do my job because of regular daycare closures and quarantines." Another stated, "I had my sons home with me and working full time - I am exhausted." However, a majority of the respondents focused more on adapting their work and responses to the stresses their students experienced, who tend to be full-time educators who work in schools and have to adapt their instruction, policies, and processes in response to the pandemic. Program coordinators noted substantial increases in student issues, including the need for more time on assignments, increases in incompletes, requesting leaves of absence, delays in graduations, providing more time for student advising, supports, and counseling. Program coordinators made comments, such as, "Huge increase in student-related issues," "More conversations with candidates who are stressed with their job; so little time for coursework and family," and "Students need more attention and emotional support." Another stated:

> COVID-19 has created challenges for my students that transcend far beyond their work as graduate students. They are struggling to lead schools and districts under conditions I never experienced as a practitioner. I have found it challenging but critical to support them in whatever way I can.

One program coordinator commented that some stressors wrought by the pandemic affect both students and faculty alike, noting that "the stress of family members getting sick, dying, etc. is a lot to bear."

Table 6.10

COVID-19 Impacts

Code	Example(s)	Frequency
Adapting for Stress	"My students, who are primarily P–12 teachers, are under a great deal of stress in the current environment and I am doing whatever I can to help/accommodate them through this difficult time."	29
Online	"We had to shift our Ph.D. program to online instruction."	23
Recruitment	"Hard to recruit students. Our educators are exhausted. They are not in the market to begin a master's or certificate program at this time."	16
Communication	"Challenges of communication internally and externally."	11

(Table continued on next page)

Table 6.10 (Continued)

COVID-19 Impacts

Code	Example(s)	Frequency
Isolation	"I struggle with the inability to see my colleagues on a regular basis. I am grateful that Zoom has become a second-nature tool in my work; however, it does not replace the face-to-face interactions."	7
Workload	"The workload increased significantly."	7
Engagement	"Everyone (instructors, students, and me) are personally impacted by COVID, which impacts their engagement with the program."	5
Lack of collaboration	"All meetings are online; way fewer opportunities to chat and troubleshoot with colleagues."	5
Adapting Outreach Efforts	"Increasing our electronic outreach through webinars and social media mechanisms." "It's been (understandably) MUCH harder to communicate with and coordinate with K–12 systems—we're not a priority for them at the moment, and that has very much negatively impacted partnership work."	5
Wellbeing	"Keeping mentally and physically healthy."	5
Teaching	"Moving courses virtually and supporting faculty in teaching virtually with limited knowledge/desire to do so."	5
Navigating Returns to Campus	"Managing the return to in person/hybrid to maintain program approval status."	3
Internships	"Supervision of internship has been complicated by COVID."	2
Short-staffed	"We've also had a few retirements, but those lines have gone unfilled."	2

Another commonly reported impact of the pandemic on program coordination was the need to adapt face-to-face graduate instruction to online delivery. Most were simple statements of fact, such as the pandemic required "Moving in-person program online," "Everything is remote so more difficult to coordinate at times," and "Working out online instruction and COVID protocols." Others were more descriptive, such as one program coordinator who described the move to online delivery, its perceived impacts on doctoral student learning, and the interaction of stresses students faced at home and work, stating:

> Instruction suffered during the move to online, creating gaps in Ed.D. students' knowledge of study design/academic writing and thinking. Students are also way more stressed and stretched thin, hindering their academic performance and also leading to more interpersonal conflicts because they rarely saw each other in person. I think we also need to include racial reckoning and trauma into the stresses they feel and how they interact with each other.

As if transitioning to online delivery and navigating these associated policies were not enough, program coordinators also reported the challenge of transitioning returns back to campus. As one program coordinator noted, "Many of my colleagues feel it is fine to not have to return to work. They want the paycheck but don't want to show up to work because we are fully face-to-face."

Program coordinators also discussed specific stresses that the pandemic caused, such as the difficulties of recruiting students during a pandemic and the subsequent impacts on budgets and scheduling. As one program coordinator explained, "Our enrollment numbers have declined as well as current students have needed additional support and counseling due to the pandemic." Another noted the "Challenges with getting international students into the US."

Parallel to the shift to online instruction, program coordinators noted the changes in communication (e.g., moving from face-to-face on online program meetings), feeling isolated and missing opportunities to collaborate with colleagues and districts, and perceiving decreased levels of engagement among both students and fellow faculty members. Program coordinators noted that the pandemic necessitated that communications among program faculty and with their students also move online. Not all program coordinators bemoaned this. One noted an improvement in faculty attendance with online program meetings. Another noted that they "moved most meetings online—this isn't necessarily a bad thing." However, seven program coordinators lamented the professional isolation of program coordination and faculty life during the pandemic. One stated, "All meetings, programmatic and individual, have to be virtual, reducing the ability to collaborate with faculty." Another said, "All meetings are now online. Limited connection with faculty members." Similar to the discussions of faculty stress, six program coordinators indicated their workload increased dramatically due to the pandemic. One stated:

> The workload increased significantly, especially in terms of helping faculty members move their courses to fully online platforms, as well as troubleshooting tech-related issues that have surfaced, upon which I have no expertise in handling. I also believe that this increase in work was overshadowed

> by university administration and not factored into a possible reduction in teaching loads.

Another program coordinator was particularly bitter in their response, stating:

> After my department chair told me that he had advice for how I could be a better program coordinator, an unfunded, unsupported, unasked-for position that in no way supports my tenure materials, I seriously debated quitting the profession. The PC position during COVID is horrible nonsense.

Yet another decried that it has been "harder to facilitate work bcz of lack of interaction. Also, faculty are burned out and don't wanna help, but shit still gotta get done."

Program coordinators reported having to adapt their outreach efforts in terms of recruitment of individual students and with specific districts due to the pandemic. Capturing these difficulties is one program coordinator's response, stating:

> More difficulty in recruiting students. Much of it was in-person meetings and conversations prior to COVID-19. In addition, district leaders are stretched thin and time is critical for them. It is more difficult to meet with them about succession planning and supporting their needs in the district.

Another noted, "It's been (understandably) MUCH harder to communicate with and coordinate with K–12 systems. We're not a priority for them at the moment, and that has very much negatively impacted partnership work." One particular district partnership component that program coordinators discussed as adversely affected by COVID-19 was student internships, due to their limited opportunities during online P–12 instruction.

A few program coordinators noted being short-staffed—which ties back to the perceptions of stress and increased workload. The pandemic complicated, or even mitigated, their institution's staffing efforts due to decreased enrollments and subsequent budget concerns. One program coordinator noted being fortunate to staff positions but cited the challenges of orienting new staff members during the pandemic. This program coordinator said, "Another challenge has been training up and working with new staff hired during the pandemic. That was difficult to do entirely online."

DISCUSSION AND IMPLICATIONS

Our quantitative analysis yielded some consistent trends in data collected in 2017 (prior to the pandemic) and in 2022 (during the pandemic).

In terms of the characteristics of our convenience sample, more female program coordinators than males completed our survey, but the number of females serving in the role increased in 2022. Like in our previous study, an overwhelming majority of respondents were White and in public state universities. Among our findings, 79.1 % of respondents reported that research responsibilities received less attention due to program coordination responsibilities. Interestingly, the average number of responsibilities decreased slightly from approximately 18 in 2017 to 17 in 2022 and the percentage of respondents reporting at least 11–15 hours weekly on program coordination decreased from 60.8% in 2017 to 47.7% in 2022. The number of respondents who indicated that family responsibilities received less attention due to assuming program coordination increased from 80.5% in 2017 to 87.1% in 2022.

While most of our inferential analyses yielded insignificant differences, such as our comparing the average number of responsibilities between male and female program coordinators, program coordinators at public versus private institutions, White and non-White program coordinators, and tenured versus non-tenured program coordinators, we did identify a significant difference between White/non-White program coordinators ($p > .05$), such that minority program coordinators reported receiving significantly fewer incentives than their White counterparts. As was the case in prior studies using the PCS, our present study is limited by convenient sampling and only generalizable to the sample of respondents and the time period in which the survey was issued. This significant finding may be the result of the vagaries of a relatively small sample and who opted to respond. That said, any real or potential disadvantaging of non-White program coordinators in terms of incentives should not occur at any UCEA-member institution, an organization that prides itself on its commitment to social justice and its provision of graduate student professional development opportunities that seek to diversify the professoriate in the field of educational leadership; most notably, its Jackson Scholars Network. Racial discrimination also can exacerbate faculty dissatisfaction, which could lead to faculty of color leaving the profession (Hesli & Lee, 2013), which is a loss from both a human capital perspective and from a social justice perspective.

Our analysis of open-ended responses revealed that current respondents, like those in 2017, continued to find their program coordinator work rewarding, especially when it involved supporting students, leading quality programs, and collaborating with colleagues and districts. They talked about enjoying relationships, making a difference, helping, and nurturing. All of these rewards are similar to other faculty job satisfaction constructs (Janik, 2015), and are perhaps especially relevant to those in the education field, which is service-oriented and people-oriented (Karpouza & Emvalotis, 2019; Klassen et al., 2012).

Our analysis also revealed challenges of program coordination, which were similar to those from our previous study. Time, or lack thereof, was once again the most cited challenge, with program coordinators reporting that their duties took more time than they felt was possible to do a good job, with their coordinator responsibilities taking attention from their research and from their families. Challenges reported here echo previous research on role conflict (Schwab et al., 1986), where faculty are expected to hold two time-intensive roles (i.e., research and program coordination), and on work-family conflict (Carlson et al., 2019), where work responsibilities take time away from personal or family responsibilities. Both situations may lead to job dissatisfaction. In addition, coordinators wrote about the lack of resources to do their jobs (de Lange et al., 2008; Lambert et al., 2018), such as recruiting students, and the misunderstanding of their colleagues and supervisors of what their job is or should be (Abramis, 1994; Bauwens et al., 2019). Again, both of these situations may lead to job dissatisfaction (Sabagh et al., 2018).

Program coordinators, like other employees, might weigh the rewards of their job versus the challenges of it, and decide whether to continue in the job based on that reward-challenge weighing, while also factoring in other personal characteristics or contingencies. No job is perfect, after all. However, the COVID-19 pandemic exacerbated the challenges for program coordinators. The rewards of the job, such as supporting students, or collaborating with colleagues, became challenges instead of rewards. Program coordinator workload increased significantly, with even more hours required to support students and to adapt to online delivery. And while these two responsibilities intensified, administrative demands for recruiting students—especially in order to keep budgets stable—continued, even though coordinators reported that their students were not in a financial or emotional position to join programs, it was difficult to recruit online, and institutional resources for recruiting were scarce.

Much has been written in higher education about the expected turnover of staff and faculty, as well as about faculty burnout. The stresses wrought by the pandemic may contribute to program coordinator turnover and complicate efforts to ensure quality educational leadership preparation and create sustainable cultures that foster transformative change around diversity, equity, and inclusion. The pandemic certainly made the program coordinator job more difficult. However, our research from 2017 to now indicates that most of the rewards and challenges for program coordinators are the same. What was rewarding before the pandemic is rewarding now, and what was challenging before the pandemic is challenging now, though much more so. It remains to be seen whether program coordinators will once again absorb and adapt to those challenges or join the national "great resignation" (Gittleman, 2022).

Returning to the rationale for our study—the crisis of the COVID-19 pandemic—Marshall et al. (2020) identified four critical leadership skills and behaviors needed in a higher education leader during the pandemic: providing clear direction, communicating effectively, working collaboratively, and engaging in adaptive leadership. With regard to the first, program directors identified ensuring program quality and direction as a theme of what they perceive as a reward of the job, but leading at the program-level is challenged when their institutions fail to provide adequate supports, incentives, or role clarity. Indeed, our respondents reveal that they have had to engage in adaptive leadership throughout the pandemic, adapting their communication and instruction with their fellow faculty and students in response to the pandemic and adapting their district outreach and recruitment efforts. Collaboration was a reward of the job prior to and during the pandemic, but collaboration, like so many things, was complicated by the pandemic. Researchers, such as Kruse et al. (2020), note an ongoing disconnect between the scope and difficulty of department chairs' work and the ways in which their work is recognized and supported. We would add program coordinators as subject to the same disconnects.

REFERENCES

Abramis, D. J. (1994). Work role ambiguity, job satisfaction, and job performance: Meta-analyses and review. *Psychological Reports, 75*(3_suppl), 1411–1433. https://doi.org/10.2466/pr0.1994.75.3f.1411

Alford, J., & Head, B. W. (2017). Wicked and less wicked problems: A typology and a contingency framework. *Policy and Society, 36*(3), 397–413. https://doi.org/10.1080/14494035.2017.1361634

Anfara, V. A., Jr., Brown, K. M., & Mangione, T. L. (2002). Qualitative analysis on stage: Making the research process more public. *Educational Researcher, 31*(7), 28–38. http://www.aera.net/pubs/er/pdf/vol31_07/AERA310706.pdf

Barkhuizen, N., Rothmann, S., & van de Vijver, F. J. R. (2014). Burnout and work engagement of academics in higher education institutions: Effects of dispositional optimism: Burnout and work engagement in higher education institutions. *Stress and Health, 30*(4), 322–332. https://doi.org/10.1002/smi.2520

Barroso, A., & Horowitz, J. M. (2021). The pandemic has highlighted many challenges for mothers, but they aren't necessarily new. *FactTank*. https://www.pewresearch.org/fact-tank/2021/03/17/the-pandemic-has-highlighted-many-challenges-for-mothers-but-they-arent-necessarily-new/

Bataille, G. M., & Cordova, D. I. (2014). *Managing the unthinkable: Crisis preparation and response for campus leaders.* Stylus.

Bauwens, R., Audenaert, M., Huisman, J., & Decramer, A. (2019). Performance management fairness and burnout: Implications for organizational citizenship behaviors. *Studies in Higher Education, 44*(3), 584–598. https://doi.org/10.1080/03075079.2017.1389878

Blumenstyk, G. (2014). *American higher education in crisis? What everyone needs to know.* Oxford University Press.

Brennan, J. A., & Stern, E. K. (2017). Leading a campus through crisis: The role of college and university presidents. *Journal of Education Advancement & Marketing, 2*(2), 120–134.

Brooks, S. K., Webster, R. K., Smith, L. E., Woodland, L., Wessely, S. Greenberg, N., & Rubin, G. J. (2020). The psychological impact of quarantine and how to reduce it: Rapid review of the evidence. *Lancet, 395*, 912–920. https://doi.org/10.1016/S0140-6736(20)30460-8

Carlson, D. S., Thompson, M. J., & Kacmar, K. M. (2019). Double crossed: The spillover and crossover effects of work demands on work outcomes through the family. *Journal of Applied Psychology, 104*(2), 214–228. https://doi.org/10.1037/apl0000348

Converso, D., Loera, B., Molinengo, G., Viotti, S., & Guidetti, G. (2018). Not all academics are alike: First validation of the academics' quality of life at work scale (AQoLW). *Frontiers in Psychology, 9*, 2408–2408. https://doi.org/10.3389/fpsyg.2018.02408

Cooper, D., & Hickey, S. M. (2022). *Raising pay in public K–12 schools is critical to solving staffing shortages*. https://www.epi.org/publication/solving-k-12-staffing-shortages/

Corder, G. W., & Foreman, D. I. (2014). *Nonparametric statistics: A step-by-step approach* (2nd ed.). Wiley.

Craig, L. (2020). Coronavirus, domestic labour and care: Gendered roles locked down. *Journal of Sociology, 56*(4), 684–692. https://doi.org/10.1177/1440783320942413

Creswell, J. W. (2013), *Research design: Qualitative, quantitative, and mixed methods approaches* (3rd ed.). SAGE.

de Lange, A. H., De Witte, H., & Notelaers, G. (2008). Should I stay or should I go? Examining longitudinal relations among job resources and work engagement for stayers versus movers. *Work and Stress, 22*(3), 201–223. https://doi.org/10.1080/02678370802390132

Diliberti, M. K., & Schwartz, H. L. (2022). *Districts continue to struggle with staffing, political polarization, and unfinished instruction: Selected findings from the Fifth American School District Panel Survey.* https://www.rand.org/pubs/research_reports/RRA956-13.html

Donovan, D. (2022, May 17). *U.S. officially surpasses 1 million COVID-19 deaths*. Johns Hopkins Coronavirus Resource Center. https://coronavirus.jhu.edu/from-our-experts/u-s-officially-surpasses-1-million-covid-19-deaths

Fagell, P. L. (2020). Teacher wonders how to help students during coronavirus shutdown. *Phi Delta Kappan, 101*(8), 67–68. https://doi.org/10.1177/0031721720923799

Filho, W. L., Wall, T., Rayman-Bacchus, L., Mifsud, M., Pritchard, D. J., Lovren, V. O., Farinha, C., Petrovic, D. S., & Balogun, A. (2021). Impacts of COVID-19 and social isolation on academic staff and students at universities: A cross-sectional study. *BMC Public Health, 21*(1213), 1–19. https://doi.org/10.1186/s12889-021-11040-z

Gerich, J., & Weber, C. (2019). The ambivalent appraisal of job demands and the moderating role of job control and social support for burnout and job satisfaction. *Social Indicators Research, 148*(1), 251–280. https://doi.org/10.1007/s11205-019-02195-9

Gigliotti, R. A. (2020). *Crisis leadership in higher education: Theory and practice.* Rutgers University Press.

Gigliotti, R. A. (2021). The impact of COVID-19 on academic department chairs: Heightened complexity, accentuated liminality, and competing perceptions of reinvention. *Innovative Higher Education, 46*, 429–444. https://doi.org/10.1007/s10755-021-09545-x

Gittleman, M. (2022, July). The "Great Resignation" in perspective. *Monthly Labor Review*. Bureau of Labor Statistics. https://doi.org/10.21916/mlr.2022.20

Hemmer, L., & Elliff, D. S. (2020). Leaders in action: The experiences of seven Texas superintendents before, during, and after Hurricane Harvey. *Educational Management Administration and Leadership, 48*(6), 964–985.

Hesli, V. L., & Lee, J. M. (2013). Job satisfaction in academia: Why are some faculty members happier than others? *PS: Political Science & Politics, 46*(2), 339–354. https://doi.org/doi:10.1017/S1049096513000048

Hoffman, J. A., & Miller, E. A. (2020). Addressing the consequences of school closure due to COVID-19 on children's physical and mental well-being. *World Medical and Health Policy, 12*(3), 300–310. https://doi.org/10.1002/wmh3.365

Ingle, W. K., Marshall, J. M., & Hackmann, D. G. (2020). The leaders of leadership preparation programs: A study of program coordinators at UCEA-member institutions. *Journal of Research on Leadership Education, 15*(2), 120–149.

Ingle, W. K., Worth, J, Marshall, J. M., & Hackmann, D. G. (2018). The incentives and costs of program coordination in P-12 educational leadership programs. *Journal of Education Finance, 44*(2), 175–198.

Janik, M. (2015). Meaningful work and secondary school teachers' intention to leave. *South African Journal of Education, 35*(2), 1008–1008.

Johnson, M. M. (2022). Self-care is not enough! *ASCD*. https://www.ascd.org/el/articles/self-care-is-not-enough

Kaden, U. (2020). COVID-19 school closure-related changes to the professional life of a K–12 teacher. *Education Sciences, 10*(165), 1–13. https://doi.org/10.3390/educsci10060165

Karpouza, E., & Emvalotis, A. (2019). Exploring the teacher-student relationship in graduate education: A constructivist grounded theory. *Teaching in Higher Education, 24*(2), 121–140. https://doi.org/10.1080/13562517.2018.1468319

Kaufman, J. H., Diliberti, M. K., & Hamilton, L. S. (2022). How principals' perceived resource needs and job demands are related to their dissatisfaction and intention to leave their schools during the COVID-19 pandemic. *AERA Open, 8*. https://doi.org/10.1177/23328584221081234

Klassen, R. M., Perry, N. E., & Frenzel, A. C. (2012). Teachers' relatedness with students: An underemphasized component of teachers' basic psychological needs. *Journal of Educational Psychology, 104*(1), 150–165. https://doi.org/10.1037/a0026253

Kruse, S. D., Hackmann, D. G., & Lindle, J. C. (2020). Academic leadership during a pandemic: Department heads leading with a focus on equity. *Frontiers in Education, 5,* 1–14. https://doi.org/10.3389/feduc.2020.614641

Lambert, R., Fitchett, P., McCarthy, C., & Eyal, M. (2018). Examining elementary teachers' risk for occupational stress: Associations with teacher, school, and state policy variables. *Teachers College Record, 120*(12), 1–42.

Marshall, J., Roache, D., & Moody-Marshall, R. (2020). Crisis leadership: A critical examination of educational leadership in higher education in the midst of the COVID-19 pandemic. *International Studies in Educational Administration, 48*(3), 30–37.

Maxwell, J. A. (2005). *Qualitative research design: An interactive approach* (2nd ed.). SAGE.

Mutch, C. (2018). The role of schools in helping communities cope with earthquake disasters: The case of the 2010-2011 New Zealand earthquakes. *Environmental Hazards, 17*(4), 331-351. https://doi.org/10.1080/17477891.2018.1485547

National Association of Secondary School Principals. (2021, December 8). *NASSP survey signals a looming mass exodus of principals from schools.* https://www.nassp.org/news/nassp-survey-signals-a-looming-mass-exodus-of-principals-from-schools/

O'Meara, K., Lennartz, C. J., Kuvaeva, A., Jaeger, A., & Misra, J. (2019). Department conditions and practices associated with faculty workload satisfaction and perceptions of equity. *The Journal of Higher Education, 90*(5), 744–772.

Phelps, C., & Sperry, L. L. (2020). Children and the COVID-19 pandemic. *Psychological Trauma: Theory, Research, Practice, and Policy, 12*(1), 273–275. https://doi.org/10.1037/tra0000861

Piotrowski, C., & King, C. (2020). COVID-19: Challenges and implications for higher education. *Education, 141*(2), 61–66.

Reich, J., & Mahta, J. (2021). *Healing, community, and humanity: How students and teachers want to reinvent schools post-COVID.* https://edarxiv.org/nd52b

Sabagh, Z., Hall, N. C., & Saroyan, A. (2018). Antecedents, correlates and consequences of faculty burnout. *Educational Research, 60*(2), 131–156. https://doi.org/10.1080/00131881.2018.1461573

Schwab, R. L., Jackson, S. E., & Shuler, R. S. (1986). Educator burnout: Sources and consequences. *Educational Research Quarterly, 10*(3), 14–29.

Schwartz, H. L., & Diliberti, M. K. (2022a). *Flux in the educator labor market: Acute Staff Shortages and Projected Superintendent Departures: Selected Findings from the Fourth American School District Panel Survey*. RAND. https://www.rand.org/pubs/research_reports/RRA956-9.html

Schwartz, H. L., & Diliberti, M. K. (2022b). *State of the superintendent; High job satisfaction and a projected normal turnover rate: Selected findings from the Fifth American School District Panel Survey*. RAND. https://www.rand.org/pubs/research_reports/RRA956-12.html

Shaw, M. (2018). Teaching campus crisis management through case studies: Moving between theory and practice. *Journal of Student Affairs Research and Practice, 55*(3), 308–320, https://doi.org/10.1080/19496591.2018.1399894

Strauss, A., & Corbin, J. (1990). *Basics of qualitative research: Grounded theory procedures and techniques*. SAGE.

Striepe, M., & Cunningham, C. (2022). Understanding educational leadership during times of crises: A scoping review. *Journal of Educational Administration, 60*(2), 133–147. https://doi.org/10.1108/JEA-03-2021-0057

Torres-Pagán, L., & Terepka, A. (2020). School-based health centers during academic disruption: Challenges and opportunity in urban mental health. *Psychological Trauma: Theory, Research, Practice, and Policy, 12*(S1), S276–S278. http://dx.doi.org/10.1037/tra0000611

Trinidad, J. E. (2021). Equity, engagement, and health: School organisational issues and priorities during COVID-19. *Journal of Educational Administration and History, 53*(1), 67–80. https://doi.org/10.1080/00220620.2020.1858764

UCEA. (n.d.) *About UCEA*. http://www.ucea.org/about-ucea/

Van Lancker, W., & Parolin, Z. (2020). COVID-19 school closures and child poverty: A social crisis in the making. *Lancet, 5*(5), E243–E244. https://doi.org/10.1016/S2468-2667(20)30084-0

Woo, A., & Steiner, E. D. (2022). *The well-being of secondary school principals one year into the COVID-19 pandemic*. RAND. https://www.rand.org/pubs/research_reports/RRA827-6.html

Zamarro, G., Camp, A., Fuchsman, D., & McGee, J. B. (2022). *Understanding how COVID-19 has changed teachers' chances of remaining in the classroom*. https://www.edworkingpapers.com/sites/default/files/ai22-542.pdf

ENDNOTE

1. The instrument was not included in the manuscript due to the added length its inclusion would entail, but is available upon request from the corresponding author.

CHAPTER 7

SUCCESSES, CHALLENGES, AND HOPES OF AN EDUCATIONAL LEADERSHIP PROGRAM COORDINATOR

Balancing the Self and Others

Barbara L. Pazey
University of North Texas

ABSTRACT

The program coordinator (PC) for the educational leadership program wears numerous hats and serves as a referee, at times, in helping to craft the vision and purpose of the program. In the university setting, those who oversee, teach, and serve within the Master's in Education (MEd) degree/principal certification, the Education Doctorate (EdD) or the Doctor of Philosophy (PhD) degrees, and superintendent certification possess a varied set of experiences, knowledge, understanding, and skills. Some are more closely aligned with policy and research with little to no actual leadership experience in schools or districts. Others bring a vast array of leadership experiences that are relevant to school-level and/or district-level leadership positions. Additional factors relate to the various philosophies of how schools and districts should operate and function and the policies and politics of higher education. The PC must address each of these factors within the program while navigating, adjusting

Navigating the Ubiquitous, Misunderstood, and Evolving Role of the Educational Leadership Program Coordinator in Higher Education, pp. 135–157

to, and balancing the expectations of leaders in one's department, college, university, EC-12 surrounding school districts, and the multiple perspectives of the students the program serves. This chapter focuses on the successes, challenges, and hopes of a PC at a Tier 1 university as I attempted to reestablish and maintain unity and cohesion among members of the educational leadership program between 2019 and 2022, prior to, during, and following the pandemic and some of the events that occurred within that timeframe.

Keywords: program coordinator, educational leadership, politics and policies, higher education, academic freedom, spirituality

In 2017, I arrived at my current institution to fulfill the role of associate professor in educational leadership. The educational leadership (EDLE) program was thriving with a mix of faculty who had strong roots in leadership experience ranging from building-level leadership positions at the early childhood (EC) and elementary, middle school, and high school levels to district-level leadership as superintendent, associate or assistant superintendent, and executive director positions, and higher education senior-level administrative positions. The Master's in Education (MEd) and principal certification program boasted record numbers and a nationally ranked reputation due to its online presence and its reach across the state, other states, and international audiences. The superintendent certification program had an established partnership with a regional service center to offer face-to-face certification courses and had just received approval to offer classes via online delivery, enabling the program to recruit students from a wider geographic area. The Education Doctorate (EdD) and the Doctor of Philosophy (PhD) degree programs had numerous cohorts meeting at various locations across the region with promising opportunities for continued growth in the area. The EDLE program embraced their relatively new membership with the Carnegie Project for the Education Doctorate (CPED) and the University Council for Educational Administration (UCEA) professional organizations.

In the first few months of the fall 2017 semester, the new and former faculty shared a celebratory mindset and strong professional learning community, despite various differences in value systems and approaches to leadership that existed within the program. I soon discovered that certain rifts among the faculty had developed through their effort to redesign the EDLE program to accommodate the move to create an EdD degree program, adjust the PhD program so some of their courses corresponded with the PhD program, and lesson the number of hours for the completion of both degrees. Some of the EDLE faculty preferred to uphold the long-held tradition of offering management-oriented leadership preparation courses while other EDLE faculty supported an advocacy-oriented approach to leadership preparation, emphasizing the importance of arming the master's and doctoral students with a social justice, equity-oriented mindset and approach to their scholarship and leadership practice (Ezzani & Paufler, 2018). These types of challenges, while typical when faculty endeavor to redesign their degree programs (Perry et al., 2020), remained under the surface, but bubbled up on occasion in some of our EDLE program faculty meetings.

As the doctoral program facilitator for the EdD and PhD doctoral degree programs for two years, I worked in concert with the facilitator of the MEd and principal certification program, the superintendent certification program facilitator, and the EDLE program coordinator (PC), a tenured professor with prior college- and department-level leadership experience. The PC worked to strengthen each of our efforts and solidify the faculty into a cohesive unit. There were bumps along the way due to occasional differences in perspectives and situations that needed to heal predicated on events that occurred prior to my arrival. Meeting together regularly, face-to-face, and attending conferences together helped to advance the newer faculty toward meeting the PC's goals. Nevertheless, several faculty members who helped to build the EDLE program prior to the newer faculty's arrival continued to struggle with the philosophical and curricular shift in which the EDLE program was headed. They believed the former PC failed to honor their voices and took advantage of the newer faculty and the relationship held with the former department chair to push through a different agenda. Wounds remained and tempers flared on several occasions; however, the PC achieved a sense of unity and camaraderie among us all. Coming from a former institution and department where I witnessed these types of philosophical distinctions and heated arguments among the faculty, I believed we could overcome the differences and achieve the goals set forth by the PC.

During the 2018–2019 academic year, four EDLE faculty and three research assistants conducted a mixed methods program evaluation study with EDLE doctoral students, admitted since 2012, for continuous improvement purposes (Paufler et al., 2020). Based on the survey results and focus group participants' responses generated across five cohorts, we decided to maintain specific aspects of the program that students indicated they liked and began to strategize ways in which we could address some of the students' suggestions in concert with the EDLE faculty during the 2019–2020 academic year. Regrettably, the plans to move forward and take the necessary steps to begin the conversation to improve the program structure and instructional delivery came to a screeching halt as a result of the pandemic.

TRANSITIONING TO THE ROLE OF EDLE PC

In summer/fall 2019, two years after my arrival, the EDLE program lost two assistant professors who accepted positions at other institutions and the leadership of a full professor who stepped down as the EDLE PC due to a decision to relocate and leave the program the following year. The program's full-time faculty immediately went into triage mode as two tenured professors in the program, three tenure-track faculty, and six non-tenure-track faculty came together to serve the master's, doctoral, and leadership certification-seeking students in the program. A large number of doctoral students pursuing the EdD or PhD degree needed new advisors to assist them in the various stages of their doctoral journey and dissertation. At that time, five tenured, tenure-track faculty members were asked to absorb the students affected by the exiting faculty. The master's program, one of the largest programs at the university, lost three of the lead instructors for one or more of the masters-level courses, and the remaining faculty needed to ensure class sections would be covered by qualified adjunct leadership faculty. Although a national search to fill the vacancies of three of the four positions was put in force, we knew we had to pull up our bootstraps and embrace an all-or-nothing mentality to make the 2019–2020 academic year work.

In the midst of the chaos, the newly appointed department chair requested that I serve as the PC for the program, adding to my duties as the EdD and PhD doctoral program facilitator. Regrettably, a job description for serving as PC did not exist. The lack of a position description for educational leadership PCs aligns with Hackmann and Wanat's (2008, 2016) research findings, based on the perspectives of educational leadership PCs. With no formal description to guide me and no suggestions for who I might reach out to for assistance, it did not take long for me to realize the complexities inherent in performing the PC role and the journey that laid ahead. In this chapter, I focus on the challenges, lessons learned, and successes that I experienced as a PC of the EDLE program at a Tier 1 university as I attempted to reestablish and maintain unity and cohesion among members of the program between 2019 and 2022, prior to, during, and following the pandemic, the subsequent events that have occurred within that timeframe, and my hopes in terms of recommendations for future practice and research to make the role of the PC a respected role within the arena of educational leadership preparation programs.

POSITIONALITY: A CRITICAL CONSIDERATION IN ONE'S ABILITY TO FUNCTION AS PROGRAM COORDINATOR

One of the most critical components in terms of fulfilling a particular position or role in one's career requires a consideration of the individual's positionality and the interplay between the expectations and demands of the position itself and the background, experiences, and held beliefs and perspectives that undergird the profile of that individual. I am a White female and a member of the Baby Boomer generation with an invisible dis/ability. My previous experience in education spans serving as a K–12 music teacher, a musical director for several professional organizations, a K–12 special education teacher, a high school principal, and a faculty member and/or higher education administrator in teacher education, special education and special education administration, and educational leadership and policy.

Due to the more recent stereotyping and negative portrayal of individuals who profess to be a Christian by certain groups, I am hesitant to lump myself into such a category. For me, an earlier claim made regarding the position that no one accepted definition of social justice existed (North, 2008) applies to the multiple portrayals and definitions that swirl around those individuals who identify themselves as being a Christian. For that reason, I choose to describe myself as a person who embraces Jesus Christ as my Lord and Savior and attempt to live in accordance with the Word of God and be led by the Holy Spirit. I acknowledge that my successes and failures are a product of my dependence on Him, while still learning how to navigate and, at times, battle the thoughts, emotions, and pressures of daily life. Regrettably, I sometimes try to handle my battles through the weakness of my own self and flesh; therefore, I admit that I am far from the attainment of what God, my Lord and Savior, the Word of God, and Holy Spirit call for me to be. Acknowledging the frailties of self and juxtaposed against the reality that I may fall short in reaching any goal of perfection in Him, I strive to forget whatever things are behind so I can press toward those things that lay ahead of me with the goal of obtaining the "prize of the upward call of God in Christ Jesus" (New King James Bible, 2022, Philippians 3:14).

Regarding the other aspects of self, due to my premature birth status and the medical attention given in association with being kept alive, my natural self, on and off, has had to fight against bouts of anxiety, depression, and doubts about my own ability. These battles were tightly connected to living with an invisible dis/ability and striving to manage or control such challenges over the course of the first 26 years of my life. I finally admitted my need to turn to a higher power other than myself to navigate who I am and what I believe in my own work as well as in my work with others in the current and previous positions held. As much as I would like to say that the battles have subsided, they still exist. With that in mind, I realize this narrative of the successes, challenges, and future hopes that I possess about serving as the PC of an EDLE program may not represent other PCs. Nevertheless, similar to what I surmise applies to other PCs, the need to balance who I am while working with individuals from multiple generations with multiple perspectives, expectations, and demands may raise more questions than answers. My prayer is that the level of transparency provided may enable all of us, as PCs and educational leaders, to highlight the realities of serving as a PC that have been overlooked by university, college-level, and departmental administrators as well as by the faculty, staff, and graduate students that EDLE programs serve.

ROLE, RESPONSIBILITIES, AND SUPPORTS

Similar to the findings of Hackmann and McCarthy (2011), the EDLE program is housed within a larger department, combining multiple teacher education programs with educational leadership. The former and current department chair's academic expertise is aligned with the curriculum and instruction side of the department, necessitating the selection of an EDLE faculty member to facilitate the bulk of the responsibilities for the various needs of the EDLE program. My practitioner experience as a former school principal has equipped me with the ability to provide "oversight to everything" (Hackmann & Wanat, 2016, p. 102) that takes place in the EDLE program. Typically, I complete the tasks individually; however, I am increasingly trying to distribute certain "assignments among willing faculty within the program" (Hackmann & Wanat, 2008, p. 65). In most cases, however, I serve as the initial point of contact for inquiries about the EDLE doctoral degree programs and, in some cases, the master's and principal and superintendent licensure programs. I also facilitate program meetings monthly and serve as the conduit between the voice of the EDLE faculty, the department chair, the dean of the College of Education, and as graduate advisor for the doctoral students, the administration, and staff of the Graduate School.

Ingle et al. (2018) highlighted several disincentives for serving as the PC in accord with Hackmann and Wanat (2016): "lack of time, diminished scholarly productivity, lack of formal authority, colleagues' unwillingness to engage with the work of the program, and lack of empathy and support from department chairs" (p. 181) as well as a lack of training for PCs. Each of these disincentives correspond with my own experience as the EDLE PC at my institution. No financial benefits, administrative appointments, or salary increases are applied for serving in the PC role; however, one course release per year is provided (Ingle et al., 2018).

Based on my observations of the behaviors and actions of the EDLE program faculty at two different institutions, they appeared to assume that the PC would complete most tasks and reports on their own. In my experience as PC and based on the research cited above, such an assumption can denigrate the level of support that PCs tend to feel in their role, subjugating them to feeling as though their peers view them and their needs as irrelevant to themselves and thus, unimportant. The emotions that accompany these perceptions, for me, have caused me to rethink the value of serving as PC, particularly in terms of the sacrifice of self and inability to focus on my own research agenda. Over the past three years, the EDLE program has been populated primarily by tenure-track assistant professors who have been protected from the expectation to provide additional service to the program and non-tenure track faculty whose primarily responsibility is teaching, without the towering demands to publish. At times, I found myself battling against the temptation to shift my thinking toward a negative, envious, or resentful attitude toward my colleagues. Within the current semester, however, I have noticed a renewed willingness to step in and assist emerging, a change that has taken away some of the stress and impending symptoms of burnout that were knocking at my door.

According to Hackmann and Wanat (2016), a major role of the PC is to "maintain relationships with local school districts, regional education agencies, local and state administrative organizations, and state education departments" (p. 100). Fortunately, the EDLE program employs two non-tenure track faculty to teach and handle the details of the principal and superintendent certification programs. Their contributions allow me to focus on the details of the EdD and PhD doctoral programs and the coordination of all the degree and certification programs when communicating with the department chair about the various concerns of the program faculty. Considering the multiple concerns of the program that involve a repeated review of the course curriculum, recruiting, and admitting students, determining teaching assignments to full-time and adjunct faculty, ensuring national accreditation reports are submitted annually, the facilitators of the master's/principal program and superintendent program are invaluable to my ability to fulfill my PC and doctoral program facilitator responsibilities.

The master's/principal program facilitator understands the intricacies of the principalship certification, taking the pressure off of me to make sure these students are adequately cared for. She also prepares the national accreditation report for the master's program which leaves me with completing the reports for the two doctoral programs. The masters' principal program facilitator benefits from several support staff assigned to assist her with the informational and admissions process of students and the administration of the online program. As a result, the master's program continues to stand out as one of the top programs in the state.

Due to his experience as a superintendent, networking capabilities, and familiarity with the leaders of school districts within the area as well as the regional and state agencies pertinent to educational leadership, the superintendent facilitator as the executive-in-residence is expected to take the lead on establishing a larger presence to support our program and communicating the mission and vision of the EDLE program. He is also the point person in helping me as well as other faculty within the EDLE and department develop partnerships with EC–12 school districts (Coleman & Reames, 2020) for individual or collaborative research and grant-writing opportunities. For the doctoral programs on both sides of the department—teacher education and educational leadership—the department provides both program coordinators with an administrative assistant who answers doctoral students' questions and assists us with the various administrative and technological functions of the position.

The willingness of the department to provide these types of supports represents a commitment to our EDLE program which, until I started examining the scant research findings of the types of support PCs receive at other institutions, made me appreciate the positive aspects of serving as the EDLE PC. Nevertheless, the underlying challenges inherent in navigating the internal and external barriers related to the role of the PC can contribute to the creation of a much more complicated picture, particularly in light of the events that have taken place between 2019 and 2022. While not inclusive of the challenges faced, those addressed in this chapter include (a) the need to react and respond to the unexpected events, concerns, and opportunities that tend to surface along the way, (b) the diverse leadership backgrounds and experiences of the faculty, (c) the various philosophies about how districts and schools should operate and function, (d) the politics and policies in higher education at various hierarchical levels that correspond with or are in conflict with those within our program area, and (e) the challenges involved in trying to balance care for self and others and the shifting aspects of the my positionality as I endeavored to fulfill the role of the EDLE PC .

Need to React and Respond to Unexpected Events, Concerns, and Opportunities

During the 2019–2020 academic year, we welcomed a new department chair whose expertise was related to the teacher education side of the department. As our own subunit, the EDLE program faculty coalesced around a common theme and purpose: to work together to ensure the program maintained or even exceeded the quality of instruction and supports that existed during the previous two years. The EDLE faculty rallied around me as the newly appointed PC to make sure we could accomplish that goal. Fortunately, due to the facilitators of the master's/

principal certification program and superintendent certification program, both programs functioned as smooth-running operations.

Filling in the Gap of Faculty Advisors

The largest concern involved the need to fill in the gaps for students who were left by exiting faculty without a chair or advisor to assist them in their doctoral and dissertation journeys. We met and discussed students and, due to the previous assistance provided by two non-tenure track faculty, everyone was willing to take on the extra load of students, making the transition possible. Other incidents that required immediate attention in 2019 involved the loss of a third assistant professor who accepted a district-level position for the fall semester and the additional reassignments of doctoral students. One of the greatest challenges for me as PC was trying to assuage the concerns of some of the doctoral students who felt as though the rug had been pulled out from under them after establishing a strong relationship with the professors who left. In addition, I endeavored to search for ways to ease the overwhelming burden placed on our EDLE faculty to make up the hedge for these students while continuing to recruit students, support a search for three new faculty members, and learn how to function in the role as PC. Considering that I had recently submitted my materials for tenure and knew I needed to continue to be productive regarding my research agenda and scholarship, the EDLE faculty became my greatest support group.

The Onset and Overall Effects of the COVID-19 Pandemic

When things seemed to be settling down in March 2020, the COVID-19 pandemic uprooted the slight level of calm that the EDLE faculty were experiencing. Because many of our classes were already online, the adjustments that needed to be made for instructors were minimal. We had just finished conducting a search for three faculty and hired a new assistant professor for the next year, creating a positive attitude despite not being able to hire three faculty. We moved our EDLE faculty meetings online, as well, and the camaraderie that we established during the first seven months of the year remained intact. In reality, many of the faculty expressed a preference for virtual meetings over face-to-face meetings due to the travel distance, inconvenience of coming to campus, and concern for their health. Recruitment efforts were held strictly through weekly online information sessions, as well, and as PC, these meetings became an additional function of my role for the EDLE doctoral programs.

The largest hurdle during 2020 involved the need to respond to the heavy burdens that were placed on our EDLE students as classroom teachers, building administrators, and district-level leaders. The students put in innumerable hours to develop ways to make sure their schools continued to function with the total shutdown of their districts. In the process, they suffered from Zoom fatigue due to the immediate shift to an online platform for required meetings and the need to conduct their administrative responsibilities online. For the master's and principal certification-seeking students, the ability to complete their work without having to meet face-to-face reduced some of the pressure. For those who were expected to show up for synchronous, face-to-face classes, however, the 5:30 p.m. time slot for a three-hour course at the end of their workday presented an additional burden and level of stress on their abilities to focus and concentrate on the discussions related to the weekly topic, course content, and requirements for class. As PC, I relayed their concerns to the EDLE faculty and we agreed that a level of grace, understanding, and flexibility in expectations and demands would guide our approach.

Continuing into the fall semester of the 2020–2021 school year, most of our students were required to physically return to their positions and arrange for and manage a combination of face-to-face and online course delivery options, the multiple COVID-19 protocols, and all other activities associated with working with students and parents to ensure a safe learning environment for their school and classrooms. A majority of students reached out to me and the other facilitators, thankful that the EDLE online and hybrid courses were handled virtually. The physical and emotional toll on our students began to have an effect on their level of enthusiasm for completing some of their coursework, engaging in discussions and, for doctoral students, meeting at the allotted time slots. Other students, on the other hand, noted that they missed meeting face-to-face and being able to network with one another through their physically present conversations. Reconciling the differences and inconveniences of having to balance their work-life demands with their course demands, exacerbated by the COVID-19 pandemic, continued to be a major concern to facilitate through the spring and summer sessions. Due to the complexities of their job requirements and the added stress placed on them to handle the requirements of their positions, however, most of the students admitted that going home from work to attend class online rather than having to travel to a specific location for their courses at the end of their workday served as a blessing.

Another item that emerged was the slowness of administrative processes at the university due to everything moving online. Review of applications to the graduate school, prior to being able to be reviewed by EDLE faculty to consider their admission to our various degree and certification programs, were stalled, causing us to lose a number of candidates to other institutions.

The Institutional Review Board was short-staffed, causing delays in many of our doctoral students' and faculty members' abilities to receive approval to conduct their research. In a number of cases, students' research and graduation timelines were set back by one or more semesters. Working with the department chair to resolve these issues, we soon discovered that our hands were tied due to staff shortages and the new replacements having to learn the ropes, the backlog of IRB applications that existed prior to the pandemic, and the additional number of IRB applications that continued to be submitted by faculty and students. Administrators from the graduate school informed us of these shortages and the accompanying challenges inherent in onboarding those new the position. In my role as PC, students looked to me to solve dilemmas like these. Because I could not correct the situation, my priority became helping students maintain positive attitudes to help them persevere while defending the university, college, department, and program when necessary.

For the 2021–2022 school year, the university reopened with strict protocols for mask-wearing in place and requirements for proof of vaccine or testing for COVID-19 in place. Due to a state mandate from the governor, mandatory vaccines and masking requirements could not be put into force. As PC, I fielded numerous complaints from students or faculty who had students who did not want to wear masks or were concerned about the closeness of the room and lack of social distancing available in crowded classrooms. Other students who were accustomed to online classes indicated their displeasure that they had to travel to several locations for classes. Online only students and faculty questioned the documentation requirements to demonstrate proof of vaccine or vaccine testing results.

A clear pattern of concerns emerging because of the switch from online to hybrid classes with face-to-face requirements caused us to rethink the semester classes requiring students to travel to one or more campuses for classes. As a PC, I anticipate having to mediate the direction we should take due to the mixed feelings among faculty and students. These conversations are ones that can be challenging, especially when different leadership backgrounds and experiences exist among faculty.

DIFFERENCES IN LEADERSHIP BACKGROUND AND EXPERIENCES OF FACULTY

Prior to 2020, the position description postings for EDLE faculty noted the importance of school- or district-level leadership experience to support the preparation of educational leaders. Traditionally, those who were admitted to our EDLE program were aspiring teacher-leaders, principals, district-level administrators, or superintendents, regardless of the degree they were seeking. The EDLE faculty held to this expectation for the students we admitted as well as the faculty who were hired. The dean of the college and department chair, however, shifted toward a preference for research faculty due to the Tier 1 status of the university, replacing the expectation for leadership experience with a related-experience expectation. These distinctions were discussed within our program faculty meetings with some concern and disagreement.

In 2020 and 2021, we hired three assistant professors with stronger backgrounds in teacher leadership, educational policy, and research and an additional executive-in-residence faculty member to assist with the recruitment of teaching of master's and doctoral students. We continue to highlight the preparation of educational leaders due to our principal and superintendent certification programs and scholarly practitioner via the EdD degree program. With the addition of the new assistant professors, however, we are also emphasizing the opportunity to pursue a career in academia through our PhD degree program. Until recently, courses required as part of the PhD degree mirrored the same required courses for the EdD degree, differentiated by the requirement to take one additional research course and an additional core course with a strong research component. The superintendent certification courses as a concentration area continue to be available as hours pursued for the PhD degree, an option we are trying to discourage our students from pursuing due to the importance of acquiring a stronger knowledge base in research-, policy-, and specialization courses relevant to a career in academia. Working together to ensure the most appropriate courses are embedded in or made available to students within the EdD and PhD degree, according to their current and future career trajectory and intentions, continues to be an important function for the PC to facilitate, especially in light of future discussions necessary to ensure a distinction between the courses required for earning an EdD versus a PhD.

Philosophical views of faculty are united in terms of many aspects of where we are headed as a program, especially in terms of embracing an equity-oriented leadership preparation focus. However, the expertise needed to prepare future school leaders, oversee their internships, and teach certain classes related to building- and district-level leadership are relegated primarily to faculty who have EC–12 experience, while the expertise needed to work with students with a greater interest in pursuing academia and policy-oriented careers includes the newer faculty and additional faculty who have acquired knowledge due to their various leadership experiences. During the 2021–2022 academic year, we engaged in discussions about how we might support certain initiatives advanced by the university, college, and department as well as how we might share the load of doctoral students as their advisor or chair. Hard conversations and, at times, misunderstandings and hurt feelings occurred. Despite my attempts as PC to manage these types of conversations and follow up with those involved, some individuals chose to report their concerns to the department chair. The department chair took the liberty to speak with others in the program rather than discussing the situation with me as PC which then led to further mistrust among various EDLE faculty who felt the situation should have remained within the program area.

While we have reconciled the situation, it is important to note that the PC role and the continual changes that occur within the program require a recognition and appreciation of the reality that differences in philosophies among faculty can and do occur. The need for an established level of trust and collegiality and a protocol for how to discuss topics and potential changes when different philosophical viewpoints are present is imperative. Further, the importance of knowing when to involve individuals from outside of the program area and how to work within the confines of one's authority and positional role need to be clearly defined and communicated upfront. After these incidents occurred, we revisited the norms we established as a department: (a) speak your truth and respect the opinions of others, (b) seek to understand, (c) lean into discomfort, and (d) expect and accept a lack of closure. We also talked about the importance of having the hard one-on-one conversations with the individual(s) to clarify any potential mixed messages prior to moving to the next level of authority, a process commonly followed in leadership circles. We moved toward a more formal approach to our program area meetings as a result, utilizing a modified version of the rules of order to ensure everyone's voice is heard and sharing the responsibility for facilitating the meeting with another faculty member. Admitting the need to move in this direction was a humbling experience albeit one that reconnected us to work together for the betterment of the EDLE program and the individuals we serve.

POLITICS AND POLICIES PERTAINING TO HOW EC–12 DISTRICTS AND SCHOOLS SHOULD FUNCTION AND WHAT STUDENTS SHOULD LEARN

Across the State of Texas, the views and perspectives of state, district, and school leaders; parents, families, and their children; faculty and students; and other constituents who are directly or indirectly tied to the EDLE program vary widely. The policies and perspectives of state officials as well as the state legislature, state education agency, and governing state board of education correspond to or are in conflict with the perspectives of those they oversee or represent. Some of the most highly contested areas of concern are related to various philosophies about how schools and districts should operate and function which includes a consideration of what should be taught in EC–12 schools and classrooms and what EC–12 students should learn and be able to do as they traverse through their school careers. Moreover, families send their children to EC–12 schools with the belief that their children will be exposed to the grade-level content and specific real-world experiences that will best prepare them for the future. What is deemed necessary and critical to prepare students for the future, however, depends on the perspectives that are promulgated between and among each of these groups. Each of these topics and concerns cross over into the role of the PC and the facilitation of EDLE program discussions and items for consideration.

In 2021, the Texas 87th legislative session introduced House Bill 3979 (87(2)), later updated by Senate Bill 3 (87(2)), to provide specific "requirements and prohibitions related to instructional content" (Texas Education Agency, 2022, para. 1). Creating a new section of the Texas Education Code (TEC) §28.0022, the bill was enacted and went into effect on December 2, 2021, impacting school districts and open enrollment charter schools. Essentially, the bill applies to "any course or subject" (S.B No. 3, Sec. 28.0022) for students in K–12. No teacher can be "compelled to discuss a widely debated" or "controversial issue of public policy or social affairs" (1) and if the teacher chooses to do so, the topic must be explored "objectively and in a manner free from political bias" (2). The bill further prohibits the "inculcation" within the content of any course that "one race or sex is inherently superior to another race or sex" (4A(i) as well as the concept that any individual, based on their race or sex, "is inherently racist, sexist, or oppressive, whether consciously or unconsciously" (ii). Additional language contained within the bill bans the teaching that (a) a person be "discriminated against or receive adverse treatment" in light of their race or sex (4A(iii); (b) a person's "moral character, standing, or worth" should be based on their race or sex (iv); (c) a person, due to their race or sex, should bear "responsibility, blame, or built for actions committed by other members of the same race or sex" (v); and (d) that "meritocracy" or traits that highlight "a hard work ethic are racist or sexist or created by members of a particular race to oppress members of another race" (vi). Beyond additional statements contrasting slavery and racism against American values, naming them as "deviations from, betrayals of, or failures" to align with the "founding principles of the United States which included liberty and equality" (viii), the bill specified that no administrator, teacher, or staff member within the state agency, a school district, or charter school could be taught to adopt any of the fore-mentioned concepts.

Several news stories brought attention to the bill, raising questions and concerns expressed by districts, educators, and parents. The Texas Tribune headline read, "Texas educators worry bill limiting the teaching of current events and historic racism would 'whitewash history'" (McGee, 2021) while other media outlets connected the bill to critical race theory (CRT) (KVUE News Staff, 2021; Tietz, 2021; Zeeble, 2021; Zou, 2021). Tietz (2021), an education reporter for the *Daily Caller*, a conservative news outlet, claimed that proponents of CRT "pursue 'antiracism' through the end of merit, objective truth and the adoption of race-based policies" (para. 3).

On the heels of the passage of the Senate Bill 3 (2021), Governor Gregg Abbott pitched a proposed amendment to the Texas Constitution, granting parents more rights and solidifying the concept that parents should be viewed by schools and districts as the predominant decision-makers for their children (Lopez, 2022a). According to Lopez, however, the TEC already offers parents a "wide range of access and veto powers" pertaining to their children (para. 13). Shortly thereafter, in May 2022, the north Texas region caught the attention of state and national news outlets due to the number of conservatives who swept the school board elections, winning seats to replace school board members across the state, particularly in the north Texas region. Richman (2022a, 2022b) attributed the victory to culture wars, relevant to what students should be learning in public schools, parental rights and choice, library books, and race and gender issues, fueled by efforts of the Republican party and conservative political action committees. According to Richman (2022b), "conservative pundits" (para. 21) have tied education leaders' attempts to address a "range of diversity and inclusion efforts" to disrupt "long-standing academic disparities" (para. 22) and discipline outcomes, particularly in terms of race, to CRT in negative ways. Regardless of the position taken, school board members have shifted their attention toward issues related to what should and what should not be taught in schools with both conservative and liberal viewpoints and partisan politics taking center stage (Anderson, 2022; Mitchell, 2022).

The Texas State Board of Education dictates what approximately 5.5 million Texas students within 1,200 public school districts are expected to learn in Texas' public schools as they are responsible for setting the state's curriculum (Lopez, 2022b). For the November 2022 midterm elections, all 15 seats were open due to redistricting that took place the previous year. Although the state board consisted of 10 Republicans and 5 Democrats, two Republican incumbents were replaced by candidates who promised "to get critical race theory out of classrooms" (para. 5) although, according to Lopez, CRT is not taught in elementary or secondary Texas schools. Based on the results of the election, one more Republican seat was added to the board, with several candidates who ran in opposition to CRT, with a close race in favor of a potential second Republican still in question.

Within the EDLE program, the issue of how K–12 districts and schools should function and what students should learn within the larger context of what current and future educational leaders and policymakers need to take forward in their educational practice and scholarship has been repeatedly discussed and revisited. In some conversations, we have paid close attention to the traditional expectations inherent in preparing school and district-level leaders including topics such as school law, finance, personnel, school facilities, instructional leadership, curriculum development and supervision, superintendent, and principal competencies, and so forth. In other ways, we have addressed cultural, ethical, and equity-oriented themes within a number of other courses that include race, class, gender, dis/ability, language, and other intersectional identities. Within higher education and the context of serving as PC of the EDLE program, the department, the college, the university; and the policies and politics that are often linked to these and other conversations, reaching consensus is not necessarily accomplished without encountering some messiness and, at times, controversy. In the next section, I share some of the conflicts and concerns that arose and continue to exist in association with the politics and policies of higher education and my role as PC.

POLITICS AND POLICIES OF HIGHER EDUCATION

During the spring 2020 semester, the department began to engage in deeper conversations about diversity and equity with a predominant focus on race. In our searches for new faculty at the EDLE assistant, associate, and/or full professor level, we endeavored to hire individuals with educational leadership experience who brought a strong research agenda that would complement the expertise of EDLE faculty and fill some of the gaps created by those who left in fall 2019. At the same time, we realized that we would have to honor the vision and expectations of the University, COE Dean, and TE&A Department Chair which was premised on the need to hire faculty of color whose research agenda pertained to historically minoritized populations and communities with a lesser focus on hiring faculty with previous leadership experience. The distinction between the two views became apparent during the hiring process, particularly when a large number of teacher education faculty attended the prospective research faculty's research presentations and favored the faculty, via their questions, who embraced a diversity, equity, and inclusion agenda, regardless of whether their research specifically focused on an educational leadership topic.

As PC and a member of several of the search committees, I leaned more toward those candidates who had a previous publication record that pertained to educational leadership, however. The majority of EDLE faculty recognized the value of both in terms of background, scholarship, and research; however, the majority of the faculty voiced a preference for faculty candidates whose research would contribute to the leadership side of the program. In several situations, I had to quell the concerns of those in the program that those who would be making the final hiring decision seemed to be ignoring the needs of the program and the students and districts we served. We were successful in hiring a candidate for one of the three positions with a strong balance in terms of research and leadership. Due to the COVID pandemic and other extenuating circumstances, the search for the remaining two candidates was closed. The following year, we reopened the search and were successful in hiring two additional faculty as assistant professors. The decision to close the search for an associate/full professor without consulting with the faculty on the search committee, however, caused EDLE faculty to question the administration's level of commitment to the EDLE program. Whether accurate or not, numerous one-on-one and group conversations, trying to heal some of the damage done in the process, took up much of my time as PC.

During the 2020–2021 academic year, we formed an ad-hoc committee to discuss how we could redesign the EdD degree program and differentiate it from the PhD degree program. Individual faculty members held closely to the courses they traditionally taught. When we presented the proposed purpose and vision for new EdD degree program to members of the superintendency advisory committee, they underscored the larger need to focus our attention on preparing district and school leaders who could establish strong district and school cultures and navigate the challenges faced in light of COVID 19. Specific areas of concern included the mental health needs of teachers and students, teacher shortages, learning loss, and the ability to respond to the demands of parents and the larger school community. The impetus to incorporate courses that focused on diversity, equity, inclusion, and access with a larger focus on an anti-racist agenda was recognized as valid, although those topics were not deemed to be as critical as those the superintendents identified as more immediate needs. In light of the fact that the department, at the time, was advertising and mandating an anti-racist focus in all our courses and expecting us to document such a focus, we realized we would need to find a way to balance the two seemingly competing agendas. As EDLE faculty, we were able to come to a form of mutual agreement in the changes to be made to satisfy the preferences of those representing our area school districts as well as those of the department. Nevertheless, certain glitches along the way caused a delay in our ability to move forward due to a total turnover of departmental and program area staff. As PC, working with those who sacrificed their efforts to see this work move forward, it seemed as though we were taking one step forward and two steps backward.

Over the course of the past two to three academic years since I became PC, the university has increased their attention toward issues related to diversity, equity, and inclusion and, more recently, access. In concert with the Division of Inclusion, Diversity, Equity, and Access, the university requires its employees to complete a specific number of learning and development hours each year, dedicated to "the development of a socially just and intentionally inclusive environment for the university community." During the 2021–2022 academic year, much of the training spilled over into in-depth conversations and emphases toward making sure we, as a program, department, and college, are interrogating our own attitudes and values and incorporating instructional approaches that honor and represent the multiple identities of faculty and staff, students, and the larger community we serve. While many of the conversations that take place within our program area honor these goals, there have been occasions when individuals shared a perspective that deviated from the message being advanced. In other instances, what was being said versus what was actually meant was miscommunicated or misunderstood. Certain incidents were influenced by an individual's value system that was different from the one being advanced by those in charge. In some cases, certain faculty chose to discuss what they perceived to be taking place with individuals outside of our program area, causing individuals to jump to conclusions, take certain reported actions, and ignore the possible divisions within the EDLE program that might occur. Incidents similar to these and others are par for the course in nearly every organization. Trying to balance the perspectives of self and others in ameliorating the subsequent consequences and occasional fallout that can occur along the way, however, posed a different challenge than what existed prior to the COVID-19 pandemic; the heightened attention paid to diversity, equity, inclusion, and access concerns; and subsequent politics and policies evolving within the higher education setting.

BALANCING CARE FOR SELF AND OTHERS

Amidst the political climate of higher education, coupled with the policies and subsequent interpretive actions in response to such policies that tend to follow, Marshall and Scribner's (1991) seminal article addressing the micropolitics of education that stated, "It's All Political" holds true 30 plus years later. Within the overarching realm of educational leadership and preparation programs, we must not only adhere to the politics and policies of higher education. We are also expected to consider how we interact with the politics and policies that direct, guide, and impact our partners in EC–12 education.

As PC, I embrace the mindset that individuals have the right to hold to their own belief systems and should be allowed to discuss their perspective in a safe and comfortable work environment. In higher education settings, some of the politics and policies being advanced by educational leadership, teacher education, and other departments and colleges—more specifically—to critique, disrupt, and replace the various systems that currently exist and commit to take an activist approach toward change have caused me to rethink my role as PC. I am concerned that we are headed in a particular direction where those who choose to advocate for the rights of those whose perspectives and beliefs differ from the ones being advanced by others—often, the majority—may be in danger of censorship and forced to silence by their critics. Our U.S. Constitution and the principle of academic freedom, which grant the right to share one's perspective and hold to one's belief system, no matter where it falls on the spectrum of liberal to conservative, appears to be in jeopardy.

Regardless of the political climate within our nation, state, EC–12 districts and schools, and higher education, I do not believe any one entity has the right to impose their belief systems upon another individual or require them to compromise what they believe to fit into the system. As a woman of faith with a hidden dis/ability, my own beliefs and perspectives have not necessarily aligned with those advanced by others in my program area as well as the larger field of educational leadership and educational policy. Serving as PC within the EDLE program and housed within a department and college and university setting that requires us to examine ourselves and challenge our perspectives has, at times, been unsettling. Do we, within the higher education setting and, more specifically, educational leadership and other related fields of education, wish to advance an agenda that argues for a one-size-fits-all perspective? Were we created to mimic the voice of the majority, or bow down to a perspective that embraces a philosophy of life and action that violates our own consciences and what we believe? As I commit personally and spiritually to walk according to the truth of God's Word, guidance of the Holy Spirit, and Lordship of Jesus Christ, serving as PC within the current climate of higher education and educational leadership has, at times, been difficult. By the same token, I know the challenges I am encountering may not be that much different from what many of my colleagues are experiencing, albeit in different ways. Nevertheless, as both PC and an academic, I am concerned about the direction in which those of us in higher education and educational leadership appear to be headed, unless we commit to a wide berth of acceptance and rethink what we believe equity, diversity, inclusion, and access are all about. For that reason, I am a member of the Academic Freedom Alliance (AFA).

The AFA (n.d.) consists of faculty "who are dedicated to upholding the principle of academic freedom" with members "from across the political spectrum" (para. 1). They commit to defend the rights of faculty to engage in "freedom of thought and expression" in "their work as researchers and writers" and "their lives as citizens, within established ethical and legal bounds" (para. 2). According to the AFA (2022), many academics are being placed in an environment where they are expected to pledge a level of conformity to a particular belief system to "accommodate the perceived ideological preferences of an institution" despite the "actual beliefs or commitments of those forced to speak" (para. 2). The AFA further claims that requiring individuals to pledge allegiance to a particular value system "enlists academics into a political movement, erasing the distinction between academic expertise and ideological conformity" and "encourages cynicism and dishonesty" (para. 3). In their full statement, the AFA acknowledges that "such skepticism exists across a wide ideological range that includes not only right-leaning scholars but left-leaning scholars as well" (para. 5). They further state: "Fortunately, there are signs that increasing numbers of academics are becoming aware of the need to respond with candor and determination to procedures that might seem to be innocuous but that are detrimental to core values of higher education" (para. 5).

At times, I grapple with the radical approaches and behaviors of individuals who stand on both sides of the political spectrum and the policies advanced within Texas, higher education, educational leadership, and the EC–12 districts, schools, and leaders we, in effect, are expected to serve. In certain incidents serving as PC, I have played out my inner thoughts and subsequent actions in ways that required me to step back and reassess how I should lead. Within the larger context of higher education and how I believe EDLE programs and the PC must function, we must continue to fight for the right to freedom of expression so multiple perspectives are honored. In the midst of differing viewpoints about how we believe we should proceed and move forward, as the PC of the EDLE program, I admit that I have not necessarily reacted according to what I profess. Coming to grips with such a realization has caused me to draw even closer to God, in hopes that He will lead and guide me as I strive to fulfill my role as the PC during these turbulent times.

REFLECTIONS AND CONCLUSIONS

As I reflect on my experiences serving as PC within the various context represented in this narrative, my positionality has shifted several times due to my renewed spiritual commitment. In the process of adjusting to the departure of EDLE faculty, filling the positions with new faculty, and advancing in the midst and aftermath of the COVID-19 pandemic, it became apparent that the PC serves as a middle manager. Fulfilling the PC role, carrying out the various responsibilities inherent in leading the EDLE program, working with faculty with diverse viewpoints and experiences to meet the needs of the students in the program, and answering to the expectations and demands of those in charge of the department, college, and university continue to come with numerous challenges. With no actual guidance for PCs in the research literature, most PCs have had to learn how to perform their role without any actual guidance within the research literature or from their institution. Further, as noted by Ladyshewsky and Flavell (2011), PCs are not necessarily prepared for the leadership demands and are expected to lead without any "line management authority," requiring them to "build their influence through collegiality and informal relationships" (p. 12) which occurs more frequently at the program area level with their academic peers. I am grateful for the renewed support of the EDLE faculty and that we, as an EDLE program, have embraced a distributed leadership model and approach, making my role as PC an enjoyable and worthwhile experience.

Clearly, the role of the EDLE PC needs to be further defined and additional supports and leadership training is needed to ensure the PC can function successfully without attempting to fulfill the role on their own, with little to no guidance. A leadership development program dedicated to the PC role, with strong PC mentoring and coaching, is recommended. Additional research to determine the actual design of such a program is also needed and could be initiated by examining the experiences and expertise shared by the chapter authors within these two volumes. Beyond the imperative to provide additional supports and training, however, the paramount importance of recognizing the reality of the EDLE PC's need to be able to balance between the self and others and honor the individual right to hold true to one's perspective and beliefs, cannot be ignored. Otherwise, we risk losing the essence of what those of us in equity-oriented educational leadership programs claim to embrace and advance.

REFERENCES

Academic Freedom Alliance (n.d.). *Mission of the Academic Freedom Alliance.* https://academicfreedom.org/about/

Academic Freedom Alliance (2022, August 22). *AFA calls for end to required diversity statements.* https://academicfreedom.org/afa-calls-for-an-end-to-required-diversity-statements/

Anderson, E. (2022, May 9). *Parent movement scores big wins in north Texas school board races.* https://texasscorecard.com/local/parent-movement-scores-big-wins-in-north-texas-school-board-races/

Coleman, L. B., & Reames, E. (2020). The role of the educational leadership program coordinator (PC) in university-K-12 school district partnership development. *Journal of Research on Leadership Education, 15*(4) 241–260. https://doi.org/10.1177/1942775118803335

Ezzani, M. D., & Paufler, N. A. (2018). Doctoral program in education leadership redesign: Utilizing a multicriteria framework. *Impacting Education, 3*(2), 11–16. https://doi.org/10.5195/ie.2018.70

Hackmann, D. G., & McCarthy, M. M. (2011). At a crossroads: The educational leadership professoriate in the 21st century. *UCEA leadership series*. Information Age Publishing.

Hackmann, D. G., & Wanat, C. L. (2008). The role of the educational leadership program coordinator: A distributed leadership perspective. *International Journal of Educational Reform, 17*(1), 64–88. https://doi.org/10.1177/105678790801700105

Hackmann, D. G., & Wanat, C. L. (2016). Doing the work or sharing the work? The educational leadership program coordinator's role. *International Journal of Educational Reform, 25*(2), 100–124. https://doi.org/10.1177/105678791602500201

Ingle, W. K., Worth, J. J., Marshall, J. M., & Hackmann, D. G. (2018). The incentives and costs of program coordination in P-12 educational leadership programs. *Journal of Education Finance, 44*(2), 175–198. http://www.jstor.org/stable/45095013

KVUE News Staff. (2021, July 16). Critical race theory bill SB3 passes in Texas Senate by 18-4 vote. *KVUE-ABC*. https://www.kvue.com/article/news/politics/texas-legislature/critical-race-theory-senate-texas-legislature/269-9e40d158-a700-437b-8bf0-8d8a2aaeec92

Ladyshewsky, R. K., & Flavell, H. (2011). Transfer of training in an academic leadership development program for program coordinators. *Educational Management Administration & Leadership, 40*(1), 127–147. https://doi.org/10.1177/1741143211420615

Lopez, B. (2022a, January 26). Gov. Gregg Abbott taps into parent anger to fuel reelection campaign. *The Texas Tribune*. https://www.texastribune.org/2022/01/26/greg-abbott-parental-bill-of-rights/

Lopez, B. (2022b, November 9). Texas Republicans against "critical race theory" win seats on the State Board of Education, strengthening its GOP majority. *The Texas Tribune*. https://www.texastribune.org/2022/11/08/texas-state-board-education-election-results/

McGee, K. (2021, May 26). Texas educators worry bill limiting the teaching of current events and historic racism would "whitewash history." *The Texas Tribune*. https://www.texastribune.org/2021/05/26/texas-teachers-critical-race-theory-legislature/

Marshall, C., & Scribner, J. D. (1991). "It's all political": Inquiry into the micropolitics of education. *Education and Urban Society, 23*(4), 347–355. https://doi.org/10.1177/0013124591023004001

Mitchell, I. (2022, May 10). Conservative trend emerges in May school board races in Texas. *The Texan*. https://www.dallasnews.com/news/education/2022/05/05/big-money-texas-school-board-races-the-new-norm-as-conservative-spending-ramps-up/

New King James Bible. (2022). Blue Letter Bible Online. https://www.blueletterbible.org/nkjv/phl/3/14/s_1106014

North, C. E. (2008). What is all this talk about "social justice"?: Mapping the terrain of education's latest catchphrase. *Teachers College Record, 110*(6), 1182–1206. https://doi.org/10.1177/016146810811000607

Paufler, N., Ezzani, M., Viamontes, J., Murakami, E. & Pazey, B. L. (2020). Educational leadership doctoral program evaluation: Student voice as the litmus test. *Journal of Research on Leadership Education, 17*(3), 215–242. https://doi.org/10.1177/1942775120976705

Perry, J. A., Zambo, D., & Abruzzo, E. (2020). Faculty leaders challenges and strategies in redesigning EdD programs. *Impacting Education, 5,* 1–6. https://doi.org/10.5195/ie.2020.143

Richman, T. (2002a, May 5). Big-money Texas school board races the 'new norm' as conservative spending ramps up? *The Dallas Morning News.* https://www.dallasnews.com/news/education/2022/05/05/big-money-texas-school-board-races-the-new-norm-as-conservative-spending-ramps-up/

Richman, T. (2022b, May 9). GOP leaders point to North Texas school board wins as strike against CRT. *The Dallas Morning News.* https://www.dallasnews.com/news/education/2022/05/10/gop-leaders-point-to-north-texas-school-board-wins-as-strike-against-crt/

S.B.3 No. 3. (2021). *An act.* https://legiscan.com/TX/text/SB3/id/2431439/Texas-2021-SB3-Enrolled.html

Texas Education Agency. (2022). *Senate Bill 3, 87th Texas legislature, second called session: Update to instructional requirements and prohibitions.* https://tea.texas.gov/about-tea/news-and-multimedia/correspondence/taa-letters/senate-bill-3-87th-texas-legislature-second-called-session-update-to-instructional-requirements-and-prohibitions

Tietz, K. (2021, June 16). Texas governor signs bill that prohibits schools from teaching an individual to feel 'anguish' or 'guilt' due to their race or gender. *Daily Caller.* https://dailycaller.com/2021/06/16/texas-bill-prohibits-schools-from-teaching-due-to-race-or-gender/

Zeeble, B. (2021, July 9). The Texas legislature has targeted critical race theory, but is it being taught in public schools? *Texas Standard: The National Daily News Show of Texas.* https://www.texasstandard.org/stories/the-texas-legislature-has-targeted-critical-race-theory-but-is-it-being-taught-in-public-schools/

Zou, I. (2021, July 9). Texas Senate bill seeks to strip required lessons on people of color and women from "critical race theory" law. *The Texas Tribune.* https://www.texastribune.org/2021/07/09/texas-critical-race-theory-schools-legislation/

SECTION III

CHAPTER 8

"WE'RE LUCKY TO HAVE EACH OTHER"

Solo Leadership Faculty as Program Coordinators

Wesley Henry
Central Connecticut State University

Ann E. Blankenship-Knox
University of Redlands

Sarah M. Jouganatos
Sacramento State University

Lori Rhodes
Stamford Public Schools

ABSTRACT

This study explores the work of four principal preparation program coordinators (PCs) who were the only tenure-track, full-time educational leadership faculty at their institutions as they engaged in program redesign to emphasize equity-focused leadership preparation. Findings explore the role of solo-faculty PCs as agents of change as they sought to build capacity for greater focus on equity through a response to state-level changes in

Navigating the Ubiquitous, Misunderstood, and Evolving Role of the Educational Leadership Program Coordinator in Higher Education, pp. 161–182

www.infoagepub.com

administrator credentialing requirements. PCs were able to accelerate change within their individual institutions by leveraging their collective capacity through collaborative redesign. This study offers implications for solo-faculty PCs, for leadership preparation programs with small faculties, and for administrators seeking to better support addressing the challenges facing solo-faculty PCs.

REVIEW OF RELEVANT LITERATURE

Educational leaders are responsible for myriad boundary spanning duties within the schools and communities they serve (Miller, 2007, 2008). The dual pandemics of racial injustice and COVID-19 have amplified the important role leaders play in fostering a positive culture that supports student success (Kraft et al., 2020). Educational leadership preparation programs have a key role to play in helping future administrators respond to unforeseen challenges in ways that promote equity and well-being (Cunningham et al., 2019). The necessary focus on fostering leaders who will champion equity and inclusion adds another layer of complexity for educational leadership program coordinators (PCs) who already have wide ranging duties that eclipse those of coordinators for programs in other disciplines (Ingle et al., 2020; Reames, 2016).

Educational leadership PCs are responsible for matters on-campus (e.g., scheduling courses), but their coordination work extends far beyond campus with responsibilities including nurturing relationships with districts, overseeing administrative internship placements, and tending to credentialing requirement updates (Reames, 2016). This outreach is critically important to ensure strong partnerships with districts (Coleman & Reames, 2020; Hackman & Wanat, 2016; Ingle et al., 2020; Reames, 2016) and to engage in advocacy at the state-level related to changes in administrator certification (Hackman & Malin, 2016; Reames, 2016).

By engaging in this broad portfolio of duties, PCs collaborate with a variety of stakeholders, and some of these stakeholders may have competing interests or lack an understanding of the needs of other stakeholders (e.g., department chairs, district partners, state officials responsible for credentialing). The quasi-official capacity of the role often means that PCs are responsible for many duties but have little authority within universities (Hackman & Wanat, 2016). Additionally, the extraordinary amount of time, effort, and energy required to successfully coordinate an educational leadership program is well documented (Coleman & Reames, 2020; Hackman & Malin, 2016; Hackman & Wanat, 2016; Ingle et al., 2020). Leading change within programs and advocating for change at other levels within the institution are key factors in the work in which PCs engage (Ingle et al., 2020). The commitment of time and effort is amplified for PCs shepherding program redesign efforts with on- and off-campus stakeholders (Coleman & Reames, 2020). This is particularly true as PCs endeavor to redesign programs to achieve a sharper focus on issues of diversity, equity, and inclusion.

A body of scholarship underscores the role that the design and delivery of educational leadership preparation programming plays in fostering more equitable schools. For example, extant literature highlights the power of fostering university-district partnerships in the pursuit of equity-focused leadership preparation (Davis, 2016; Fusarelli et al., 2019; Hitt et al., 2012), supporting the development of culturally competent leaders (Barakat et al., 2019), and engaging in deliberate program evolution to meet the needs of diverse educator and PreK–12 student populations (Honig & Donaldson-Walsh, 2019). Indeed, steering coherent program redesign rooted in equity principles is a cornerstone of the work of educational leadership faculty (Henry & Cobb, 2021). A growing body of literature explores the design of high-quality educational leadership preparation programs that emphasize equity-focused learning experiences (e.g., Cunningham et al., 2019; Young, 2015) and purposeful collaboration of educational leadership faculty within and across institutions (e.g., Coleman & Reames, 2020; Hackman & Malin, 2016; Thornton et al., 2022). Scholarship also emphasizes the importance of high-quality faculty (Jacobson et al., 2015; Young et al., 2016). Yet, limited research regarding the role of educational leadership PCs exists, and extant literature tends to investigate the role of PCs at research-focused institutions (e.g., Hackman & Wanat, 2016; Ingle et al., 2020). In addition, the sources cited above underscore the importance of collaboration between educational leadership faculty within an institution in the dual processes of program improvement and delivery, yet not all educational leadership preparation programs have a robust faculty to support in this work.

STUDY BACKGROUND AND CONTEXT

The purpose of this study was to investigate the experiences of program coordinators from four different institutions within the same large state to better understand the work and role of PCs who are the only tenure-track educational leadership faculty at their institutions. Three of the four institutions are part of the same state university system with over 20 campuses and the remaining institution is a highly ranked, private regional university. We first met as members of a larger consortium of leadership preparation programs of various sizes, including those housed within public and private institutions as well as local education authorities (LEAs) which can certify educators in this state. This consortium was a three-year, grant-funded initiative intended to support the implementation of a multi-cycle performance assessment that principal candidates must pass before receiving a credential. This policy change required a full redesign of the programs across our four institutions, and it also provided PCs with an opportunity to collaborate beyond the scope of the mandate to redesign curriculum, improve field experiences, and expand district-partnership initiatives.

Over the course of the three-year initiative, representatives from this consortium came together in person once or twice each year with regular collaboration online between in-person meetings. Remote meetings became more frequent during the COVID-19 pandemic when university campuses and LEA offices were shuttered. Prior to the pandemic, the four co-authors formed a more intimate, informal faculty network within this consortium. Early in this work, we bonded over the challenges of serving as the only full-time and/or tenure-track educational leadership faculty at our institutions while also responsible for leading the principal preparation program. As we explore further below, having a group of colleagues working within similar contextual demands was a valued dynamic and resource. In fact, following the implementation of the redesigned programs and once the implications of the pandemic on credentialing requirements stabilized, we continued collaborating as a means for program improvement and professional support.

CONCEPTUAL PERSPECTIVE

This study utilizes grounded theory to conceptualize a framework for the role of solo faculty program coordinators. A key characteristic of grounded theory studies is that they do not include a predetermined conceptual framework but instead leverage data collected for the study to present findings (e.g., Charmaz, 2014; Corbin & Strauss, 2008). Therefore, this study was designed to better understand the role of educational leadership PCs who are also the only tenure-track educational leadership faculty at their institutions. Specifically, these research questions guided our collective inquiry:

- How do solo faculty PCs navigate the dual demands of tenure-track productivity expectations and program coordination work?
- What specific contributions, if any, did PC collaboration across institutions contribute to local program coordination and/or redesign efforts?
- What specific contributions, if any, did PC collaboration across institutions contribute to faculty work not related to program coordination responsibilities?

METHODOLOGY

This study seeks to ground the development of theories in rich data (Charmaz, 2014; Corbin & Strauss, 2008). To that end, we employed a collaborative autoethnography (CAE) study design (Chang et al., 2013). CAE is methodologically related to autoethnography in that it is a qualitative method that relies on the lived experience of the researchers; researchers analyze and interpret their experiences through an ethnographic process to make meaning of and to gain a sociocultural understanding of shared experience (Anderson, 2006; Chang, 2008; Ellis, 2004). CAE "invites community to investigate shared stories and balances the individual narrative with the collective experiences" (Blalock & Akehi, 2018, p. 94). Chang et al. (2013) argue that because CAE relies on multiple data sources from the scholars themselves, it may be more reliable than an autoethnography.

CAE may include a wide variety of data sources, including but not limited to personal memory data, mutual interviews, and archival data. The process is not linear and may occur over long periods of time (Chang et al., 2013). The methodology is democratic in nature, equally valuing each member's lived experiences. This process may be logistically, relationally, and ethically challenging, depending on the size of the CAE team and their dynamic (Hernandez et al., 2017).

Research Context and Participants

Each author was a PC (or served in an equivalent position with coordinator responsibilities) of a principal preparation credential program in the same large state. We each started our time as program leaders as tenure-track, assistant professors and managed the program at our institutions individually. There were no other full-time faculty devoted to supporting the educational leadership program. We initially connected through a professional organization for professors of educational leadership and remained connected through state-run training workshops and other collaborative opportunities. Specifically, we were all members of a grant-funded consortium designed to provide collaborative opportunities for managers of education administration programs as they engaged with program revisions to align with new state program requirements.

Individually and through our collaboration, we were actively engaged in program redesign efforts that ultimately created new knowledge to be shared with one another. We had similar needs and faced similar challenges, so we endeavored to treat our work like action research cycles (Merriam & Tisdell, 2016). As we engaged in program improvement efforts, we strove to capture data and details to add context to our successes and failures to help those in the group with similar needs. This approach encouraged us to document and reflect on our work in ways that supported sharing our work with one another. Through CAE inquiry, we investigated the "beliefs, values, and attitudes" (Merriam & Tisdell, 2016, p. 29) that informed our work at our institutions as well as our collective work through a consortium.

Data Collection and Analysis

We collected data over a period of four years of collaboration (three years as a part of the grant-funded consortium and one additional year). Key data sources included targeted transcription of consortium meetings (with information for other participants removed), field notes from consortium meetings and breakout sessions between the research group included here, extensive field notes and analytic memos from the research team's time in their respective PC positions, program specific documents, and the administration of a multiphase participatory action research semi-structured interview protocol used by the research team to guide each other through reflective interviews and journaling.

We engaged in open, axial, and selective coding in tandem with the constant comparative method (Glaser & Strauss, 1967; Saldaña, 2012) to move from lower-level codes to categories and overarching themes present within the data. Additionally, as themes crystalized, we shared a summary of emerging findings with select colleges within our institutions. This allowed us to check for our own biases by triangulating our perspectives with those who were engaged in departmental conversations and processes.

FINDINGS

Findings underscore the role of the PC as an agent of change for equity-focused leadership preparation. In addition, the PC must advocate for resources, flexibility, and visibility for educational leadership programs. Four distinct but interconnected themes emerged from this study:

1. PCs bridged and buffered the influence of their department, college, campus, and external entities.
2. PCs engaged in a significant amount of capacity building to educate colleagues and administrators about leadership preparation and advocate for programs in the context of individual institutions.
3. The demands of attending to PC duties and engaging in program improvement initiatives served as a distraction from working toward tenure.

4. The nature of the solo-faculty PC role contributed to sustainability challenges for faculty and for the products of PCs' efforts, such as district partnerships.

Bridging and Buffering

As PCs, we all worked to bridge and buffer influences external to leadership programs within our institutions and beyond. Within departments and colleges, we navigated institutional challenges, such as strict scheduling policies and university supervision processes developed to serve teacher education programs. This was the case for all PCs, but the impact of teacher preparation-centric logistics and faculty mindsets varied somewhat between institutions. The educational leadership programs we oversaw were housed in departments that covered a variety of content areas (e.g., educational leadership and higher education; educational leadership and special education; and one department housing teacher credentialing, special education, school psychology, speech pathology, and educational leadership). While PCs at two of the institutions were able to drive decision making about program matters independently, the other two institutions required shared governance of the educational leadership programs with input from faculty with no educational leadership experience or expertise.

The two PCs who did not need to navigate extensive departmental micropolitics to pursue changes that would increase program quality still engaged in relationship-building and education efforts within their college and institution. As one PC explained, "building relationships was key. I made conscious efforts to engage in conversations with leadership, other faculty, and state agency individuals. By having these connections, I was trusted to make changes or ask for resources that were needed." Similarly, the other PC in this position mentioned,

> while many of my colleagues had experience with credentialing specifically, I was one of few faculty or staff who had extensive knowledge about our [leadership] program and how it met standards. I worked to bring others into that conversation so there was more shared knowledge.

The two PCs who worked within a shared decision-making structure that included non-leadership faculty engaged in a significant amount of capacity building within their department (explored in more detail in the next section), but such capacity building was done to craft a common understanding of the work necessary for leading an educational leadership program aligned with emerging knowledge about exemplary leadership preparation.

The emphasis on building shared knowledge with stakeholders on campus and beyond was relevant for all of us. A common theme emerged that underscored the importance of the PC role in working proactively to build shared knowledge with district partners and field experience mentors. All PCs, regardless of how established their programs were, worked to build new partnerships with local districts and/or expanded existing partnerships. Across the institutions, these relationships had not existed prior to our efforts to foster engagement with local districts in ways that might support educational leader preparation. This work was especially relevant for all four programs during redesign efforts to ensure that curricular changes and program improvements could reflect the shared needs of local schools and districts. Additionally, fostering relationships with districts was particularly critical for the success of the redesigned programs because, in most cases, district administrators and field experience mentors learned about the credentialing changes directly from PCs. These relationships were important because the performance assessment required a new degree of active engagement from candidates' principals and other administrators and sustained communication between preparation programs and districts.

Bridging and buffering was also common with nonlocal, off-campus entities exerting influence on leadership programs. Most significantly, as the new performance assessment cycles were introduced, we served as a liaison between our campuses and the state educator credentialing agency. This required traveling for several in-person meetings and engaging in monthly webinars to learn about the new requirements as well as assessment scoring, the submission system, and other administrative components. The performance assessment launched after the start of the 2018–2019 academic year as a requirement for all candidates starting a program during the inaugural year, but it was not consequential, meaning candidates were not required to meet a passing standard. The first consequential year for the performance assessment was the 2019–2020 academic year. This meant that the performance assessment and our program redesign efforts were still relatively new when the COVID-19 pandemic closed schools and university campuses. During this turbulent time, a key component of our PC role was to act as an information funnel for university credentialing analysts, districts, and multiple cohorts of students. This represented work typically supported by university credentialing analysts for teacher preparation programs at these institutions. Therefore, as we attempted to bridge and buffer by acting as a central hub for information during the implementation of the performance assessment, we assumed additional duties that were not asked of PC colleagues overseeing other educator preparation programs.

Finally, we endeavored to bridge the collective expertise and knowledge we gained through a variety of professional organizations. The California Association of Professors of Educational Administration (CAPEA) provided a venue for learning and sharing with institutions and LEAs who were also engaged in programmatic efforts to embed the performance assessment. Other professional organizations, especially the American Educational Research Association (AERA), the International Council of Professors of Educational Leadership (ICPEL), and the University Council for Educational Administration (UCEA) highlighted emerging research-based best practices for educational leadership preparation. These organizations' conferences and publications provided inspiration for incorporating powerful learning experiences (Cunningham et al., 2019; Young, 2015) that would challenge principal candidates' thinking about diversity, equity, and inclusion and prepare them for the complex nature of leadership positions.

We were all engaged with these professional organizations, but we came together for close collaboration through the three-year grant-funded initiative mentioned above. This consortium of programs enabled sharing ideas across programs with a diversity of enrollment, geographic location, and organizational structure (e.g., public and private universities and local education agencies). Yet, it was the relationship forged between us as solo-faculty PCs that held the most significant impact for our program leadership work. We were able to collaborate with one another and to act as critical friends as we navigated the challenges of serving as a solo-faculty PC. We were also able to leverage the opportunity to cocreate curriculum and learning experiences as we engaged in program redesign. This allowed us to customize collaborative products to meet local priorities rather than starting from scratch with each task.

Building Capacity

Each of us devoted significant time and energy to engage in capacity building efforts that would support our institution's leadership programs. As suggested above, we built capacity within our departments and/or colleges to help differentiate leadership programs from other programs with more faculty, students, and/or history. This advocacy included requesting time on meeting agendas to facilitate meaningful conversation with departmental stakeholders, delineating decision-making authority within the department and/or college regarding program-specific changes, and helping colleagues understand the implications of policy changes (e.g., the new performance assessment and policy responses to the COVID-19 pandemic).

At the two institutions with decision-making powers shared by faculty from other education related disciplines, PCs attempted to build the capacity of faculty colleagues to understand changes necessitated by the performance assessment and, more generally, best practices and trends in educational leadership preparation. Faculty from areas outside of educational leadership had limited or no exposure to state or national leadership preparation standards, credentialing expectations, and so on. The most significant potential for tension in these cases was rooted in PCs' desires to incorporate research-based leadership preparation practices, but non-leadership faculty colleagues, including administrators, were sometimes resistant to changes. A frequent response from these stakeholders was that programs approved or accredited by the state educator credentialing agency met all necessary state standards and the performance assessment should be layered on top of the work already underway. Interestingly, such a static approach was not adopted for the programs in which these faculty taught. Additionally, many documents and processes at these two institutions initially mirrored teacher preparation operations already in place, and PCs worked to adjust processes within their first year to be responsive to the different nature of leadership preparation. As the PC who was hired to implement the launch of a newly approved educational leadership program shared,

> While reorienting the materials approved for the program, I was replacing mentions of "teacher candidates." I realized materials for the [principal preparation program] were modeled from other programs and syllabi were borrowed from other institutions. As conceived, our admin candidates would only work on three leadership standards within their internship fall semester and the other three during spring. That's not how school leadership works.

Each of us voiced navigating micropolitics within our departments and colleges; however, this was more difficult at the institutions where faculty from other disciplines held decision-making power. In those cases, non-leadership faculty were more engaged with programmatic intricacies that were left to the PCs at the other institutions to determine based on their content expertise.

As we worked to increase equity-focused content, learning experiences, and district partnerships we often found that we were challenging the traditional norms about "how things are done." Faculty colleagues across all institutions were sometimes resistant to endorse change, but this was particularly relevant to the programs that shared a graduate degree with the other programs in the department. These programs extended beyond credential coursework for master's program completion. Introducing changes within these umbrella degrees had potential knock-on effects for central administration (e.g., the registrar's office) that PCs worked to navigate on behalf of their programs. PCs at the two institutions where shared degrees created administrative challenges (e.g., processing graduation requests) ultimately led to the process of creating a stand-alone educational leadership master's degree. As one PC reflected,

> This took a lot of patience and energy. One gatekeeper [in the provost's office] suggested that all master's students should take the same core and then decide if they want to be a teacher or a principal and finish the appropriate pathway. I have limited authority to push past these barriers, but I'm expected to take care of this work. It's demoralizing.

These conversations within the department and across the institution required building relationships that would demonstrate the need for changes and to foster capacity for changes to curriculum, scheduling, and program structure.

One of the initial reasons we were so eager to collaborate with each other was our shared stance that educator preparation—especially leadership preparation—should encompass more than a high-quality, standards-based curriculum. To that end, within the programs we coordinated, we completely redesigned all of the learning experiences (e.g., admissions, orientation, coursework, and field experience). As explained by one PC:

> [within our program] we did a lot of self-evaluation, of our program, pedagogy, and delivery, to ensure that it aligned with best practices and the needs of our surrounding educational communities.... These efforts are sometimes difficult to sustain because they take a lot of energy and one party generally is the driving force, expending all of the energy. It's easier to create change in a silo but it never produces the best result.

Despite departmental or institutional influences and approval processes, the work of incorporating the performance assessment, specifically, and program redesign, more broadly, was done within a silo at our institutions. The close network we formed enabled us to deconstruct that silo by sharing ideas with one another, serving as sounding boards, and adapting materials and processes between our institutions. In this way, we were consistently focused on building capacity within our own programs and building our collective capacity. As one PC remarked during a mutual interview, "we're lucky to have each other. Answers, ideas, commiseration, and encouragement are always just a text [message] away."

Because of the bond we formed and the products of our collaboration, we presented at conferences and were noticed by leaders within the state educator credentialing agency who asked us to deliver professional development for educational leadership PCs throughout the state. As a result, we built capacity for change at our institutions and sought to support statewide efforts to build capacity for educator preparation rooted in principles of equity and inclusion. Building collective capacity had a positive impact on our redesign efforts, and the work associated with program improvement was never ending. As one PC explained,

> the scope of what I needed to do just got more and more complex as time went on. It started with curriculum revisions, and then real program improvement took on its own life. It was the snowball effect, and it was a lot.

Another PC underscored, "the key here is collaboration. This work cannot be done alone. It took many hours to increase my own knowledge on all of the entities needed for revision, and this time was outside of my regular responsibilities."

Time and Tenure Implications

Release time for coordination duties differed across the four institutions from no course release to a full course release and summer compensation for curriculum redesign. Working as solo leadership faculty members and PCs required advocacy to department chairs and deans for adequate resourcing in addition to the capacity building discussed previously. The necessity to advocate for change and additional resources led to conversations with deans, chairs, and other administrators that had the potential to be difficult given our status as assistant professors. Therefore, serving in this capacity posed an additional layer of micropolitical navigation for pre-tenured faculty. Administrators across the four campuses had varied responses to requests for release time and additional resources. Two PCs felt that their department chairs, who came from non-educational leadership backgrounds, sought to block petitions for support from reaching the dean. Both PCs served under several deans at their institution in the span of three years and felt that the leadership structure at their institutions prevented PCs from engaging in important conversations beyond the department.

Three of the four PCs started their time as a program leader without any coordination release. Two were able to secure coordination support over the course of their time in the role. To secure this workload credit they engaged in advocacy efforts with their deans and sought to understand what other programs (e.g., teacher credentialing, school counselor credentialing, and so on) received as coordination credit. Of the remaining two coordinators, one had release time and was given twenty paid summer days by the dean to engage in redesign efforts. This PC remarked, "I realized how lucky I was when I looked at the situation on other campuses. I think my first dean's background in educational leadership was a key reason for the support I had for coordination and curriculum updates." Yet, this was an institution where multiple deans were appointed over three years and where the department chair acted as a strong filter for access to the dean. Support for coordination was not sustained at such a high level.

The final coordinator had no release time to build or administer the new educational leadership program but was able to secure ten paid summer days for administrative work (e.g., admissions and program updates). Initially, this PC was told that they were not officially a PC since the credential was under the umbrella of a larger, generalized master's degree, yet this faculty member was expected to perform the same tasks as teacher credential PCs. Release time for the educational leadership program did not change when that program became a standalone credential or when a separate educational leadership master's degree was implemented to address administrative issues. Eventually, this faculty member co-coordinated the umbrella master's program with five distinct pathways, but no additional release was extended to account for the work needed to continue coordinating the educational leadership program. At all points, this faculty member was viewed as a coordinator by the state educator credentialing agency and was responsible for implementing the performance assessment, preparing for the state accreditation visit, working with part-time lecturers, running admissions for the educational leadership program, and so on.

A PC who eventually received release time reflected, "this was actually one of the things I did that highlighted our leadership program to our own college. I made my efforts and work known, and when I did that, the college leadership supported my efforts a bit more." The other PC who did eventually receive release time for coordination reflected that,

> the work fell to the person who felt most accountable for the outcomes ... it was difficult to juggle teaching obligations, research to stay on track for tenure, and program leadership responsibilities. Honestly, I was in way over my head several times, and it certainly took a toll.

The release time we were granted for coordination duties, especially those related to the program redesign necessitated by the new performance assessment, represented the most significant variation across our institutions. This was particularly interesting as three of the four PCs were part of the same state university system and represented by the same collective bargaining agreement. Despite the variation in support for program coordination, we each expressed concern that program coordination duties pulled us away from focusing on teaching and research, which were the most important factors for tenure at our institutions. Not only did coordination duties stretch us, but they were also counterproductive for seeking contract renewal and tenure because we were expected to engage in typical service activities (e.g., committees, work in the field, and so on).

We each indicated that our work was necessary for the success of the program. Simply stated, if we did not do this work, it would not happen. Through our reflective interviews, we returned to one key theme related to time and tenure challenges: these tasks were about more than administering a program. As one PC explained, "This is about kids in schools for me. Our graduates will lead schools. Just meeting the state standards won't help our graduates change systems. We have such a pronounced need [in this region], and our kids deserve better." We felt strongly that our work had the potential to contribute to fostering more equitable schools in our areas, and we sought to leverage the performance assessment for holistic program improvement that would center on equity for all students.

Program Leadership Sustainability

A variety of issues related to sustainability were shared across institutional contexts. First, we note that two of the PCs are no longer at their institutions. One left the professoriate for a district leadership position but continued as full-time faculty for a year. The other left for a non-tenure track faculty position elsewhere but continued with their initial institution as a lecturer to teach core administrative preparation courses and oversee the performance assessment. In both cases, these participants felt a responsibility to bridge the transition to a new faculty member for their institution because no other faculty member at those institutions had taught the core curriculum or were familiar with the new performance assessment. The final two participants are no longer officially PCs because they have taken on more significant administrative positions (e.g., chair of graduate studies and department chair prior to being named associate dean). Therefore, this collective inquiry surfaces issues of sustainability in program leadership and the initiatives championed by PCs.

Despite the variety of our pathways away from the PC role, the implications for relationships with schools, districts, and other community stakeholders were strikingly similar. The two former PCs who remained with their institution continued to support new PCs well past the transition period. One of these PCs remarked, "I have not been the program coordinator for more than two years, and I am still doing some program coordination duties because I care about them, and they would not get done otherwise." PC transitions impacted recruitment, marketing, and other outreach efforts including program advisory boards. Relationships shifted between programs and district partners across all four institutions. Specifically, when PCs were no longer doing this work individually, some of these efforts simply stopped.

A key challenge for solo-faculty PCs that emerged was rooted in planning for succession and program continuity. This dynamic applied to internal and external relationships. Internally, relationships with students, graduates, other programs, and the university in general were impacted.

Externally, relationships with advisory boards, partners, and the state educator credentialing agency were also impacted. These challenges underscored the unique role the solo-faculty PC fills, particularly that we were responsible for brokering relationships, ensuring compliance, and maintaining or growing a program. As a result, we held all institutional knowledge, and this knowledge was lost despite efforts to onboard and/or support replacements. As the PC who returned to a district leadership position remarked, "when all knowledge rests with one person, that's not really a sustainable model." Finally, the two PCs no longer with their institutions discussed efforts, noted elsewhere in this chapter, to carve out a space for the unique aspects of educational leadership preparation at their institutions. According to former colleagues, some of the gains they made for program autonomy diminished upon their departures. This connects to a reflection we each surfaced multiple times during our collaboration: across our institutions, the PC role was opaque. Specific expectations of PCs were not documented, but we were told that certain tasks were required of us. We also knew that additional work was necessary to provide a high-quality educational leadership program, and we had to determine how to balance these responsibilities.

DISCUSSION

As the findings demonstrate, serving in the PC role as the only full-time and/or tenure-track faculty member at our institutions necessitated our ability to navigate competing demands on our time. Program coordination diverted focus and energy away from our institution's key tenets for retention, promotion, and tenure (mainly teaching and research). In addition to general program management, additional effort was required to meet the demands of the new performance assessment. Finally, because we were committed to engaging in equity-focused preparation, we leveraged reorienting our programs to align with the credentialing change as an opening to emphasize the development of equity-focused leaders (see Figure 8.1 for a visual conceptualization of this work).

Making sense of policy informed program improvement, and improvement efforts influenced and were influenced by collaboration with stakeholders. These efforts continued even when we were not responding to policy updates. Of course, the work of identifying and implementing promising practices for equitable leadership education is not linear, but we understood these efforts to be rooted in the cyclical nature of seeking program improvement through collaboration. Additionally, we found that while we engaged in many bridging and buffering activities, we primarily bridged knowledge from professional organizations and partners in the

Figure 8.1

Conceptualization of PC Efforts for Equity-Focused Continuous Improvement

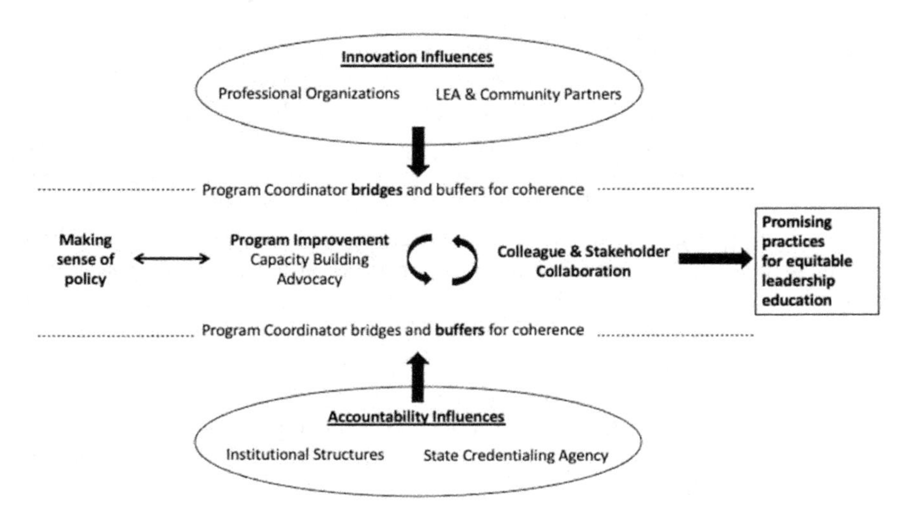

field in ways that championed innovation within programs. Conversely, we found that we sought to buffer accountability influences, such as our institutions and the state educator credentialing agency. We attempted to make sense of the policies these entities imposed and found that they were often rooted in compliance requirements to be met as a part of more significant continuous improvement efforts.

Pursuing Program Coherence

We sought to create coherent programs that would guide the development of candidates as educational leaders by providing them with experiences tailored to be responsive to their contexts. Our candidates were educators in a wide variety of settings including urban and rural communities spanning from coastal towns to the desert; therefore, despite our close collaboration, we sometimes found it necessary to diverge to meet specific needs of students within the communities they served. We all partnered with districts where most of our students worked to better understand their pressing challenges and official or unofficial equity and improvement agendas and adjusted course materials, assignments, and performance assessment support to target learning toward districts' greatest priorities. The work necessary for equity and inclusion initiatives was different across our regions, and we sought to meet our students where they were in their journey as equity-focused leaders with the intention of building their capacity from that point. This dynamic ultimately strengthened the consortium collaboration, and it especially bolstered our more intimate collaboration. As Fullan and Quinn (2016) posit, "there is only one way to achieve greater coherence, and that is through purposeful action and interaction, working on capacity, clarity, precision of practice, transparency, monitoring of progress, and continuous correction" (p. 2). As they explain, this requires "the press for progress within supportive and focused cultures," and this mixture of "pressure and support" is what we provided for each other (p. 2). As we sought greater coherence within the programs we coordinated, we also forged collective coherence between our programs.

We endeavored to refine programs with coherent curriculum and complimentary learning experiences that could challenge and inform candidates' conceptions of equity and inclusion (Cunningham et al., 2019; Young, 2015). While engaging in this work, a significant amount of time was devoted to buffering the impact of external forces on- and off-campus. Implementing the new performance assessment provided valuable political cover in this endeavor. Additionally, although it was sometimes a challenge to be the only individual on campus familiar with this credentialing requirement, we were able to use this dynamic to our advantage. For example, coursework for all our programs had been determined to meet the state standards during a program approval or accreditation process, but we recognized that coursework needed to change. Revising courses to embed the performance assessment and to have a more explicit focus on equity allowed us to expedite the equity-focused work we hoped to accomplish. Hackman and Wanat (2016) note that department chairs who hold no educational leadership expertise or experience are not well-positioned to guide leadership programs. Therefore, folding broad program redesign work into the process of performance assessment implementation was a useful lever for building the capacity of non-leadership faculty and administrators who held decision-making power over program changes. In turn, curriculum changes provided additional justification for making changes to program operations, such as program length, course sequence, and course scheduling. Many of these conversations stretched over multiple semesters or years and included both buffering and capacity-building efforts.

Implications for Faculty Time, Tenure, and Sustainability

Program management and improvement require time, effort, and resources to foster positive change and sustained impact. Literature demonstrates the importance of providing PCs with sufficient support and/or course release to engage in program leadership work (e.g., Hackman & Wanat, 2016; Milstein et al., 1999), yet three of us started PC duties without any course release, and one program continues to lack release time for the faculty member tasked with leadership duties. The policies governing coordination course release vary from one institution to another, but it is important to underscore that educational leadership PCs must attend to constituencies beyond those of traditional program management. For example, off-campus duties consistently range from partnership support in local schools to frequent engagement with state education agencies (Coleman & Reames, 2020; Hackman & Malin, 2016; Reames, 2016).

Coleman and Reames (2020) argued that the duties associated with program leadership and the time these duties consume are too great for a tenure-track faculty member to assume alone. Our experiences working as solo-faculty PCs validate this assertion. The solo-faculty PC role places a great burden on that faculty member. As we demonstrated, this can lead to sustainability challenges for individual faculty and programs. Requiring solo-faculty PCs to perform duties that stretch in all directions may also have implications for program quality. We made personal and professional sacrifices due to our collective commitment for rooting the programs we oversaw in learning experiences, curriculum, and partnerships that would build leadership candidates' capacities for leading diversity, equity, and inclusion work.

Our commitment to equity-focused preparation aligned with research-based best practices for leadership preparation but did not factor into the retention or tenure and promotion process at our institutions. The outsized responsibilities of program coordination (Coleman & Reames, 2020; Hackman & Malin, 2016; Hackman & Wanat, 2016; Ingle et al., 2020) were amplified for us as solo-faculty, assistant professor PCs. As the findings surfaced, this dynamic created challenges for balancing program leadership and improvement duties with the activities most valued by our institutions in the tenure process (e.g., teaching and scholarship). As Ingle et al. (2020) explain, "the addition of program coordination responsibilities in the nascent stages of one's academic career can add undue stress to an already stressful process" (p. 141). In addition to issues of balance, program coordination by untenured faculty places those faculty in a vulnerable position (Ingle et al., 2020). The hierarchical structure of the academy placed us in a subordinate position as assistant professors and this impacted our ability to drive equity-focused program improvement. We each needed to challenge the status quo to move program improvement efforts forward, and this forced difficult conversations with administrators and colleagues who influenced our futures within our institutions. Finally, we assumed expansive duties as solo-faculty PCs but were expected to meet the same standards as peers who had not taken on these additional duties. Coordination did not supplant additional service expectations (e.g., service on committees, assisting with department operations, and supporting student engagement initiatives).

Implications for Solo-Faculty Program Coordinators

These sustainability challenges for all four PCs hold implications for those serving in the solo-faculty PC role and their institutions. Solo-faculty PCs must take care to balance the realities of their positions with their own best interests for longevity, tenure, and a rewarding research agenda. Solo-faculty PCs, especially pre-tenure faculty, require resources that will aid program leadership and pathways to advocate for these supports. Course release for coordination is key, but resources may also include support personnel to assist with the additional work required for educational leadership coordination (Hackman & Wanat, 2016). Additionally, tenure and promotion expectations should reflect the complex nature of program leadership work including working with partner districts (Cosner, 2019). Again, this is critical for pre-tenure faculty.

Participation in professional organizations helped facilitate the emphasis on equity, inclusion, and coherence we hoped to achieve in the programs we oversaw. The relationships we fostered in these networks and the knowledge we obtained through these connections empowered building capacity for program redesign on our individual campuses. By leveraging this knowledge, we were able to incorporate promising practices and emphasize research-based educational leadership program design. We sought to infuse the fruits of this learning and collaboration in ways that might supersede a narrow programmatic response to changing expectations for educational leader credentialing. Therefore, we underscore the value of these venues and the importance of providing PCs with resources to collaborate with peers from their state and from around the country.

Finally, the opportunity to engage in deep, sustained, and relevant collaboration with each other was a key driver for program improvement efforts within our individual programs. This collaboration provided a space that fostered collegial support for duties beyond program coordination. We grew into a close-knit network of colleagues over the course of our collaboration, and these relationships were valuable to us as we navigated the challenges of serving as a solo-faculty PC. Our roles have shifted since we began this collaboration, but these relationships remain important to us on personal and professional levels. We encourage those serving in the solo-faculty PC role, and indeed any faculty, to seek and leverage these types of collaborative communities.

CONCLUSION

This chapter explored the realities facing solo-faculty PCs and offered a conceptualization of the ways in which we came to understand our work to improve leadership preparation programs. We surfaced the essential role of collaboration between solo-faculty PCs in our program improvement efforts. Therefore, we emphasize the importance of this collaboration for the success of the programs we led and our own successes as PCs and as faculty members.

The collaborative community detailed here was formed over the course of several years and supplemented the structural and emotional support often lacking for PCs (Ingle et al., 2020). We could not address structural support deficits on each other's campuses, but we were able to collaboratively troubleshoot these challenges. Genuine friendships grew out of our sustained collaboration to provide emotional support that extended beyond PC duties. These experiences suggest how educational leadership PCs, particularly those who have limited opportunities for collaboration within their institutions, might seek to collaboratively engage in leadership and continuous improvement efforts that prioritize preparing equity-focused leaders.

REFERENCES

Anderson, L. (2006). Analytic autoethnography. *Journal of Contemporary Ethnography, 35*, 373–395.

Barakat, M., Reames, E., & Kensler, L. A. W. (2019). Leadership preparation programs: Preparing culturally competent educational leaders. *Journal of Research on Leadership Education, 14*(3), 212–235. https://doi.org/10.1177/1942775118759070

Blalock, A.E., & Akehi, M. (2018). Collaborative autoethnography as a pathway for transformative learning. *Journal of Transformative Education, 16*(2), 89–107.

Charmaz, K. (2014). *Constructing grounded theory* (2nd ed.). SAGE.

Chang, H. (2008). *Autoethnography as method.* Left Coast Press.

Chang, H., Ngunjiri, F., & Hernandez, K. (2013). *Collaborative autoethnography.* Left Coast Press.

Coleman, L., & Reames, E. (2020). The role of the educational leadership program coordinator (PC) in university–K-12 school district partnership development. *Journal of Research on Leadership Education, 15*(4), 241–260. https://doi.org/10.1177/1942775118803335

Corbin, J., & Strauss, A. (2008). *Basics of qualitative research* (3rd ed.). SAGE.

Cosner, S. (2019). What makes a leadership preparation program exemplary? *Journal of Research on Leadership Education, 14*(1), 98–115. https://doi.org/10.1177/1942775115569420.

Cunningham, K. M. W., VanGronigen, B. A., Tucker, P. D., & Young, M. D. (2019). Using powerful learning experiences to prepare school leaders. *Journal of Research on Leadership Education, 14*(1), 74–97. https://doi.org/10.1177/1942775118819672

Davis, J. (2016). *Improving university principal preparation programs: Five themes from the field.* The Wallace Foundation. https://www.wallacefoundation.org/knowledge-center/Documents/Improving-University-Principal-Preparation-Programs.pdf

Ellis, C. (2004). *The ethnographic I: A methodological novel about autoethnography.* AltaMira Press.

Fullan, M. & Quinn, J. (2016). *Coherence: The right drivers in action for schools, districts, and systems.* Corwin.

Fusarelli, B., Fusarelli, L. D., & Drake, T. A. (2019). NC State's principal leadership academies: Context, challenges, and promising practices. *Journal of Research on Leadership Education, 14*(1), 11–30. https://doi.org/10.1177/1942775118819678

Glaser, B. G., & Strauss, A. L. (1967). *The discovery of grounded theory: Strategies for qualitative research.* Aldine.

Hackmann, D. G., & Malin, J. R. (2016). If you build it, will they come? Educational leadership program coordinators' perceptions of principal preparation redesign in Illinois. *International Journal of Educational Reform, 25*(4), 338–360. https://doi.org/10.1177/105678791602500401

Hackmann, D. G., & Wanat, C. L. (2016). Doing the work or sharing the work? The educational leadership program coordinator's role. *International Journal of Educational Reform, 25*(2), 100–124. https://doi.org/10.1177/105678791602500201

Henry W., & Cobb C. (2020). Social justice leadership design: Reorienting university preparation programs. In C. A. Mullen (Ed.), *Handbook of social justice interventions in education. Springer International handbooks of education.* Springer. https://doi.org/10.1007/978-3-030-29553-0_63-1

Hernandez, K. C., Chang, H., & Ngunjiri, F. W. (2017). Collaborative autoethnography as multivocal, relational, and democratic research: Opportunities, challenges, and aspirations. *a/b: Auto/Biography Studies, 32*(2), 251–254.

Hitt, D. H., Tucker, P. D., & Young, M. D. (2012). *The professional pipeline for educational leadership.* University Council for Educational Administration. https://files.eric.ed.gov/fulltext/ED533487.pdf

Honig, M., & Donaldson Walsh, E. (2019). Learning to lead the learning of leaders: The evolution of the University of Washington's education doctorate. *Journal of Research on Leadership Education, 14*(1), 51–73. https://doi.org/10.1177/1942775118819673

Ingle, K., Marshall, J. M., & Hackmann, D. G. (2020). The leaders of leadership preparation programs: A study of program coordinators at UCEA-member institutions. *Journal of Research on Leadership Education, 15*(2), 120–149. https://doi.org/10.1177/1942775118803334

Jacobson, S., McCarthy, M., & Pounder, D. G. (2015). What makes a leadership preparation program exemplary? *Journal of Research on Leadership Education, 10*, 63–76. https://doi.org/10.1177/1942775115569420

Kraft, M. A., Simon, N. S., & Arnold Lyon, M. (2020). Sustaining a sense of success: The importance of teacher working conditions during the COVID-19 pandemic (EdWorkingPaper: 20-279). Annenberg Institute.

Merriam, S. B., & Tisdell, E. J. (2016). *Qualitative research: A guide to design and implementation* (4th ed.). Jossey-Bass.

Miller, P. M. (2007). Examining boundary-spanning leadership in university-school-community partnerships. *Journal of School Public Relations, 28*(2), 189–211. https://doi.org/10.3138/jspr.28.2.189

Miller, P. M. (2008). Examining the work of boundary spanning leaders in community contexts. *International Journal of Leadership in Education, 11*(4), 353–377. https://doi.org/10.1080/13603120802317875

Milstein, M. M. (1999). *Changing the way we prepare educational leaders: The Danforth experience*. Corwin.

Reames, E. H. (2016). From coordination to compliance: The program coordinator's changing role during redesign. *Planning and Changing, 47*, 263–278.

Saldaña, J. (2012). *The coding manual for qualitative researchers.* SAGE.

Thornton, M., Barakat, M., Grooms, A. A., Locke, L. A., & Reyes-Guerra, D. (2022). Revolutionary perspectives for leadership preparation: A case of a networked improvement community. *Journal of Research on Leadership Education, 17*(1), 90–108. https://doi.org/10.1177/1942775120945356

Young, M. D. (2015). The leadership challenge: Supporting the learning of all students. *Leadership and Policy in Schools, 14*, 389–410. https://doi.org/10.1080/15700763.2015.1073330.

Young, M. D., Crow, G. M., Murphy, J., & Ogawa, R. (Eds.). (2016). *Handbook of research on the education of school leaders.* Routledge.

CHAPTER 9

THE ROLE OF THE CLINICAL PROFESSOR

Program Coordination and Partnership Development

William A. Bergeron, Yvette Bynum, and Brenda Mendiola
University of Alabama

While tenure-track jobs have been the norm in academia, there has been a decline in the last four decades (Asali, 2019) with the increasing number of non-tenure-track positions (Curtis, 2005). Non-tenure track faculty in the United State have increased from 22% in 1969 to 63% in 2019 (American Association of University Professors [AAUP], 2021; Finkelstein et al., 2016). The position of clinical professor is one example of an emerging, non-tenure track position finding its place in educational leadership departments. The clinical professor or professor of practice is someone who provides the students with practical instruction in the field as opposed to tenure track faculty who maintain a heavier focus on scholarship and research. Additionally, the clinical professors have the advantage of practical experience and creditability that is critical when developing partnerships with schools and school districts. Clinical professors are typically hired on a contract basis with no tenure-earning status. They have often distinguished themselves in their fields, and they provide an integrated instructional approach combining traditional scholarship and practical experience

Navigating the Ubiquitous, Misunderstood, and Evolving Role of the Educational Leadership Program Coordinator in Higher Education, pp. 183–195

(Professor of Practice, 2022). The real significance of the clinical professor is based on the difference between the theory of education and education in action (Holland, 1999). While clinical professors often have full professorial responsibilities, the expectation is that these professors will provide a necessary bridge between theory and practical application in the school setting (Cornbleth & Ellsworth, 1994) and provide an avenue to developing strong partnerships as a result of this combination of theory and practical experience.

Non-tenure track faculty usually do not participate in shared governance (AAUP, 2019; Kezar & Lester, 2009). Faculty senate, university committees, and leadership roles are generally reserved for tenured faculty, however, institutions are advised to develop specific guidelines, policies, or amended practices for the inclusion of all faculty types. Besosa (20011) advocated for the establishment of a non-tenure track faculty committee to advocate for leadership positions, and bargain for equal rights, benefits, retirement, and other related issues, priorities, and needs. A valid argument for including the clinical professor in the university setting is to provide a voice from the front lines and add credibility to the preparation of future teachers, school leaders, and partnerships.

THE EMERGENCE OF THE CLINICAL PROFESSOR IN EDUCATION

The first clinical faculty appeared in about 1839 in Lexington, Massachusetts (Herbst, 1989). However, during the early half of the twentieth century, the use of clinical professors declined as a result of the schools/colleges of education working to be seen as more scholarly and research-driven, thus distancing themselves from the practical day-to-day operations of teaching in schools (Clifford & Guthrie, 1988; Cornbleth & Ellsworth, 1994; Judge, 1982). The post-World War II baby boom and the corresponding increase in school-aged children led to the need to employ adjunct faculty to meet the demand. According to Cornbleth and Ellsworth (1994), the resulting "rising educational levels of elementary and secondary teachers ... contributed to their acceptability as cooperating teachers and, soon after, as clinical faculty" (p. 57). By the early 1950s, an exchange program was developed in which a classroom teacher and a college faculty member would rotate with each other. The classroom teacher taught at the university and the college professor taught at the school. By the 1980s, the idea of the clinical faculty was revived once again as a result of the need to improve the creditability of the Schools/Colleges of Education by establishing a closer connection to the classroom (Cornbleth & Ellsworth,

1994) and developing the critical partnerships to ensure quality teacher/administrator preparation programs.

THE BENEFITS OF EDUCATIONAL CLINICAL FACULTY AS PROGRAM COORDINATORS

The program coordinator within the university structure is much like the Teacher Leader within the PreK–12 schools throughout this nation. Program coordinators have no formal authority (Ingle et al., 2018). The role of the program coordinator is ill-defined and has no approved job description (Coleman & Reames, 2020; Ingle et al., 2018; Reames, 2016). Clinical Faculty that are also program coordinators, much like the teacher leader, can lead or coordinate the program as a result of their reputation and the trust and confidence their colleagues place in their abilities. The benefit of using a clinical or professor of practice as the program coordinator is the instant credibility and partnerships they have with key stakeholders of the university's leadership preparation program. Clinical faculty may be appropriately assigned as program coordinators and may be willing to serve in this capacity because of their desire to serve the students and develop lasting partnerships while also improving the quality of the leadership preparation program.

Educational leadership faculty with experience in the field have practiced servant leadership and are thus well-positioned to serve in the program coordinator role. What is a servant leader? "servant leaders do not solve organizational issues by identifying and diagnosing broken "cogs" with their authority or expertise. Instead, they facilitate problem-solving by helping others confront their values" (Wicks, 2019, p. 67). Servant leadership is focused on the well-being, development, and success of students above the professors' personal goals or ambitions. Individuals will follow a servant leader because they work to build trust and ensure their people that they are important to the success of the organization. The key traits of servant leaders include: being a positive role model, listening to individuals, providing the scaffolding necessary to ensure individuals reach their full potential, providing effective communications, and providing direction for individuals and the organization (Aboramadan et al., 2000) all of which are critical in the development of partnerships. Clinical professors serving as program coordinators cannot only teach the necessary educational theories but also provide a practical application with real-life examples and situations due to their lived experiences. As the title of Covey's (2012) book suggests, we must "seek first to understand, then to be understood." Being a positive role model requires the servant leader to have the ability to listen to their constituents. As experienced school leaders, clinical professors who are program coordinators have had extensive experience in being active listeners and have likely made more than a few mistakes along the way. Additionally, as experienced administrators, they have learned to create and perfect their answers before speaking. This hard-earned experience provides the clinical professor with the unique ability to model this skill when working with students, faculty members, and other stakeholders.

Educational leadership students in particular benefit from having clinical faculty in the educational leadership program coordinator position due to their ability, resulting from lived experiences, to provide the necessary scaffolding, empathy, and direction to ensure that they develop to their full potential while developing the necessary self-confidence to be successful school leaders. This would be difficult for a professor serving in the coordinator role who has never been in the trenches of running a successful school or school system.

The clinical professor's ability to have empathy for the students in the program is the result of their understanding of the position the students are in currently; they are full-time working professionals with many responsibilities other than teaching, they often have families, and they are graduate students at an R-1 university. The clinical professor has likely experienced the same plight as the students, many of whom continue until the completion of their terminal degree of PhD or EdD. The clinical professor works to ensure the rigor required of an R-1 university while having the empathy necessary to ensure the students do not lose hope and leave the program. This is especially important during the program coordinator's advising time with the students. A critical issue for many program coordinators is the need to ensure a healthy work-life balance (Burke, 2002). This is a critical skill that the clinical professor serving as the program coordinator can pass on to their students. The ability to have an acceptable level of work/life balance is important for a school leader to avoid burnout and stagnation. Students often need to be cautioned about overloading themselves. Steven Covey (1989) noted that leaders need to begin with the end in mind. As clinical professors, it is critical that we ensure our students do not lose sight of their ultimate goals and that they take time to see and understand the big picture. Additionally, Covey reminds us that we need to take time to recharge ourselves or, as he writes, to "sharpen the saw." Just as very few people would allow their cell phone batteries to drain down to zero, we need to ensure our students take the time to recharge themselves. Modeling this behavior for students will help them see the need to both practice recharging their batteries and also model this behavior for their staff and faculty. As servant leaders, our students must realize that poor decision-making and burnout may be the result of failing to manage the work-life balance.

A clinical professor as servant leader provides the students the support they need by listening to their concerns and problems both within the program and within their professional lives, providing the guidance and direction that can only come from the lived experiences of the clinical professor, and ensuring the students are recharging their batteries consistently. It is only the real-world, lived experiences of the clinical professor that provide authentic activities that help the students develop a sense of ownership of their knowledge, abilities, and self-confidence to ensure the student is fully prepared for the real work of running a school.

One final thought about the clinical professor as the program coordinator - many practitioners left the PreK–12 arena to get away from the paperwork of accountability and program leadership. The program coordinator position places them right back into the type of administrative role they may have been trying to escape. Many moved to the academy to conduct research and help improve teaching and learning. The role of program coordinator takes time away from their research and teaching, proving once again that they are truly servant leaders remaining focused on what is best for their students, educational partners, and key stakeholders.

ONE UNIVERSITY'S STORY

To gain a clearer picture of how the clinical professor as program coordinator might work in a real-life setting, consider how the program coordinator position evolved in one large research institution. A 12-year review of the educational leadership program reveals an ever-changing structure that grew and expanded to reflect the growth of programs and the development of partnerships, not necessarily in number, but in complexity due to the increase of tasks placed on program coordinators by both internal and external forces. At the beginning of the twelve-year review, the department structure was simple. There was a department head representing educational leadership, policy, and technology studies (ELPTS). During the period reported, the department head had expertise in a field other than educational leadership and as a result, programmatic responsibilities were assigned to program faculty with expertise in educational leadership. This arrangement is not atypical as noted by Hackmann and Wanat (2016) in their study on the role of the educational leadership program coordinator. Each of the five programs had a program coordinator selected by the members of the program. The educational leadership (EL) coordinator's primary duties included scheduling and facilitating program meetings, maintaining records of meetings, assigning professors to courses, meeting with other program coordinators, and seeing that university, college, and program reports were completed (if not by them, then by another member of the program faculty). Except for higher education, program coordinators were tenure-track faculty members. In return for serving as a program coordinator, a one-course reduction per year was awarded to the coordinator. In addition to an educational leadership program coordinator, within the program, there was also a designee to manage responsibilities associated with the Master of Arts (MA) in Educational Leadership with Class a Instructional Leadership (IL) state certification and Educational Specialist (EdS) in Educational Leadership with Class AA Instructional Leadership (IL) state certification and to develop the necessary partnerships. The program organizational chart is depicted in Figure 9.1.

Educational leadership program responsibilities increased after the restructuring of educational leadership programs prompted by the 2004 Governor's Congress on School Leadership that shifted the focus of school leadership from school administration to instructional leadership. The result was a redesign of educational leadership programs in the state with 2010 marking the year for the first cohort to complete the program described in this chapter. The redesign resulted in a more rigorous application process, alignment with leadership standards, mentoring, university district partnerships, and rigorous coursework with field-based and residency experiences (Coleman & Reames, 2020; Reames, 2010; Schmidt-Davis, et al. (2010). These components added to the work expected of educational leadership program coordinators. These tasks were assigned to the MA and EdS designees, both clinical faculty members with prior K–12 administrator experience, by the department chair and

Figure 9.1

Program Organizational Chart

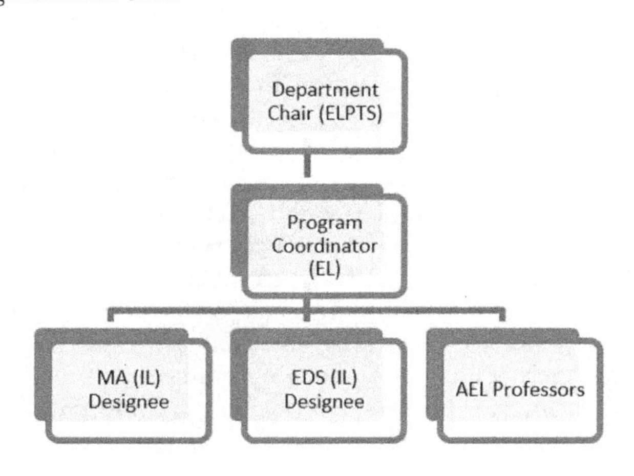

program coordinator. These designees carried most of the administrative tasks associated with the degrees but did not lead program meetings or determine which courses would be offered, when they would be taught, or who would teach them.

In addition to changes at the state level, accreditation agencies such as the Council for the Accreditation of Educator Preparation (CAEP) and the Southern Association of Colleges and School Commission on Colleges (SACSCOC) placed increased pressure on the educational leadership program to meet established accreditation standards. Portfolio reviews, multiple assessments, and plans for continuous improvement were pushed to program coordinators to facilitate. Pressures to convert programs from in-person to online, to increase grant application and participation, and to increase the status of the college on annual rankings, created additional responsibilities for coordinators. The university's designation as an R-1 research institution according to the Carnegie Classification of Institutions of Higher Education (2018) confirmed the university's focus on research. Competition for students increased the need for recruitment, and program expansion that included the reduced hour certificate only option and the Educational Specialist Teacher Leader degree with Class AA state IL certification added to the workload.

Program responsibilities were eventually split between tenure track and clinical faculty members with tenure track faculty members primarily responsible for the doctoral programs (EdD and PhD in Educational Leadership) and clinical faculty members primarily responsible for coordinating the MA, RHO, and EdS programs. The clinical faculty members are former school leaders with extensive experience in the field. The new program arrangement features three program coordinators with equal status and all responsibilities associated with the degrees assigned to them by mutual agreement between members of the Educational Leadership program and by the department chair. Program coordinators take turns running program meetings and determine courses taught, when, and by whom for the degrees for which they are responsible. Figure 9.2 illustrates the current program structure.

A CAUTIONARY TALE

Taken as a whole, program coordinator tasks, many of them administrative rather than academic, have the potential to pull professors away from the mission of the college and university where the focus is on teaching, research, and service with service beyond the boundaries of the institution expected for promotion. Time spent on coordinator activities varies with one study reporting an average of 17 hours a week (Ingle et al., 2018)

Figure 9.2

Current Program Structure

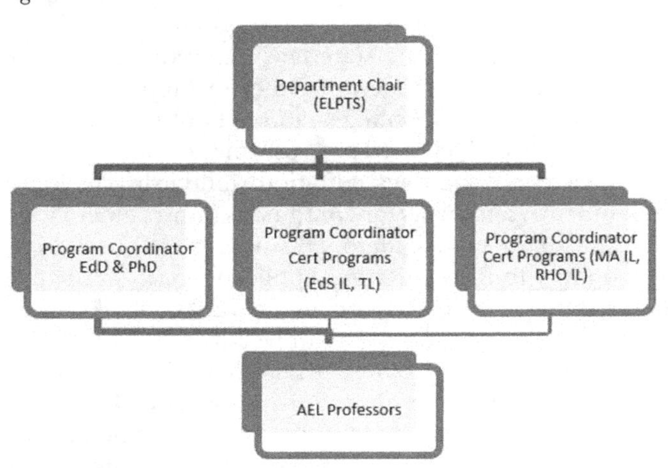

and another reporting 20-35 hours weekly during the academic year (Hackmann & Wanat, 2016). Whether 17 or 35, the time involved can keep tenure-track professors from meeting their research and publication goals. At first glance, the addition of multiple program coordinators, tenure track, and clinical, all with equal status, would appear to resolve the issue of work overload for the program coordinator.

With the measures of success for tenure track faculty members focused primarily on teaching (40%) and research (40%) with 20% for service, delegating coordinator responsibilities to clinical faculty who may have a higher percentage of their work norm assigned to service makes sense. Workloads are assigned by the department head and contract faculty may negotiate their research and service norms; however, clinical faculty desiring to conduct research may find it difficult to negotiate increased research time when department heads are faced with a shortage of faculty members willing to complete administrative tasks that result in little reward and recognition either for merit or promotion. Since by nature, clinical faculty have no tenure and with the continuation of their appointment dependent upon meeting the standards set forth by the department and college, clinical faculty may have little choice about taking on tasks assigned by the department head whereas tenure-track faculty members may opt-out of program coordinator roles because research productivity may be impacted. Coordinators, unlike department heads, have no "formal authority within the university organization" (Hackmann & Wanat, 2016, p. 101). Given the lack of formal authority, program coordinators must rely on the goodwill of their colleagues to share program responsibilities. Placing a clinical faculty member in a coordinator position with no real authority puts them in a vulnerable position—especially with tenured faculty members who may see their roles and responsibilities as divergent rather than overlapping (Hackmann & Wanat, 2016).

Having more coordinators with leadership roles exemplifies the distributed leadership theory, a theory that promotes the empowerment of others through leadership opportunities. Hackmann and Wanat (2016) propose distributed leadership as an appropriate framework for examining the coordinator position. Distributed leadership will not prevent questions of equitable labor that may arise if power is not equally distributed. Some faculty members may perceive that they work more and harder than others with little recognition for their efforts (O'Meara et al., 2019). Often little is done to invest, value, and support non-tenure track faculty (Haviland et al., 2017) whose positions are the least secure, lowest renumerated (AAUP, 2021), and seen as expendable and voiceless (Alleman et.al., 2020). These "invisible laborers" feel they are contributing their energies and talents to an organization that does not see them or their impact on the organization (Gordon et al., 2022). This is especially true for non-tenure track faculty when they are the "heavy lifters" of the organization but are treated as "second-class citizens" (Ochoa, 2011). Some studies cite differences in workload based on gender and race (Guarino & Borden, 2017; Misra et al., 2011; O'Meara et al., 2017). Care must be taken to ensure that women and underrepresented minorities are not unfairly relied on to complete tasks that remove them from academia and hinder research and consequently tenure, promotion, and merit.

Another issue that may arise when coordinator roles are split is the possibility that coordinators will work in isolation rather than in collaboration. Power struggles, disagreements over resource allocation, and failure to focus on common goals may lead to a weakened and disjointed program. Conflicts may arise between tenure track and contract or clinical faculty serving as program coordinators who may not see their roles and status as equal. For department heads, having more than one program coordinator may add to the complexity of the position, especially when coordinators are not working collaboratively.

RECOMMENDATIONS

There is not a one size fits all approach that works for every educational leadership program. The number and type of degrees and certificates offered, whether programs are offered in-person or online, the research status of the university, the number of students served, and the number and types of faculty members (tenure track and clinical), are all factors that may drive the selection of one or more program coordinators and the division of labor in a program. Careful thought should be given to arrangements that have the potential to not only divide tasks but divide faculty in a way that hinders their achievement of common goals. Given the tenuous nature of placing non-tenured track faculty members in the coordinator's role, consideration should be given to the following:

Professional Development

Conferences and professional development opportunities can help non-tenure track faculty create networks of like-minded people. Likewise, campus-wide networks such as a professional development center cultivate and promote a collaborative professional development community (Kezar & Lester, 2009).

Mentoring

The value of mentoring relationships cannot be underestimated; however, mentoring is seen as an informal process on many campuses. Typically, non-tenure track faculty receive little mentoring, no annual reviews (Tolbert, 1998), and little substantive feedback (Baldwin & Chronister, 2001). A more intentional and formal process needs to be developed to foster leadership and to help non-tenure track faculty learn how to navigate resistance, obstacles, and barriers (Kezar & Lester, 2009). Drake et al. (2019) recommend that more experienced full-time non-tenure track faculty members mentor, advocate, and guide newer non-tenure track faculty.

Terminology

The terms used to describe non-tenure track faculty are extremely important and may be the first step to removing the label of "invisibility." Terminology such as "invisible faculty," "contract faculty," or "clinical faculty" often denotes a less than desirable term. Returning to the general term "faculty" is perhaps the most desirable approach.

Rotating Roles

Given the time the coordinator role is likely to take, the nature of the position as contributing little to merit or promotion, the lack of authority in the position, and the pull away from other more fulfilling work, an organized system of rotation where all program members can serve in a coordinator position may alleviate some feelings of unfair workload assignments for a few select faculty members.

Promoting Collaboration

Drake et al. (2019) suggest that departments should encourage sharing of best practices, current research, and curriculum among all faculty members to promote collaboration and prevent the disconnect that may occur between non-tenure-track and tenure-track faculty.

REFERENCES

Aboramadan, M., Dahleez, K., & Hamad, M. (2000). Servant leadership and academics' engagement in higher education: Mediation analysis. *Journal of Higher Education Policy and Management, 46*(2), 617–633. https://doi.org/10.1080/1360080X.2020.1774036

Alleman, N., Allen, C. C., & Haviland, D. (2020). Full time, non-tenure track faculty, service, and organizational commitment. *Journal of the Professoriate, 11*(1), 48–77

American Association of University Professors. (2019). *Annual report on the economic status of the profession*. https://www.aaup.org/our-work/research/FCS

American Association of University Professors. (2021). *Annual report on the economic status of the profession*. https://www.aaup.org/our-work/research/FCS

Asali, M. (2019). A tale of two tracks. *Education Economics, 27*(3), 323–337.

Baldwin, R., & Chronister, J. (2001*). Teaching without tenure: Policies and practices for a new era*. Johns Hopkins University Press.

Besosa, M. (2011). Ways to organize non-tenure-track faculty. *Academe, 97*(6), 46.

Burke, R. (2002). Organizational culture: A key to the success of work and family programs. In R. D. Burke & D. L. Nelson (Eds.), *Advancing women's careers: Research and practice* (pp. 287–309). Blackwell.

Clifford, G., & Guthrie, G. W. (1988). *Ed school: A brief for professional educaton*. University of Chicago Press.

Coleman, L. B., & Reames, E. (2020). The role of the educational leadership program coordinator (PC) in university–K–12 school district partnership development. *Journal of Research on Leadership Education, 15*(4), 241–260.

Cornbleth, C., & Ellsworth, J. (1994). Teachers in teacher education: Clinical faculty roles and relationships. *American Educational Research Journal, 31*(1), 49–70. Retrieved October 28, 2022, from https://doi.org/10.2307/1163266

Covey, S. (1989). *The seven habits of highly effective people*. Simon and Schuster.

Covey, S. R. (2012). The wisdom and teachings of Stephen R. Covey. Simon and Schuster.

Curtis, J. W. (2005). inequities persist for women and non-tenure-track faculty. *Academe, 91*(2), 20–98. https://doi-org.libdata.lib.ua.edu/10.2307/40253410

Drake, A., Struve, L. Meghani, S. A., & Bukoski, B. (2019). Invisible labor, visible change: Non-tenure-track faculty agency in a research university. *The Review of Higher Education, 42*(4), 1635–1664.

Finkelstein, M. J., Conley, V. M., & Schuster, J. H. (2016). *The faculty factor: Reassessing the American Academy in a turbulent era*. John Hopkins University Press.

Gordon, H. R., Willink, K., & Hunter, K. (2022). Invisible labor and the Associate Professor: Identify and workload inequity. *Journal of Diversity in Higher Education*. Advance online publication. http://dx.doi.10.1037/dhe0000414

Guarino, C. M., & Borden, V. M. (2017). Faculty service loads and gender: Are women taking care of the academic family? *Research in Higher Education, 58*(6), 672–694. https://doi.org/10.1007/s11162-017-9454-2

Hackmann, D. G., & Wanat, C. L. (2016). Doing the work or sharing the work? The educational leadership program coordinator's role. *International Journal of Educational Reform, 25*(2). https://doi.org/10.1177/105678791602500201

Haviland, D., Alleman, N. F., & Cliburn Allen, C. (2017). "Separate but Not Quite Equal": Collegiality experiences of full-time non-tenure-track faculty members. *Journal of Higher Education, 88*(4), 505–528. https://doi-org.libdata.lib.ua.edu/10.1080/00221546.2016.127232

Herbst, J. (1989). *And sadly teach: Teacher education and professional American culture*. University of Wisconsin Press.

Holland, L. G. (1999). Invading the Ivory Tower: The history of clinical education at Yale Law School. *Journal of Legal Education, 49*(4), 504–534. Retrieved October 30, 2022, from http://www.jstor.org/stable/42898276

Judge, H. (1982). *American Graduate Schools of Education: A view from abroad.* Ford Foundation.

Ingle, K., Worth, J., Marshall, J., & Hackmann, D. (2018). The incentives and costs of program coordination in P-12 educational leadership programs. *Journal of Education Finance, 44*(2), 175–198.

Kezar, A., & Lester, J. (2009). Supporting faculty grassroots leadership. *Research in Higher Education, 50*, 715–740.

Misra, J., Lundquist, J. H., Dahlberg Holmes, E., & Agiomavritis, S. (2011). The ivory ceiling of service work. *Academe, 97*, 2–6.

O'Meara, K., Kuvaeva, A., & Nuns, G. (2017a). Constrained choices: A view of campus service inequality from annual faculty reports. *The Journal of Higher Education, 88*(5), 672–700. https://doi.org/10.1080/00221546.2016.1257312

O'Meara, K., Lennartz, C.J., Kuvaeva, A., Jaeger, A. & Misra, J. (2019). Department conditions and practices associated with faculty workload satisfaction and perceptions of equity. *The Journal of Higher Education, 90*(5), 744–772. https://doi.org/10.1080/00221546.2019.1584025

Ochoa, X. (2011). *Learnometrics: Metrics for learning objects.* ACM International Conference Proceeding Series. https://doi.org/10.1145/2090116.2090117

Professor of Practice. (2022, October 30). Retrieved from University of California, Santa Barbara: https://ap.ucsb.edu/policies.and.procedures/red.binder/sections/%5B5_20%5D%20Professor%20of%20Practice.pdf

Reames, E. H. (2010). Shifting Paradigms: Redesigning a principal preparation program's curriculum. *Journal of Research on Leadership Education, 5*(2). https://files.eric.ed.gov/fulltext/EJ913598.pdf

Schmidt-Davis, J., Bussey, L. H., O-Neill, K., & Bottoms, G. (2010). *School leadership change emerging in Alabama.* Southern Regional Education Board.
The Carnegie Classification of Institutions of Higher Education. (n.d.) *Classification descriptions.* http://carnegieclassifications.iu.edu/descriptions/basic.php. carnegie@acenet.edu
Tolbert, P. S. (1998). Two-tiered faculty systems and organizational outcomes. *New Directions for Higher Education, 104,* 71–80.
Wicks, J. W. (2019). Servant leadership, the college bubble, and saving higher. *College and University, 94*(4), 67–69. Retrieved October 30, 2022, from https://www.proquest.com/scholarly-journals/servant-leadership-college-bubble-saving-higher/docview/2323343811/se-2

CHAPTER 10

RECRUITING AND PARTNERSHIP EXPERIENCES OF THE GRADUATE ASSISTANT TO THE PROGRAM COORDINATOR

Angela C. Adair
Auburn University

Defining the Role of Graduate Assistant

The role of the graduate assistant varies from program to program in each university. In this chapter, the graduate assistant is a graduate student who works for the educational leadership program and serves as an assistant to the educational leadership program coordinator. The graduate assistant works for 20 hours per week which is considered a full-time position for a graduate assistant due to the university's understanding that the student must also dedicate hours towards research and study and receives free tuition and a modest salary in exchange for the hours dedicated to the educational leadership program.

Defining the Role of Program Coordinator

The responsibilities of the program coordinator are not always clear at higher education institutions but can include recruiting, admissions,

Navigating the Ubiquitous, Misunderstood, and Evolving Role of the Educational Leadership Program Coordinator in Higher Education, pp. 197–212

advising, scheduling, a multitude of administrative tasks, submitting documentation for accreditation and other requirements, and program and partnership development and the continuous improvement efforts necessary to achieve those ends. The responsibilities are many and are placed on program coordinators in addition to their teaching, researching, publishing, outreach, and service requirements. Because the program coordinator has so many responsibilities, having a graduate assistant who acts as assistant to the coordinator is optimal (see Table 10.1). This chapter focuses on the necessity of recruiting and building strong partnerships with K–12 institutions and other organizations because the sustainability of educational leadership programs depends upon the relationships that the university has with the organizations that benefit from the research, teaching, outreach, and service that universities provide (Kochan et al., 2021). Recruiting can be a valuable tool in building partnerships; likewise, building partnerships can be a valuable tool in the university's recruitment efforts. Placing partnerships and recruiting on the shoulders of the program coordinator without the support of a competent assistant makes the responsibilities of the role more daunting than necessary and can result in high turnover as the program coordinator position is often not one that offers additional compensation.

Mutually Beneficial Relationship

Program coordination is a complex, intensive task, especially for the program coordinator of an educational leadership principal preparation program (Ingle et al., 2020; Reames, 2016). Not all universities offer supports such as a graduate assistant, a stipend, or an annual course reduction for the faculty member who takes on the additional responsibilities required of the position (Ingle et al., 2020). A graduate student who works as an assistant to an effective program coordinator receives an excellent education above and beyond the traditional educational experience because there are no preparation classes for the role of program coordinator. While the initial learning curve is steep and vast, it is a unique experience for a student who may one day be asked to assume the responsibilities of program coordination in a higher education institution. It is an opportunity to build authentic relationships with future K–12 leaders and future higher education leadership faculty. It is also difficult to fathom that a program coordinator could effectively execute the tremendous responsibilities of the role without the assistance of a person who is not a faculty member under the pressures of teaching, research, outreach, and service.

Table 10.1

Clear Division of Responsibilities

Responsibility	Program Coordinator (PC)	Graduate Assistant (GA)
Recruiting	• Initial contact with potential students • Inform potential students of program information • Assist students in choosing the program that suits their goals • Contact university website management with necessary updates • Take advantage of all recruiting opportunities (school visits, social media, and educational conferences, workshops, and organizations) • Create and continuously improve the marketing and recruiting plan	• Create, update, and distribute handbooks, application and information packets, newsletters, flyers, and other recruiting materials • Check website and other virtual media for necessary updates • Research marketing resources that other universities or businesses are using • Send materials to recruits after initial contact by PC • Create and maintain list of potential students by program (this is ongoing as some students may enroll more than a year after initial contact) • Update PC on the status of potential recruits • Answer student questions about program information when appropriate and defer to PC when inappropriate • Take advantage of opportunities to recruit whenever possible • Assist PC in the creation and continuous improvement of the marketing and recruiting plan
Application Process	• Contact graduate program officer (GPO) when obstacles occur in process • Ask GPO for weekly list of new applicants to programs	• Assist students in application process • Continuously update PC on application status from conversations with students

(Table continued on next page)

Table 10.1 (Continued)

Clear Division of Responsibilities

Responsibility	Program Coordinator (PC)	Graduate Assistant (GA)
Admissions	• Contacts GPO when obstacles occur in process • Facilitate student interviews and writing sample sessions • Consult with faculty regarding admissions of students • Contact GPO with list of which students should be admitted to the program	• Create and update orientation presentations and agendas • Maintain notes of who has completed interviews and writing samples • Create survey for faculty to rate interviews and writing samples • Email students who have been admitted but have not accepted enrollment to ensure they have checked their emails
Registration	• Works with GA to draft advising emails for students each semester • Contacts GPO when obstacles occur in process	• Assist new students in the enrollment process • Send advising emails to students every semester with classes for registration • Inform PC of registration holds • Inform students when they need to apply for graduation or certification
Matriculation	• Provide constant support for students with questions • Check classes to ensure students have enrolled in the correct classes	• Provide constant support for students with questions • Keep lists of cohorts
K–12 and Other Partners	• Create and nurture relationships with all educational leadership university K–12 partner districts and other partnering educational organizations • Provide professional development opportunities to partners • Create and maintain advisory council	• Continuously update university partner contact information, including former program graduates • Distribute recruiting materials, university news, professional development opportunities, and newsletters to partners • Assist in workshops, conferences, and other professional developments

(Table continued on next page)

Table 10.1 (Continued)

Clear Division of Responsibilities

Responsibility	Program Coordinator (PC)	Graduate Assistant (GA)
Scheduling	• Create and update master schedule • Approve semester schedules created by GA to be posted for approval by educational leadership faculty	• Create semester schedules • Send schedules to graduate school • Create and update formatted planning worksheets
Miscellaneous	• Submit documentation for accreditation and other necessary reports	• Create surveys when necessary • Assist other graduate assistants • Send informational emails to all current graduate students • Draft evaluation forms for professional developments • Various research • Remind PC when it is time to consider internship placement, hire adjuncts, renew parking passes, etc. • Keep a chart of workflow as a way to foresee what is coming year after year

Recruiting to Build Partnerships

Recruiting is key to building relationships with K–12 institutions and is also key in building partnerships for the future. "No longer can preparation programs design and deliver learning experiences without the integral involvement of the school districts they serve" (Whitaker et al., 2004). Creating trusting relationships is important to the collaborative partnerships between K–12 and university institutions. Students who matriculate through educational leadership programs they respect and trust and from which they benefit are more likely to be those who want to give back to those programs by sending recruits and are also more open to bridging the theory to practice gap by forming partnerships with their former educational leadership programs (Russell, 2021; Wang et al., 2018). Former students who become principals, central office staff, or superintendents can serve on advisory councils that keep universities abreast of the needs of

K–12 entities and their constituents, all of whom are necessary stakeholders in the sustainability of educational leadership programs. When Bevins and Price (2014) wrote about the complex nature of partnerships regarding their experiences with two projects attempting to reduce the gap of theory to practice, they noted the following:

> It is clear to us that detailed initial planning is needed for both teachers and academics to engage in effective collaboration.... In this way we feel it is possible to avoid later realisation that the intended cooperation is doomed to failure, not through incompetence but in not recognising fundamental conditions needed to allow all participants to engage thoroughly. (p. 19)

Moreover, recruiting is necessary to produce more effective educational leaders at a time when increasing administrators are leaving the position and fewer individuals are choosing education as a career (Bottery et al., 2018). A graduate assistant to the program coordinator can be an excellent resource for recruiting because many prospective students find current students more approachable when they have questions about the program, the application process, or the registration process. Because graduate assistants can develop supportive relationships with prospective students from the beginning, they are often called upon when students finish their programs and are questioning if they should apply for the next degree program to continue their educations. As a result, a student who begins the master's degree program may continue with the university until the completion of a doctoral degree.

There are many invisible responsibilities of the program coordinator. Behind the scenes, those outside of the role may not be aware of the hours spent recruiting prospective students (Coleman & Reames, 2020; Ingle et al., 2020; Reames, 2016). Because not all programs have marketing experts or available marketing funding, the program coordinator may be tasked with developing marketing strategies to draw students to all graduate and certification programs the educational leadership program offers. This requires continuous research into what marketing strategies are working for other programs and understanding the unique needs of the prospective students for the individual program before developing a marketing plan with recruiting timelines and specific, tangible marketing recruitment tools. A graduate assistant can research other programs and assist the program coordinator with the development of the recruitment plan and the marketing recruitment tools. These marketing recruitment tools may include information and application packets, handbooks, flyers, websites, easy application guides for current students interested in transitioning to the next degree program, social media advertising, virtual open houses, videos, and so on. Often, the ability to learn the technology needed to produce these tools takes additional time (Ruffalo Noel Levitz, 2020).

Graduate assistants can research and implement the technology necessary to make the marketing recruitment tools available in aesthetically pleasing and professional formats.

Recruiting is vital to the program and should happen wherever potential students may be. Graduate assistants with a background in education typically have a network of potential students with whom they have taught. New students can be found at schools, workshops, conferences, sporting events, and even restaurants. The best recruiting tool is often current students or former graduates of the program telling their stories to prospects in their schools or professional learning communities. For this reason, it is important to make sure tangible recruiting tools are in the hands of current students and former graduates. The graduate assistant can create the recruiting tools necessary and assume the role of getting all necessary materials in the hands of potential recruits. When the program coordinator and faculty members are initially contacted by potential recruits, they can simply send emails to the recruits thanking them for their interest in the program and copy the graduate assistant on the email. The graduate assistant then adds the recruit, contact information, and program of interest to a list of potential students and emails the recruit with an information packet about the program in which they are interested. In the email, if the graduate assistant provides a telephone number and encourages the recruit to email or call with any problems or concerns in the application process, it opens more lines of communication between the university and its potential students.

Recruiting is ongoing (Ruffalo Noel Levitz, 2020). Once students have been recruited, they are often excited but intimidated by the process. Having an open line of communication throughout the process is imperative. If students do not apply within a reasonable amount of time, follow-up calls, texts, or emails may be necessary to make sure they are not having obstacles in the application process. An organized graduate assistant can be extremely effective in the maintenance of documents, recruiting tools, recruiting lists, and so on. It is helpful to keep a recruiting spreadsheet with the recruits' names, contact information, their programs of interest, the date of last contact, and the result of that contact. Once the recruit applies to the program, the same sheet can be used to track the status of the student in the application process until enrollment has been accepted.

Continuous Support

Continuous support throughout the program and beyond graduation is an often-overlooked recruiting tool. Educational leadership students are typically adults working full-time in schools who have families of their own. When the program coordinator ensures that a student's matriculation is seamless, students will be more willing to continue with their own educational journeys and to suggest the program to others. This can be achieved by sending out advising emails to make the registration process smooth and sending reminders to students to apply for graduation and certification at the appropriate times. Because of the tedious nature of scheduling and advising emails, it is best when the graduate assistant and program coordinator work together to make sure that faculty and student schedules are free from time conflicts and the correct classes are given to the right cohorts of students.

Finding the right people to recruit can be an important part of the process. Individuals who are friendly, outgoing, and have a good understanding of the university's offerings can make excellent recruiters. They should also know how to establish common ground with prospective recruits and show genuine concern that the recruit is being placed in the program that aligns with the recruit's goals (Ruffalo Noel Levitz, 2020).

Building Partnerships to Improve Recruitment Effectiveness

Creating and sustaining partnerships with K–12 districts and other organizations is often another role the program coordinator must address and is a time-consuming effort that can benefit from the help of a graduate assistant. Building lasting partnerships with K–12 districts can be a result of recruitment or the genesis of recruitment. Sanzo (2016) notes the following:

> Despite the work and uncertainty that often engulfs the world of district-university partnerships, the district stakeholders reported they felt highly valued and appreciated for all of the work they were doing to further the cause of administrator preparation. They also expressed the work provided, for them, opportunities for continuous learning and that the relationships that they developed with other stakeholders and program participants were vitally important to the success of the partnerships. (p. 16)

When universities offer quality professional developments to their K–12 partners and assist K–12 partners in growing their own leaders, a relationship of trust occurs that validates the university as an education provider in the eyes of the K–12 district. "However, partnerships today between university and K–12 teachers imply something more than an instructional relationship based on a one-way flow of information from an expert to his or her novice students. The construct of 'partnership' implies direct benefits for all parties involved" (Tomanek, 2005). This symbiotic relationship creates opportunities for the university as well as benefits for their partners. It also assists in the sustainability of the program as partners send the university aspiring leaders that one day replace veteran leadership as they enter retirement. The graduate assistant can check partners' websites often to make sure that the program coordinator has an updated list of contact information for all K–12 partners district partners and other partner educational organizations. This is especially important because of the high turnover of educational administrators. This list also provides the graduate assistant with the K–12 partners' contact information for sending out flyers and other tangible marketing materials to be distributed throughout partnering school districts.

K–12 partners can help expand the reach of the university, as well, by providing cohorts of students from remote areas in which districts are trying to grow their own leaders. The university can inquire about interest in a remote region and offer classes in that region. K–12 partners share university educational leadership information with their employees that can include an informational meeting for interested prospective students. Once enough recruits have shown interest in the program, the K–12 partner can provide space in school buildings for the university to hold classes for hybrid programs. University faculty can travel to the region for weekend classes three or four weekends per semester while allowing for all other work to be submitted online for the weeks that the face-to-face classes do not meet. Another benefit for students who have been chosen by their district to further their educations is that they begin to see themselves as teacher leaders and their district's confidence in them makes them more confident in their own abilities and more committed to taking on leadership roles (Basom & Yerkes, 2004). If there is not enough interest in the region, the university can offer distance programs that do not require students to travel to campus or university faculty members to drive to remote regions. Being flexible with program design is necessary to help K–12 partners staff their schools with effective leadership, which ultimately impacts student achievement as school leaders are considered to have the most impact on student achievement after the classroom teacher (Day et al., 2020; Huguet, 2017).

Other Benefits of Partnership

Multiple agencies, including the Wallace Foundation and the National Commission for the Advancement of Educational Leadership (NCALP), have noted the need for K–12 district and university partnerships. The importance of fostering relationships with K–12 partners should not be considered a trend but should be common practice. It is an integral part of principal preparation:

> The Wallace Foundation report (2016) argues that "strong university-district partnerships are essential to high-quality preparation but are far from universal" (p. 8). Research supports that the development of university-district partnerships can improve preparation by more closely aligning theory to practice (Davis, Darling-Hammond, Meyerson, & LaPointe, 2005; Jacobson et al., 2015; Orr, 2011). Strong partnerships can also increase the candidate's engagement in the program (Orr & Barber, 2007; Young & Crow, 2016; Young et al., 2009). In a study of high-quality programs described as exceptional, Jackson and Kelley (2002) found that those programs partnered with local districts for (a) the selection and recruitment process, (b) the continued support of program elements, and (c) the organization and development of the clinical experience. These partnerships benefit both the district and university. (Anderson et al., 2018, pp. 12–13)

Partnerships are not limited to K–12 institutions. State organizations that support educators are also key university partners and graduate assistants are often members of the organizations and may have relationships with key players. These organizations can partner with the university to offer professional development to current or aspiring school leaders. For example, the Council for Leaders in Alabama Schools (CLAS) offers aspiring leaders the opportunity to participate in mock interviews for principal and assistant principal positions through their partnerships with the University of Alabama and Auburn University. This benefits university students who are aspiring leaders, gives the universities the opportunity to network with students who may want to continue their educations with education specialist degrees or doctoral degrees, and assists CLAS in staffing effective leadership in schools all over the state.

K–12 partnerships are an avenue for research, and graduate assistants are often looking for opportunities to conduct research of their own, which could give the university additional representation at conferences like the University Council for Educational Administration (UCEA) and the American Educational Research Association (AERA). Once trusting relationships are created, partners are more likely to welcome the university to conduct research in their schools. This is important for educational leadership programs who need to stay current on what is happening in schools, especially regarding school leaders. For instance, the COVID-19 pandemic was fraught with challenges for school leaders which highlighted the need for addressing principal well-being as well as faculty, staff, and student well-being. For principal preparation programs to assist in this endeavor, it is necessary to research how or if principals have adjusted or even if they understand how to address their own well-being as well as the well-being of faculty, staff, and students. It is in the best interest of the principal preparation program and in the best interest of the school districts to address what is happening in the schools because if they do not, it could negatively impact the partnership as well as the education that students are receiving (Wang et al., 2018).

Partnerships with K–12 programs also provide opportunities for educational leadership students who need experienced mentors for clinical experiences in internships. A partnership between a university and an urban public school district in New Jersey aimed at growing their own administrators yielded favorable results: "The evaluations indicated respondents' strong program satisfaction with their preparation, a sense of program coherence, an appreciation for a rigorous and supportive internship, and a direct connection to the practice and realities of their school system" (Gutmore et al., 2009, pp. 36–37). This assists universities in finding placements for students and can be an opportunity for school districts to staff their leadership roles. In addition to the benefits it provides the university and the school districts, it can also be an incredibly engaging learning experience for the aspiring leader. An Auburn University student reported the following regarding her clinical experiences in an inner-city school system: "If I had simply been placed in a school system near my home, I would have only had the same experiences I had growing up in a rural area. I never would have had the understanding that I have from such diverse experiences." A graduate assistant can assist in the organization of the scheduling of internships and assist in keeping necessary documentation of the clinical experiences.

Partnerships can offer school leaders the opportunity to understand evidence-based strategies for effective learning, know how to recognize the characteristics of effective teaching, and see change as a collaborative process that involves all stakeholders (Goldring & Sims, 2005). Graduate assistants can help with the planning and implementation of professional development opportunities with the university's partners. Kansas State University partnered with local school districts in a program they called Professional Administrative Leadership Academy (PALA). At the conclusion of the program, a school district reported to the board of education that they had an increase in qualified applicants for administrative roles, that those in leadership positions improved their professional knowledge, that their efforts promoted school improvement and student achievement, and that the program increased the likelihood of district collaboration with the university in the future (Devin, 2004).

K–12 partnerships with universities have lasting benefits for the schools involved and for the universities; however, these partnerships require a lot of time and energy to effectively plan, recruit, budget, and evaluate, tasks that are often assumed by the program coordinator but can be somewhat alleviated by a graduate assistant. Coleman and Reames (2020) found that during the years when educational leadership roles were redefining their programs due to the call for redesign, program coordinators "were expected to develop new partnerships with K–12 school districts … required to maintain and grow existing K–12 school district partnerships … [and] expected to develop partnerships collaboratively without additional university administration resources, support, or understanding" (p. 247), which required the program coordinators to build relationships with all superintendents with whom they partnered. This required them to meet face to face at least twice per year, create and solidify formal agreements between the university and their partners, and address curriculum adjustments including getting approval for any changes to the curriculum. Reames (2016) noted the following as just a few expectations for program coordinators in Alabama:

1. Coordinating schedules for students.
2. Maintaining relationships with districts.
3. Developing and assisting with internship placements.
4. Keeping abreast of certification requirements.
5. Teaching course load of minimum of three per semester to include the feedback to students, and
6. Completing research to publish articles (as cited in Coleman & Reames, 2020, p. 256).

An effective graduate assistant can help make the role manageable by assisting in administrative tasks, research, and organizing documentation. This can include uploading important documents in a program all educational leadership faculty can access, drafting emails, attending meetings and typing meeting notes, checking links on the university website, creating orientation agendas and presentations, creating and updating formatted planning sheets, updating cohort lists, assisting applicants, creating schedules for faculty approval and finalized schedules for the graduate school, creating surveys, and more. In a special issue of the *Journal of Research on Leadership Education*, Brooks et al. (2010) state the following:

> The synergy created by the interaction among these valuable stakeholders helped create a dynamic process whereby the Instructional Leadership Program was ultimately developed. Without the vast expertise that was available to the committees, such a program would not have been possible. As the faculty and partners move forward, new information is continually made available about additional challenges and issues. The comprehensive evaluation process plus the ongoing discussion with all of the partners discussed in prior sections will provide a continuous improvement focus that is important for any type of program, but especially so for one that is trying to produce leaders for schools where continuous improvement is the key to success. (pp. 429–430)

The program coordinator who is being supported by a graduate assistant has more time available to work on creating and maintaining productive partnerships between the university and its K–12 partners. Once the systems are securely in place, they must be maintained and continually evaluated and improved, or the work and energy involved will have to be recreated once again.

Creating Successful Partnerships

In *Pedagogy of the Oppressed*, originally published in 1970, Paulo Freire (2020) wrote, "Authentic thinking, thinking that is concerned about *reality*, does not take place in ivory tower isolation, but only in communication" (p. 77). Partnerships can be formal or informal, but they must be collaborative (Gutmore et al., 2009). The graduate assistant as support to the program coordinator is a vital role in making time for the necessary collaboration that must occur between district partners and the university. "The process of developing effective district-university partnerships focused on administrator preparation must include the selection of representatives from each organization to design, build, and facilitate the partnership activities" (Sanzo, 2016). According to Chaseling et al. (2017), the K–12 and university partnership focus should be on continuous improvement though ongoing conversations, trusting relationships, sharing rather than telling, what is said rather than why it is said, reflection, and more ongoing conversations. Through literature and their study, the authors note the following as essential to successful partnerships: a shared vision, innovative thinking, collaboration with competition, trust and respect, measuring what matters, and sustainability through a positive culture (Chaseling et al., 2017). Blank et al. (2012) stated that creating a common vision, engaging stakeholders, having conversations about obstacles and solutions, being transparent with stakeholders regarding data, building central office capacity, and leveraging resources are essential strategies for building and maintaining effective partnerships. Having a graduate assistant who can take meeting notes while district leaders are in dialogue with the program coordinator allows the program coordinator to focus on what is being said throughout important conversations without the concern of losing track of what each district needs from the partnership. These partnerships can also be a rich pool from which to draw a new graduate assistant when the current graduate assistant is nearing graduation. Having the current and new graduate assistant overlap for a semester, if possible, is an opportunity for onboarding from graduate assistant to graduate assistant without putting unnecessary stress on the program coordinator.

Making the Most of a Graduate Assistant as a Resource

The program coordinator who knows how to give over some control and trust the graduate assistant to take care of necessary administrative tasks is the individual who can make the most of a graduate assistant as a resource. When the program coordinator takes time to explain to a graduate assistant why certain procedures are in place, how higher education institutions work, how the program evolved, and clarifies expectations, it creates a mentorship that has immense value for the mentor and the mentee. Not only does the graduate assistant create the time necessary for the program coordinator to focus on the important tasks of recruiting and building and sustaining partnerships, but the program coordinator provides an immeasurable value in the education provided to the graduate assistant.

Many obstacles are avoided when the program coordinator and the graduate assistant are in constant conversation with each other. A clear division of responsibilities is integral to the success of the working relationship between the program coordinator and graduate student. See Table 10.1 for an example of the division of responsibilities. The most important factor is that both parties are clear on their roles in making the program run smoothly. A program coordinator who is open to answering questions and a graduate assistant who is eager to learn can make a difference in the organization of the educational leadership program and in the lives of the students who matriculate through the program.

A program coordinator who has access to a graduate assistant can optimize the sustainability of the program by taking advantage of the help provided in recruiting, creating and sustaining partnerships, as well as assistance in other areas of the program so that the program coordinator has time to fulfill the other obligations of a faculty member regarding research, teaching, outreach, and service. It is a mutually beneficial relationship for the program coordinator and graduate assistant alike and assists in the creation and maintenance of partnerships that foster benefits for all stakeholders involved.

REFERENCES

Anderson, E., Winn, K. M., Young, M. D., Groth, C., Korach, S., Pounder, D., & Rorrer, A. K. (2018). Examining university leadership preparation: An analysis of program attributes and practices. *Journal of Research on Leadership Education, 13*(4), 375–397.

Basom, M. R., & Yerkes, D. M. (2004). A school-university partnership in administrator preparation: Learnings and subsequent questions. *Educational Leadership and Administration: Teaching and Program Development, 16*, 47–59.

Bevins, S., & Price, G. (2014). Collaboration between academics and teachers: A complex relationship. *Educational action research, 22*(2), 270–284.

Blank, M. J., Jacobson, R., & Melaville, A. (2012). *Achieving results through community school partnerships: How district and community leaders are building effective, sustainable relationships*. Center for American Progress. https://www.americanprogress.org/article/achieving-results-through-community-school-partnerships/

Bottery, M., Ping-Man, W., & Ngai, G. (2018). *Sustainable school leadership: Portraits of individuality*. Bloomsbury.

Brooks, J. S., Havard, T., Tatum, K., & Patrick, L. (2010). It takes more than a village: Inviting partners and complexity in educational leadership preparation reform. *Journal of research on leadership education, 5*(12), 418–435.

Chaseling, M., Boyd, W. E., Smith, R., Boyd, W., Shipway, B., Markopoulos, C., Foster, A., & Lembke, C. (2017). Uplifting leadership for real school improvement—The North Coast Initiative for School Improvement: An Australian telling of a Canadian story. *Alberta Journal of Educational Research, 63*(2), 160–174.

Coleman, L. B., & Reames, E. (2020). The role of the educational leadership program coordinator (PC) in university-K–12 school district partnership development. *Journal of Research on Leadership Education, 15*(4), 241–260.

Day, C., Sammons, P., & Gorgen, K. (2020). *Successful school leadership*. Education Development Trust. https://files.eric.ed.gov/fulltext/ED614324.pdf

Devin, M. (2004). Save a place for leadership in the debate on adequacy: A new model for developing leadership for schools. *Educational Considerations, 32*(1), 70–75.

Freire, P. (2020). Pedagogy of the oppressed. In J. Beck (Ed.), *Toward a sociology of education* (pp. 374–386). Routledge.

Goldring, E., & Sims, P. (2005). Modeling creative and courageous school leadership through district-community-university partnerships. *Educational Policy, 19*(1), 223–249.

Gutmore, D., Gutmore, R. F., & Strobert, B. (2009). Meeting the needs: A best practice grow your own school leader program. *AASA Journal of Scholarship and Practice, 6*(1), 33–39.

Huguet, B. C. S. (2017). Effective leadership can positively impact school performance. *On the Horizon, 25*(2), 96–102.

Ingle, K., Marshall, J. M., & Hackmann, D. G. (2020). The leaders of leadership preparation programs: A study of program coordinators at UCEA-member institutions. *Journal of Research on Leadership Education, 15*(2), 120–149. https://doi.org/10.1177/1942775118803334

Kochan, F. K., Reames, E. H., Serafini, A., & Adair, A. C. (2021). Partnerships in educational leadership preparation and development: What works and what's next? In F. Kochan, E. H. Reames, & D. Griggs (Eds.), *Partnerships for leadership preparation and development: Facilitators, barriers and models for change* (pp. 233–244). Information Age Publishing.

Reames, E. H. (2016). From coordination to compliance: The program coordinator's changing role during redesign. *Planning and Changing, 47*, 263–278.

Ruffalo Noel Levitz. (2020). *Resource Library. 2020 Marketing and Recruitment Practices for Graduate Students Report*. Retrieved October 31, 2022, from https://www.ruffalonl.com/papers-research-higher-education-fundraising/2020-marketing-and-recruitment-practices-for-graduate-students-report/

Russell, B. R. (2021). Partnering to develop school leaders: A model for success. In F. Kochan, E. H. Reames, & D. Griggs (Eds.), *Partnerships for leadership preparation and development: Facilitators, barriers and models for change* (pp. 119–135). Information Age Publishing.

Sanzo, K. L., & Wilson, J. M., III. (2016). Stakeholder experiences in district-university administrator preparation partnerships. *International Journal of Educational Leadership Preparation, 11*(2), 1–20.

Tomanek, D. (2005). Points of view: Effective partnerships between K–12 and Higher Education: Building successful partnerships between K–12 and Universities. *Cell Biology Education, 4*(1), 28–29.

Wang, E. L., Gates, S. M., Herman, R., Mean, M., Perera, R., Gerglund, T., Whipkey, K., & Andrew, M. (2018). *Launching a redesign of university principal preparation programs*. RAND.

Whitaker, K. S., King, R., & Vogel, L. R. (2004). School district-university partnerships: Graduate student perceptions of the strengths and weaknesses of a reformed leadership development program. *Planning and Changing, 35*, 209–222.

ABOUT THE AUTHORS

Angela C. Adair is a doctoral student at Auburn University who has worked as a graduate assistant for the educational leadership program for nearly four years. Her research focus is educator resilience from stress through self-care and positive psychology. In 2020 Angela wrote a book review of *Deeper Learning: How Eight Innovative Public Schools are Transforming Education in the Twenty-first Century*. Angela has authored or coauthored book chapters and journal publications to include: "Partnerships in Educational Leadership Preparation and Development: What Works and What's Next" (2020), "Data Driven Decision-Making Tools for School Leaders: Developing Tools That Enculturate Distributive Leadership and Shared Decision-Making" (2020), "Research-Based Strategies for Leading Successful High-Poverty Rural High Schools" (2021), and "Differences in Stakeholders' Perceptions of Factors That Hinder and Facilitate Student Success" (in press). She authored two chapters in this volume entitled "Recruiting and Partnership Experiences of the Graduate Assistant to the Program Coordinator" and "The Educational Leadership Program Coordinator Role: Partnerships and Recruiting."

William A. Bergeron is a clinical assistant professor of Educational Leadership at the University of Alabama. He is retired from the military and until January 2020 was a K–12 Administrator. Dr. Bergeron has a Doctorate in Educational Leadership (PhD) from Auburn University and more than 20 years of leadership experience and training in education, business, and the military. He was the principal of a large and diverse high school and the Director of Alternative Education. He also holds undergraduate degrees in Criminal Justice and Social Science Secondary Education;

master's degrees in Public Administration, Social Science Education, and Educational Leadership; and an Education Specialist (EdS) Degree in Educational Leadership. He is currently the Program Coordinator for the Educational Leadership-Teacher Leader EdS. the Educational Leadership Master of Arts and Reduced Hour Option for the initial certification of Educational Administrators. He serves as Chairperson of the University of Alabama Public Safety Committee and as a member of the College of Education's Assessment Committee.

Ann E. Blankenship Knox received her JD from the University of Tennessee in 2004 where she served as Managing Editor of the Tennessee Law Review. After practicing as a civil litigator and serving as a municipal and community development volunteer in the United States Peace Corps, she received her PhD in Educational Administration and Policy from the University of Georgia in 2013. After serving in both academic and administratice roles, Dr. Knox is currently the Associate Dean of Students at Claremont Graduate University. Dr. Knox is a researcher and scholar in the areas of education law and policy, leadership theory and practice, and educational leader training. She uses equity-based and/or critical lenses in her teaching and research.

Yvette Bynum is a Clinical Associate Professor in the Department of Educational Leadership, Policy, and Technology Studies at The University of Alabama. She serves as the program coordinator for the master's and education specialist certification programs in Instructional Leadership. Her experiences in education span more than 21 years with 9 years in higher education and 12 years in PK–12 education in Montgomery County Public Schools (AL) including 6 years in administration. In recognition of outstanding work with students, Dr. Bynum has received several college-wide service awards. She currently works as a certified mentor coach with the National Association of Elementary School Principals (NAESP), is a member of the Executive Board of the Southern Regional Council on Educational Administration (SRCEA), and a Co-Investigator on the Leadership for Character (LFC) project funded by the Kern Family Foundation and Alabama Superintendent's Academy, in addition to serving on several state and national educational leadership and program improvement committees.

Stacy Hendricks is associate dean for faculty and student services (since 2016) and program coordinator of the doctoral program in educational leadership at the James I. Perkins College of Education at Stephen F. Austin State University (SFA). She has a total of 30 years of experience as an educator. After joining SFA in 2010, she has served in numerous roles, such as director of a federal grant, program coordinator of the master's degree in educational leadership, and professor in the Department of Human Services and Educational Leadership. Before joining SFA, she spent 18 years in public education as a teacher and administrator in Texas, Mississippi, and Arkansas. Dr. Hendricks is the editor of the book, *Preparing Educators for Online Learning: A Careful Look at the Components and How to Assess Their Value*. She has published several book chapters and numerous studies in journals such as the *Journal of Interactive Online Learning, Scholarship Practitioner Quarterly, Research on Women in Education, School Leadership Review, Journal of Texas Women School Executives, Online Journal of Distance Learning Administration*, and the *Education Leadership Review*.

Wesley Henry is an assistant professor of educational leadership and policy at Central Connecticut State University. Dr. Henry began his career as a public high school teacher in the School District of Philadelphia and went on to work as a university administrator while he earned his PhD in educational leadership and policy studies from the University of Washington. He previously served as an assistant professor of educational administration and leadership at California State University Monterey Bay as the founding faculty for the principal preparation program. Dr. Henry's research interests are rooted in better understanding educator preparation, the role professional learning can play in setting organizational dynamics within educational settings, and the role of school and community leaders in equity-focused school improvement and community development.

William Kyle Ingle (PhD, Florida State University) is Professor of P–12 Educational Leadership in the Department of Educational Leadership, Evaluation, and Organizational Development at the University of Louisville. Prior to his academic appointment at the University of Louisville, Dr. Ingle served as Associate Professor and Program Coordinator for the master's program in Educational Administration and Supervision at Bowling Green State University in Ohio. Before beginning his doctoral studies, Dr. Ingle was employed by the Jackson County (Mississippi) School District. His research interests include human resource functions in education, the politics of education, and economic evaluations of education programs. His research has been published in journals, including: *American Educational Research Journal, American Journal of Education, Educational Administration Quarterly, Education and Urban Society, Education Finance and Policy, Educational Policy, Frontiers: The Interdisciplinary Journal of Study Abroad, Leadership and Policy in Schools, Midwestern Educational Researcher, Policy Studies Journal, the Journal of Educational Administration, the Journal of Education Finance, the Journal of Education Policy, Journal of Psychoeducational Assessment, the Journal of School Leadership,* and *Voices of Reform.*

Karen D. Jones is an Associate Professor and Master of School Administration Program Coordinator in the Department of Educational Leadership at East Carolina University. She has experiences as an elementary teacher, special education teacher, behavior specialist and campus administrator. Dr. Jones earned her BS in Communication Studies from the University of Texas at Austin, her MEd in Curriculum and Instruction from Texas State University, and her PhD in School Improvement from Texas State University. Dr. Jones' research focuses on preparing school leaders for success working with diverse school communities.

Sarah M. Jouganatos has over 20 years of experience working in education both in the California TK–12 system and in higher education. She currently serves as the Chair of Graduate and Professional Studies in Education at Sacramento State. Previously, she served as an associate professor and as Program Coordinator of the Educational Leadership and Policy Studies (TK–12) program. During her six years coordinating the program she developed innovative pathways, secured district partnerships, redesigned curriculum, and increased the diversity of students and faculty. Dr. Jouganatos's andragogical focus is to support and guide her students toward competency with various leadership styles, namely Transformative Leadership, an equity focused leadership style that can be used to support stakeholders and students in diverse educational systems. Specifically, she works to empower future school leaders to challenge the status quo by collaboratively constructing educationally just systems and practices.

Travis Lewis is an Assistant Professor and EdD Program Coordinator in the Department of Educational Leadership within the College of Education at East Carolina University. He earned his doctorate in education with a specialization in educational leadership from East Carolina University. His research focuses on educational leadership pedagogy, the influence of school leadership practices on K–12 teacher recruitment and retention, the effects of social and emotional learning on student outcomes and building resiliency in school-aged children.

Joanne M. Marshall is a former high school teacher and Professor in the School of Education at Iowa State University, where she researches religion and social justice pedagogy, school safety, and program coordination. She served as program coordinator of the Educational Leadership, Organizations, and Policy program at Iowa State from 2013–2020, when she stepped down to become U.S. Fulbright Scholar to the University of Namibia.

Brenda Mendiola is a clinical professor in the department of Educational Leadership, Policy, and Technology Studies at The University of Alabama (UA) where she serves as the Director of the University of Alabama Superintendent's Academy. Prior to her work at UA, Dr. Mendiola served as a K–12 educator first in New Mexico and then in Texas. Her background includes experience as a teacher, high school principal, curriculum director, and superintendent. In addition to her work with the Superintendent's Academy, Dr. Mendiola teaches leadership courses, conducts research, write grants and works with others to promote leadership development across the state. She is a Gallup-certified strength coach and a National Association of Elementary School Principal (NAESP) certified mentor. Dr. Mendiola is a Coinvestigator on the Leadership for Character (LFC) project funded by the Kern Family Foundation.

Alfred Parham currently serves as Assistant Clinical Professor for Educational Leadership and Program Coordinator at Auburn University in Auburn, Alabama. Dr. Parham recently retired March 19, 2019, as the Director of Student Services for the Muscogee County School District in Columbus, Georgia. Dr. Parham earned his Bachelor of Science Degree in Education from Delaware State University, his U.S. Army Commission from the University of Delaware, his master's degree in educational leadership from Troy University, and his Doctor of Philosophy Degree in Educational Leadership with a specialization in Secondary School Administration from Auburn University. Additionally, Dr. Parham is the current Program Coordinator for Instructional Leadership and serves as Chair for the Auburn University College of Education Clinical and Field Experiences Committee. Dr. Parham also serves as a Site Reviewer for both The Council for Accreditation of Educator Preparation (CAEP), and the Southern Association of Colleges and Schools Commission on Colleges (SACSCOC).

Noelle A. Paufler, PhD, is an Associate Professor—P–12 and the Program Coordinator for the Doctor of Education in Education Systems Improvement Science at Clemson University. She has experience as a high school social studies teacher, district administrator, and applied researcher in high-need districts and schools. Her research interests include K–12 educational policy, specifically how educational leaders enact policy into practice, its impact on teachers and students, and implications for leadership preparation. Her current research examines the lived experiences of evaluators and teachers related to the development, implementation, and impact/(un)intended consequences of teacher evaluation systems in P–12 and higher education settings. Additional areas of her research focus on doctoral leadership preparation, specifically preparing leaders who have the knowledge, skills, and systems perspective needed to effectively serve in high-need school communities. Her work has been published in premier journals including those sponsored by several prominent professional associations, such as the *American Educational Research Journal, Impacting Education: Journal for Transforming Professional Practice, Journal of Research on Leadership Education,* and *Journal of Teacher Education.*

Barbara L. Pazey is an Associate Professor of Educational Leadership at the University of North Texas. She received her PhD in Educational Administration with a specialization in Special Education Administration from The University of Texas at Austin, her Master of Arts in Music and Piano from The Ohio State University, her special education certification through the University of South Carolina and Francis Marion University, and a Bachelor of Music degree with a major in piano from Muskingum University. She has experience as a K–12 music teacher and special education teacher, musician and music director for several professional organizations, high school inclusion coordinator, high school principal, and higher education administrator. Her research centers on equity-oriented leadership, educational policy and reform, inclusive education, and the empowerment of voice for change. Her work has been published in premier journals such as the *American Educational Research Journal, Educational Administration Quarterly, Teachers College Record, Journal of School Leadership, Urban Education, Urban Education Review, Leadership and Policy in Schools, Journal of Research on Leadership Education,* among others.

Isela Peña is an Assistant Professor at the University of Texas at El Paso (UTEP). Prior to joining UTEP, she served as an Assistant Professor and Program Coordinator of the Educational Leadership Program at Sul Ross State University. Her research interests include issues of access and equity, education law and policy, principal leadership, and organizational change. With over fifteen years of experience in both K–12 public education and higher education, she has conducted numerous leadership and board member training courses and presented on a variety of educational topics at national conferences. She obtained her JD from Columbia Law School and her EdD in Educational Leadership and Administration from UTEP. While working on her EdD, she had the distinct honor of serving as a University Council for Educational Administration, Barbara Jackson Scholar from 2017– 2019.

Barbara Qualls is the coordinator of the MEd–Leadership/Advanced Certification program at the James I. Perkins College of Education at Stephen F. Austin State University (SFA). After several decades of experience in Texas schools, ranging from classroom teacher to superintendency, she joined higher education 10 years ago. She holds the E. J. Campbell Distinguished Professorship for Educational Leadership. In 2021, she was named the Human Services and Educational Leadership representative for the SFA Teaching Excellence Award. Dr. Qualls is a member of the Board of Directors for the Education Law Association. Dr. Qualls is a longtime contributor to the Yearbook of Education Law, where she is responsible for the review of Governance case law. In addition, she is the editor of the Governance section of the *Education Law Update*. Her primary research interest focuses on legal issues related to the First Amendment expression rights of both students and teachers. Recently, Dr. Qualls presented a paper at the Oxford Symposium on Religious Studies. She is a contributor and reviewer for *Research on Women in Education, School Leadership Review, the Education Leadership Review,* and *the Brigham Young University Journal of Education and Law.*

Ellen H. Reames is Professor of Educational Leadership at Auburn University in Auburn, Alabama. Her area of research is educational leadership program design. She enjoys exploring innovative ideas that promote continuous improvement in leadership preparation. Her focus in recent years includes partnership development between educational leadership preparation programs, K–12 districts, other higher education leadership preparation programs and agencies closely tied to the K–12 districts. She has published in the *Journal of Research on Leadership Education*, the *Journal of School Leadership,* and the *International Journal of Educational Reform*. She recently published a book titled, *Rural Turnaround Leadership Development: The Power of Partnerships*. A second book, *Partnerships for Leadership Preparation and Development: Facilitators, Barriers, and Models for Change,* edited by Frances Kochan, Ellen H. Reames, and Dana M. Griggs was released in 2021. Her latest work is a book called *The Art and Science of Mentoring* (2021).

Lori Rhodes is currently the Associate Superintendent for School Development for Stamford Public Schools. Prior to this, she was an Assistant Professor of Educational Leadership at Sonoma State University. Dr. Rhodes has worked in education for over 25 years. She holds a degree in curriculum and instruction from Columbia University and degrees in history and education from Stanford University, with a focus on the history of education in 20th century America and the educational experiences of Latinx youth. Dr. Rhodes began teaching in South Central Los Angeles with the Teach For America program and has served as a teacher and an administrator in public, independent, and charter schools in California, New York, and Connecticut.

Rebecca Schlosser, JD., EdD, is full professor and Director of Principal Preparation & Outreach Programs at Sul Ross State University–Alpine, Texas. Her research interests include higher education policy, education law, and 21st century standards for principal preparation programs. Dr. Schlosser's duties include the recruitment and retention of K–12 district partnerships to direct and manage Principal Preparation Academies with their district partners. Dr. Schlosser has partnered with K–12 districts for the last four years to receive the Texas Principal Residency Grant. While Dr. Schlosser has been Director, the SRSU Educational Leadership Program has been consistently awarded eligibility by the Texas Education Agency to partner with K–12 districts for the Principal Residency Grant. Dr. Schlosser recently wrote and was awarded, with a grant partner, the Cycle 5, Principal Residency Grant, $400,000.